WHAT *we* HAVE

WHAT *we* HAVE

A Memoir

A M Y   B O E S K Y

G O T H A M   B O O K S

GOTHAM BOOKS
Published by Penguin Group (USA) Inc.
375 Hudson Street, New York, New York 10014, U.S.A.
Penguin Group (Canada), 90 Eglinton Avenue East, Suite 700, Toronto, Ontario M4P 2Y3,
Canada (a division of Pearson Penguin Canada Inc.); Penguin Books Ltd, 80 Strand,
London WC2R 0RL, England; Penguin Ireland, 25 St Stephen's Green, Dublin 2, Ireland
(a division of Penguin Books Ltd); Penguin Group (Australia), 250 Camberwell Road,
Camberwell, Victoria 3124, Australia (a division of Pearson Australia Group Pty Ltd);
Penguin Books India Pvt Ltd, 11 Community Centre, Panchsheel Park,
New Delhi – 110 017, India; Penguin Group (NZ), 67 Apollo Drive, Rosedale,
North Shore 0632, New Zealand (a division of Pearson New Zealand Ltd); Penguin Books (South
Africa) (Pty) Ltd, 24 Sturdee Avenue, Rosebank, Johannesburg 2196, South Africa

Penguin Books Ltd, Registered Offices: 80 Strand, London WC2R 0RL, England

Published by Gotham Books, a member of Penguin Group (USA) Inc.

First printing, August 2010
1 3 5 7 9 10 8 6 4 2

The author wishes to make clear that while this is a work of
nonfiction, some of the names, events, and dates have been
changed in order to protect the privacy of those involved.

LIBRARY OF CONGRESS CATALOGING-IN-PUBLICATION DATA
Boesky, Amy.
What we have : a memoir / Amy Boesky.—1st ed.
p. cm.
ISBN 978-1-59240-551-0 (hardcover)
1. Boesky, Amy.   2. Cancer—Genetic aspects.   3. Genetic screening.   I. Title.
RC265.6.B64   2010
616.99'4042—dc22   2010008873

Printed in the United States of America
Set in Adobe Garamond with Bodoni BE for Display   •   Designed by Catherine Leonardo

*Penguin is committed to publishing works of quality and integrity.
In that spirit, we are proud to offer this book to our readers;
however, the story, the experiences, and the words are the author's alone.*

For Sylvia, Pody, Gail;

for my mother, Elaine;

and for the girls.

CONTENTS

Contents

PROLOGUE

ON MARCH 25, 1993, AT the end of a long, unusually snowy winter, I got a letter from the chair of the Department of Preventive Medicine and Public Health at Creighton University. They'd been following the cluster of cancers in our family since the 1980s, and they wanted to report what they'd learned. They listed statistics, numbers, names of "first-" and "second-degree" relatives. I read the letter twice. I looked down at Elisabeth, our newborn, who looked back at me with that uncanny infant mixture of myopia and focus. Sacha, our toddler, was upstairs napping.

I folded the letter up and put it away.

I knew this was big news. Even in my postpartum haze, I got that.

1

But there was a lot I couldn't fathom. I didn't realize how much the story we'd grown up with was about to change, how much of a difference it would make, rearranging what we knew—what we *thought* we knew—about our family history. Seeing connections where we hadn't before. Seeing fissures and breaks where before there'd been smooth, connecting lines.

THIS STORY IS ABOUT WHAT it's been like for one family—mine—to live with risk.

It isn't really a cancer story, or a survivor story, though it has cancer and surviving in it. Instead, it's a previvor's story. A *previvor* is someone who doesn't have cancer, but has a known (elevated) risk for it, discovered through family history or through diagnosis with a genetic mutation. That's good news. If you're a previvor, you don't have anything—at least, not yet.

The bad news is, that means you don't have anything to fix or get better from. You can diagnose being a previvor, but you can't treat it. There are things you can do, protocols to follow. But the previvor part doesn't go away. It just becomes part of who you are.

Previvors are a new group—the word hasn't been around for long—but we're growing in number every day. By the time this book is finished, there will be thousands more of us. It's peculiar and compelling, this glimpse ahead—in some ways a curse, in others, a gift.

I used to think all my favorite words began with *pre. Preface. Prepare. Prevaricate. Pregnancy* (that one doesn't belong etymologically, but still). *Pre* for "prior to; earlier than." Ahead of. I've always loved being early: the first to board the plane; the first to get a new piece of technology. The first to plan. *Preview. Premonition. Prevent.*

Would I have chosen this kind of preview on purpose?

I go back and forth. I talk about it with my sisters. Some days, the answer, emphatically, is *no*. Who wants to know her genetic destiny and have to live with the consequences? Who wants to sit down and tell her daughters about this? *Girls, guess what? We have this gene—*

Other days, I'm more upbeat. I tell myself having to live with consequences isn't the point. It's *getting* to live. Maybe even choosing to live. For that, seeing ahead is worth it.

Two different points of view, and I have both.

There's a shaped poem I've always liked by George Herbert which modern editors call "Easter Wings." Most editors lay it out vertically, so the two stanzas (shaped like triangles) stand, inverted, on a single page. Set like that, it looks like an hourglass. But if you turn the poem sideways, it looks like wings.

That's how it is for me, thinking about the future. Two different shapes. One holding time; the other escaping it. One suggesting fragility, confinement; the other, something transcendent. Turn it one way, you see an hourglass. Turn it the other way, and you see wings.

PART I

Why do we remember the past, but not the future?

—Stephen Hawking, *A Brief History of Time*

Seize the Day

MY FRIENDS FROM GRADUATE SCHOOL couldn't believe I was having a baby.

"*Now?*" they asked.

It wasn't the *what* of a baby, it was the *when*.

"Well—I guess there's never a perfect time," my friend Annie said after a pause, by which I think she really meant, *Are you insane?* Annie, who teaches Literature and Trauma at Penn, had been two years ahead of me in graduate school and was much closer than I was to turning her dissertation into a book. Mine, *Time and the Early Moderns*, was still in pieces.

She sounded mystified, though I could tell she was trying to be supportive. "I'm not exactly young for this," I reminded her. In

seventeenth-century Britain—my field—I could have been a grandmother already, having married at thirteen, with a dozen children
under my belt.

But in academia, thirty-two was considered young. I wasn't even
halfway through the six-year stretch before I came up for tenure. I
could sense Annie's unasked question: Why have a baby now, when
Jacques and I had been married less than a year?

I didn't want to get into it with Annie, but I had a reason. My
biological clock was set way ahead. I'd grown up in a high-risk cancer
family, and I'd always known if I wanted children, I had to get going.
I had a deadline, and it was looming closer all the time.

In my case, there was no question of if. I've always wanted kids.
It used to be an abstract, maybe-one-day thing. But after Jacques and
I met, I started thinking about babies in earnest. Names and potential
personalities floated through my head before sleep. I started doing all
the predictable and embarrassing things—stopping strangers to exclaim about the content of their strollers; picking up miniature-sized
shoes in Marshalls and turning them over like talismans. I even bought
a copy of *What to Expect When You're Expecting*. Good planners, those
authors. There was a whole chapter devoted to people like me called
"Before You Conceive." Vitamins to take. Chemicals to avoid. What
to expect when you expect to be expecting.

Planning wasn't the right word for this. It was more like
compulsion.

I didn't meet Jacques until I was twenty-nine, and I wanted not
just one baby (greedy girl) but *two*. In a different lifetime, with a different genetic makeup, I would have wanted more—a gaggle, a flock.
Even as it was, we needed to get going.

I had a timeline. In my family, it was all mapped out—around
age six or seven, you got glasses; around eighteen or nineteen, your
wisdom teeth came out; and by age thirty-five, it was time to take out
your ovaries. We were all on the same schedule, but my sisters (Sara,
two years older; Julie, four years younger) had been better about get-

ting their lives in order early. I was the laggard. I'd spent half my twenties in rare books libraries, which takes a toll on your social life. Besides, you can't hurry love, as the great Motown song reminds us. And as I kept reminding my mother.

Once I'd found love, though, I was good to go. I was thirty-one when Jacques and I got married. The way I saw it, we had four years— two per baby.

The trick was not to lose focus. I'm a born planner—I love thinking ahead. Jacques, on the other hand, thinks planning and over-planning are more or less the same thing. By the time I realized how great a premium he puts on spontaneity, we were already in love, and what could we do? Forget that he's from South Africa and I'm from Detroit, or that he loves numbers and newspapers, and I love poetry. The real difference between us is how we deal with the future. It's like the Montagues and the Capulets, and as long as we're together (which given that we've promised each other "till-death-do-us-part," I hope is for many, many years), this aspect of our life together will drive us both to distraction.

Jacques and I may live together, but we inhabit different time zones. Say it's twenty to eight, for instance, and we've got dinner res-ervations downtown at eight. Jacques will be upstairs dreamily flipping through the pages of the *Boston Globe*, still in his sweats, languid, oblivious to any sense of impending deadline. Whereas I'll have been ready, pacing, fingers tapping, for at least half an hour. Wherever we are and whatever we're doing, Jacques feels early and I feel late. He claims it's a northern hemisphere/southern hemisphere issue. We grew up with different frames of reference—when I think north, he thinks south; when I think winter, he thinks summer; the constellations that show up in his dreams are unfamiliar to me.

Maybe it's geographic or genetic. Maybe it's just who we are. All I know is, Jacques likes letting things unfold, and I like pinning them down. He likes to "wait and see"—his personal motto—and I like to plan. I *like* knowing where we're going on vacation next August or

how it feels, all air-conditioned and unpressured, getting to the airport an hour before you have to. Time to buy Lifesavers, to browse the
magazines. It's the *pre* in me.

Jacques is more *post* than *pre*. Maybe even *anti*.

We didn't know this about each other right away. I was actually
running late when we met, and Jacques was early. Friday afternoon
traffic had kept me trapped in a taxi three blocks from Boston's South
Station while he, fresh from the Red Line, fell into one of the last
available seats on the southbound *Yankee Clipper*.

It was a strange period for me. I was anxious about the job market, and to compensate, I'd been trying to adopt a devil-may-care
approach to the whole process. Whenever anyone asked me about it,
I was offhand, blasé. But it felt unnatural, like trying to tell a joke in
another language. After long discussions with my advisors, I sent off
applications for jobs in every English department hiring in my field—
thirty in total. There were no jobs in Boston. Most were west of the
Mississippi, in obscure locations like Lubbock, Texas, and Tempe,
Arizona. I pictured myself, the lone single woman, making my way
through Safeway with a cartful of prewashed lettuce.

Georgetown, near my sister Julie and her husband, Jon, seemed
like the ideal option on the eastern seaboard, and it happened to be
the only place I knew a single soul. Right from the start, that was the
job I wanted, even though I knew it was wrong to fixate on one position. My advisors were always reminding us not to be "bicoastal." We
were supposed to be like missionaries, grateful for any crumb. Who
cared where you lived if you got to teach seventeenth-century literature three days a week?

Actually, *I* did, but I tried to keep this to myself. Maybe it was
time for a change. I was sick of the Northeast. I was recovering from
a bad relationship with a graduate student in history who used to
make me listen while he read out loud to me from his dissertation on
war. I figured I could use a fresh start.

If I got the job in Tempe, I could buy southwestern pottery, wear turquoise. I'd reinvent myself, save up for a pony.

Bolstered by my feigned open-mindedness, I sent my applications off Express Mail and headed down to Philly to visit Annie. Friday, five o'clock, Amtrak. Rumpled and irritated, I fell into the last seat as the train was lurching away from the station—no time for Lifesavers, let alone magazines. I didn't notice Jacques, half dozing against the window, until I'd finished stuffing my book bag under the seat. Then I couldn't take my eyes off him. Dark beard, beautiful gabardine suit. He was half asleep, and I had to do a lot of throat clearing and elbow bumping to wake him up.

Once he opened his eyes, I was transfixed. He was like a magnetic field; I felt this extraordinary pull in his direction. I know this sounds crazy, but it's true: I looked at him and thought, *This is it. This is the man I'm going to marry.*

"You can't be serious," Annie said, when I told her that later. "He was *asleep.*"

"I'm telling you how I felt," I said, unapologetic. I'd been reading Petrarch that week and was steeped in neo-Platonic longing.

Besides, Jacques hadn't stayed asleep. We talked all the way from Boston to Penn Station—his stop; he was on his way to a conference in New York for the weekend. Four and a half heavenly hours. Time felt slowed down, then speeded up; everything seemed both to matter and suddenly not to. Jacques has a beautiful, lilting South African accent, and I was enchanted by his voice.

"He could've been saying anything," Julie objected, going over the encounter with me later on the phone. "He could've been talking about the weather! You're smitten with an *accent.*"

But the accent was only part of it. Mostly, I was spellbound by the sense between us of same and different. In one way, Jacques and I seemed like opposites. He worked downtown—computers and finance—and owned his own house, complete with a small yard and a pear tree. I was still in grad school, living in a dorm in exchange for writing fellowship letters for scholar-athletes. But we had an instant sense of shared values—what Malcolm Gladwell calls a "blink" moment. Jacques couldn't believe I was writing a children's book about a boy named Mordecai. Mordecai! He had an uncle named that!

We both had grandparents from Lithuania. We'd both had Labrador retrievers as children. We both loved Thai food, and political cartoons, and were both down at the Charles River early every morning—Jacques to ride his bike, me to go running.

Our birthdays were one day apart in May. A year and a day, to be exact, since he's a year older. 366 days. "Do you know what three hundred and sixty-six is?" I asked Julie, who still sounded skeptical.

"I think you're going to tell me," she said.

Three hundred and sixty-six happens to be the number of love poems Petrarch wrote to Laura in *The Canzoniere*. One for each day of the year, and then one more, to represent perfection. Perfection *plus*.

I was smitten, and it wasn't just Jacques's accent. I loved everything about him. I loved how tender he sounded when he talked about taking care of his tiny house, with its postage stamp of lawn and its burnished pears. It reminded me of the Little Prince swabbing out his miniature volcano each night, and in fact, Jacques looked to me like a dark-haired version of the Little Prince, a mop of curls and eyes an extraterrestrial shade of blue. By the time we reached New York, we'd exchanged phone numbers. When he got off at Penn Station, we waved passionately, like Yuri and Lara in *Dr. Zhivago*. The next week, back in Boston, he called me up, sounding shy, and asked me to meet him in the Square for dinner. The next night, too. By the following week, we were spending almost every evening together. "That was fast," Annie observed dryly, when I spent half my time at the English job fair that December phoning Jacques to report how my interviews had gone, and by January he was coming with me to visit universities where I had callback interviews. I didn't even pretend to be open-minded anymore. I didn't want to be in Tempe or Lubbock. I wanted to stay as close to Boston as possible. Georgetown, a short flight away, was by now my clear first choice. It also happened to be the best place for Jacques, if he were to leave Boston and come with me. That was a big if—it was way too soon for planning, as I reminded my mother and my sisters, one at a time. Sara, in a different time zone and pre-occupied with Geoff and her daughters, was long out of this phase of life. But Julie zeroed right in.

"It's too soon for any of that," I said.

"Hah," Julie said back.

She was on to me. Of course I was planning—I couldn't help myself.

I could see two different versions of the future. One was craggy and dim, hard to make out, and it scared me.

The other was lit up from underneath, sparkly. Later that spring, in a bay in St. Kitts, Jacques taught me how to snorkel. I'd never done this as a child—my father doesn't swim, and my mother hated getting her hair wet. At first I kept spluttering to the surface, afraid I was running out of air, but Jacques just held on and tugged me through the shimmery water, squeezing my hand every once in a while to signal whenever there was something just ahead. We saw fish of every gem-like hue: yellow, vermillion, sapphire blue. If you didn't think about it, if you just kept scissoring forward through the water, trusting your snorkel, there was this whole breathtaking world.

That's how I pictured the future I hoped for, being with Jacques. Luminous, shot through with sparks of unexpected color.

JACQUES CAME DOWN TO DC with me for my callback interview. The night after I gave my job talk at Georgetown, we met Julie and Jon for dinner in Adams Morgan. Halfway through the appetizers, Julie pulled me into the bathroom to tell me what she thought of him.

Julie had never liked anyone I'd gone out with before. She'd actually threatened to have me committed if I kept seeing the history grad student, who'd once spent a whole Thanksgiving dinner lecturing her on Stalin. Jacques, though . . . I waited, nervous. Julie was the first family member to meet him.

"His accent is nice," she said slowly, head to one side, as if deliberating.

I grabbed her arm. "Come on! What do you think?"

She burst out laughing. "I think he's great," she said.

She liked his twinkly eyes. And his sense of humor.

"That's important," she reminded me. "You have to have a sense of humor to survive Mom and Dad."

I nodded, afraid to agree. I didn't want to jinx this.

Julie, on the other hand, was in fast-forward mode. "You guys *have* to move here," she said. "You have to teach at Georgetown!" She'd been living in DC since law school, and she was sure we'd love it. It was a great city! Completely livable! Everything she said seemed to end in an exclamation point. They'd help us get settled! We could live with them while we were looking for a house!

Julie has always been ahead of me, planning-wise. If I'm type A minus (my mother's term), she's type A plus. "You guys can get married and get a place near us and we can raise our kids together!" she added under her breath, halfway back to the table.

To be honest, the thought had crossed my mind. But I was trying to put the brakes on. I was only here for a callback, I reminded myself. Jacques and I had only been seeing each other since October. Things couldn't happen that fast. Could they?

Sometimes, life goes your way. Miracle of miracles, I got *two* job offers. And one was from Georgetown. I was euphoric.

Back in Cambridge, one of my thesis advisors told me I had to turn Georgetown down. She closed her office door, paced back and forth, and explained that the other offer—not Lubbock, not Tempe, but a research university in the Northwest—was more prestigious. It had PhD students! She explained to me how it worked: You trained your PhD students and they went off and made a name for themselves, which reflected well on you. That was what I was supposed to be doing now—reflecting well on *her* after all her years of training me. It should have been clear to me that the bigger university was the better option. She seemed irritated with me, like I'd failed an important test. But I still had time to take the right offer and make up for it.

Up until this point, I'd always done whatever my professors told me. But I didn't want to move out West. I didn't want the big university with the lecture classes. It seemed like another planet to me: cold and distant, rimmed with phosphorescent highways.

I didn't just want a job—I wanted a whole life.

I took the Georgetown job. My first advisor stopped talking to me, but I still had my other advisor, who—her own office door closed—told me to take the job that I thought would make me happy.

Bit by bit, Jacques and I started making plans. Moving speeded everything up.

By March he was talking about coming with me, and by summer he'd sold his house (pear tree and all) and we were on our way.

We crammed a lot into a short period of time: flying to Michigan so he could meet my parents; renting a sweet, mildewy cottage on Buzzards Bay so we could practice living together; flying to South Africa and spending a week on his parents' farm north of Johannesburg, trying not to step on scorpions and watching baboons run in the hills behind their rondavel.

In August we drove down to DC, everything we owned squashed in the rented U-Haul behind us, Dave Brubeck booming on the stereo. I had a real estate agent lined up waiting to show us houses. We were in our honeymoon phase, though technically we weren't married yet, and Jacques still found my efficiency endearing. He didn't realize I was just in warm-up mode. I was only thirty—we still had lots of time.

FOR THOSE FIRST MONTHS, WASHINGTON felt charmed to us. It was a place of lucky, unasked-for coincidences—we could get good seats to shows last minute, it was easy to find parking, the people who dropped by turned into friends. The luck had to be coming from Jacques, since my family has never been lucky. But who could tell? Some of my natural anxiety seemed to be lifting. Maybe Jacques's expansive, spontaneous worldview was rubbing off on me. Moving to a new city without a place to live . . . "*Wow,*" was all Julie could say. (She and Jon, for one thing, were putting us up until the perfect spot turned up.) For my family, "last minute" has always been tantamount to chaos. Jacques, for his part, just assumed things would go our way.

And at first they did. After a short spate of house hunting we found a place we loved, a narrow town house facing the aviary in the zoo. We weren't married yet, so we set up a legal partnership, splitting everything fifty-fifty—Jacques had money from his house in Arlington, and I had the contents of my savings account—and after we signed stacks of papers, the house was ours. I couldn't get over it. I'd never owned more than a file cabinet and a futon. I loved every last stick of that house: the moldings; the sagging floorboards; even the ominous burn marks on the exposed brick in the kitchen. We met our neighbors, and to my amazement, one, Lori, turned out to be an old friend I'd known when I was studying in England. We'd lost touch, though I knew she was writing for a newspaper here. She and her husband, Dave, lived in a house that backed onto our alley, nine houses farther from the park.

It was easy to think nothing could go wrong in a place like this.

I loved my department at Georgetown. I had my own office with my name on a plaque on the door, and classrooms full of bright-eyed, attentive students who took notes on things I said. After being a graduate student for so many years, it was liberating to be an assistant professor. Students dropped by to see me and I loaned them books. I talked for hours with my colleagues. In graduate school, my advisors barely spoke to one another (or by the end, in the case of the first one, to me). Here, my colleagues met on purpose for drinks after work, sharing stories about students with a mixture of concern and genuine affection. This was a whole new world.

And people in DC were friendly! Much friendlier than in Boston. Sometimes people I didn't even know said hello on purpose.

We closed on our house and split a bottle of champagne in our empty dining room with Julie and Jon. I sent pictures of our unkempt garden to Sara. Life was good.

Granted, there were issues. For one thing, Jacques wasn't actually working in DC. Not officially. He was commuting, an arrangement that had evolved when he talked to his company over the summer about leaving his job. Every Tuesday morning he flew back to Boston for a day of meetings (US Airways, 7:00, Terminal B). Other days, he rode his bike to an office share in Foggy Bottom, where he kept flexible hours, held telephone conferences, and wrote computer code.

I worried about this. Could it last? Wasn't it tempting fate to fly so much? "It's fine," Jacques said, when I shared some of these worries with him. "What's the problem?"

Privately I call Jacques "the Optimist," and during those first months in DC his approach to life was so infectious I started adopting some of his phrases—like "what's the problem?" or "why not?"—phrases previously as unknown to me as the odd bit of Farsi or Aramaic. "It isn't like you," Annie pointed out, when she called to check on me. "You used to be so . . ." She was hunting for the word. "Skeptical," she managed, after a pause.

I could change, couldn't I?

Why not?

Secretly, though, I hated the commuting. I watched the Weather Channel every Monday night and dreaded approaching storms. I did research. Ice can collect on airplane wings at thirty-two thousand feet. Birds can be sucked into a plane's engine on takeoff. Drug-resistant infections circulate in closed cabins. The more you fly, the greater the chance of an incident.

"Nothing will happen," Jacques told me, over the static of the early morning forecast on NPR.

By spring, Jacques's one-day-a-week commute had turned into

two. He couldn't fit all the meetings in on Tuesdays. Thursdays, he said gamely, would be for "overflow."

"How," Julie asked me, "is *that* going to work?"

It was Thursday, a (new) Boston day for Jacques. Julie and I were sharing a hummus platter at Lebanese Taverna, near the Metro station.

"We're taking it one step at a time," I said, not meeting her eye. Of course, my worries had multiplied. Twice a week doubled the chance of disaster. Secretly I thought the travel was taking a toll on Jacques, who had started complaining about being tired and seemed to be losing his usual good humor. Some of his tolerance for my love of planning was wearing thin. We'd decided to get married in June, but Jacques wasn't sharing my mounting need to button down details— swatches of linens for the tables, tapes of jazz bands, and samples of butter cream frosting all elicited the same exhausted vote from him: *later.*

I didn't like it. All during the swath of ice storms and high wind that buffeted the East Coast from October till April, I kept my eyes fixed on the tiny font running along the lower edge of the TV screen, as if my anxiety alone could keep him airborne.

Premonition. Precipitation.

The phone would ring and I'd lunge for it, heart pounding— disaster! Notification of next of kin!—but it would just be my mother, curled up on the family room couch in Michigan with her before-dinner Chablis on ice and her Ancient History textbooks, checking to see how I was holding up.

My mother called each of us daily. She was emotional air traffic control, nudging us, alerting us, connecting us to one another. My sisters and I sometimes complained we didn't have to bother to catch up—we already knew each other's news inside out. With my mother, you didn't just get headlines, you got editorial and op-ed. My mother knew, for instance, that the shower in our master bath was leaking, the "good" caterer was too expensive, our next-door neighbor had a photo of himself posing with his ex-wife and Ronald Reagan that he liked so much he'd cut out a picture of his new wife's head and glued it to his old wife's body. On top of that, my mother knew the antics of our other neighbors, the ones with twin teenage daughters. One daughter climbed out the window at night to meet her boyfriend, like a twentieth-century Juliet; the other liked to squeeze her pet budgie in her mouth. "She could get diseases," my mother said, though it wasn't clear which twin she meant. My mother wasn't afraid to offer opinions on any of these stories, either to me or to Sara and Julie, who heard them secondhand, the way I heard *their* stories. Second marriages, political affiliations, curfews for teenagers, the problem with twins, hiring caterers or contractors . . . each of these, she believed, demanded advice and counsel.

If I wasn't forthcoming during these calls, my mother coaxed stories out of me, like an ace reporter. How was Jacques handling the commute? What was I having for dinner? What about Jacques—was he living on salty peanuts and Diet Coke? What was the A minus caterer like? Her ostensible worries—too much travel for Jacques, too much time alone for me—masked deeper ones. *What about tenure? Was I still looking for a position back in Boston? When would I finish the revisions on my book?*

When ran through our conversations like a mantra. None of this was ever directly stated—it was more like background noise. But trained as I'd been since childhood, like a hunting dog capable of detecting frequencies humans are deaf to, I could hear her real question loud and clear.

When were we going to have a baby?

She wasn't the only one wondering. That was on my mind, too. Constantly. I knew I was behind schedule. I needed to get going.

It was time to seize the day.

ALL THAT FIRST YEAR TOGETHER in DC, teaching, watching the Weather Channel, adopting a yellow Lab we named Bacchus, waiting for Jacques's taxi heading to or coming back from Terminal B, eating Ethiopian food with Julie and Jon, talking about flower-girl dresses for my nieces with Sara, I was thinking about babies.

I was thinking about babies all during our honeymoon in Portugal, tearing up and down the heat-mirage-laden highways of the Algarve. *Thinking* is the wrong word. It was more like channeling.

I counted backward. If we started trying next spring—

February. A Valentine's baby!

OK, problem. That would be in the middle of the semester. Not good. If we started sooner—

I counted. I did the math. I made up calendars. A May Day baby. A Fourth-of-July baby (like my mother). A Halloween baby. A Christmas baby.

I liked long, formal names with unexpected nicknames. *Alexandra. Nadia. Elisabeth.*

Maybe we could start trying now! I mentioned this to Jacques somewhere outside of Lisbon, looking for ceramics at a roadside stall.

Jacques didn't say anything. He was squinting noncommittally at a painted tureen, turning it around and around. What had looked like abstract markings from afar appeared up close to be rabbits fleeing pointy spears.

Jacques doesn't like to rush when it comes to major life choices. "A baby will change everything," he said. "Are we really ready for that?"

Ready? What is "ready"? Had I ever been anything else?

What We Knew

MY FAMILY DOESN'T DEFINE "READY" the way other people do.

Women in my family die young. For generations—as long as anyone can remember—they've all died from the same thing. Ovarian cancer. In my parents' house in Michigan, we had black-and-white photographs of all the dead aunts and grandmothers and great-aunts hanging in the hallway of our second floor. My mother had them all framed at the same time, white mats in silver, and somehow this added to the impression that the pictures were all really the same. Waiting for Sara or Julie to finish using the bathroom we shared when I was growing up, I used to walk up and down the hallway and look over this ill-fated, all-female family tree. They all looked like one another, these women, like sepia-colored ghosts, leaning on each other's arms, standing in front of antique jalopies, squinting in front of foamy spray on some unidentified beach. In one picture Sylvia, my mother's mother, five feet two and flaxen haired, had her arms linked with Pody, her younger sister. They were both laughing, their mouths wide open, maybe at something whoever was taking the picture had just said. You'd never guess, looking at them, what the future held: Sylvia dead at forty-three, Pody at forty-five. They looked so wholesome and unassailable, their gazes locked on the future like they'd never let go.

My mother was nineteen when Sylvia died. My sisters and I always knew this was the single most important thing about her. When I looked at my mother I used to picture Sylvia inside of her, like a tiny stopped clock.

Sylvia. Always Sylvia, her portrait haunting us with canny eyes. "If only you could've known Sylvia!" my father would exclaim wistfully from time to time. This was meant for my sisters and me, stuck to the present like glue. It wasn't that we didn't care. We weren't disinterested in *their* past, just in the past itself. My parents cared enough for all of us put together. They found the past mesmerizing—each had dedicated a profession to it—my mother, history; my father, psychoanalysis. The past for them was like a country they'd visited and preferred to our own. They were constantly comparing, as if our world—with its princess telephones, microwave ovens, eight-track cassette players, and color TVs—was a poor substitute for the one they'd given up. *Remember?* They'd exchange sidelong glances and we'd know an anecdote was coming. The Sylvia stories got rotated over and over again, and eventually we knew them so well we could recite them ourselves, like episodes from *I Love Lucy.* There was a whole cycle. The time Sylvia stood on a stool and yelled at my mother for using her new lipstick—Kissproof Red—without asking. She needed the stool because my mother (age fourteen) was already two inches taller than she was. Sylvia and her dancing clothes—ostrich feathers and beads. The summer Sylvia fell madly in love with a young man named Jerry at a lakeside club in

Wisconsin—he wore a white jacket, played the sax, and drank other people's whiskey. Like Scott Fitzgerald, my mother said, only Jewish. And without the novels. How they got married, Sylvia in a long ecru dress with a filmy veil. The years Jerry drank and drank and spent all their money, until one night Sylvia threw a Limoges plate at him, and another night—much later—he moved out and left them with nothing. How it was just Sylvia and my mother and their housekeeper Jennie, who lived with them. The winter Sylvia started working in a hat shop—her first job ever, she'd been a pampered first daughter— and learned to wrap parcels in brown paper with hospital corners, curling ribbon with a paring knife. The year the hat shop closed and they ran out of money but still kept Jennie with them, even when (eventually) Jennie and my mother had to share a double bed. The way Sylvia ironed her silk stockings, spitting on the iron first to test its heat. The time their cat ate tinsel hanging off their artificial Christmas tree and died in my mother's lap. Gray eyes still as stone.

My mother tried to keep Sylvia alive for us. She pointed out traits she thought we'd inherited from her: Sara's gift for watercolors, Julie's music, my love of poetry. But none of it seemed real. Sylvia was no more than a black-and-white photograph hanging in the hallway, laughing, arms linked with her younger sister, every bit as dead as she was. What could she possibly have to do with us?

Evidently, a great deal.

In the 1980s, the world began to change. My father, psychoanalyst by training and sleuth by nature, had been doing his homework. He was in touch with two different medical centers—one in upstate New York, founded when Gilda Radner died, the other at Creighton University, in Nebraska. Periodically he got bulging envelopes from one or the other of them packed with information. We knew cancer ran in our family—we just didn't know how. Now, researchers were beginning to put the pieces together.

It looked like we'd inherited more from Sylvia than a love of the arts. Dying young was another trait she'd passed on, and it was beginning to appear we were linked together in a long, fatal chain, one generation bound inextricably to the next. The only woman on my mother's side who'd made it past fifty was my great-grandmother Bea. She was a despot, but she lived to almost ninety, and Julie decided she liked her picture best. "I think I look most like Grandma Bea," she'd say hopefully, peering up in the hallway at a smudge of wavy, obsolete hair.

My mother wasn't interested in any of the information my father culled from Creighton's medical school or from the Gilda Radner Institute. She took a fatalist's point of view. "What will be, will be," she'd say with a shrug, sitting out on the deck highlighting a text on ancient Egypt for her AP students. *They freighted the boats of the dead with treasure so they would be prosperous in the afterworld.* What was the point in wasting time with worry?

My father felt differently. Medicine was the lens through which he saw misfortune. "See that man?" he asked us one night at a Chinese restaurant. He lowered his voice. "Bell's palsy," he said sadly, shaking his head. "His face is frozen that way. See how he only has half a smile?"

We saw.

Illness stalked the doorways of my childhood like Grendel. I used to thumb through the medical journals my father kept on the rattan coffee table in our family room, poring over pictures of skin ulcers that bloomed rose and apricot, like spoiled fruit. Petechiae rashes, fungi. Tumors lit up by green and vermillion dyes, like fireworks. Such vivid reminders of the body's frailties, and my father was determined to protect us from all of them.

First, he had my mother to save. He haunted her with articles gleaned from the geneticists at Creighton, urging her to have a hysterectomy from so early on I can remember no time when the word *ovary* wasn't linked for me to a sense of doom and inexplicable grief. Long before we'd gotten our periods for the first time, all three of us had been catechized: Grow up; have children fast; and get those things out of you.

Time bombs, Sara called them.

Ovary. The word was beautiful, like a poem—like things that open or encircle: *overture, oval, ovation*, but it was a sinister, destructive beauty. I pictured my ovaries inside of me like milkweeds, whispery, white pods ready to burst, and the slightest ripple or heartbeat might blow their seeds out, poisonous, to disperse their terrible harvest deep inside me. In between other things I wanted—for the Vietnam war to end, to become a judge, to write poetry—I wanted the curse on my family to be lifted. I wanted not to worry. I wanted to forget, to live my life the way other people did. And I tried. Though never exactly carefree, I pushed away worry the best I could. I had boyfriends, forgot our story for a while, then (shuddering) welcomed it back. Then pushed it away again. If I didn't think about it, it wouldn't happen. Couldn't the fates leave us alone? All the old relatives were dead, and my mother had never had a sick day in her life. I never even saw her sleeping. She was always up before us, awake after us; sharp-tongued, sharp-sighted; planning, cooking, reading, making lists. Maybe Sylvia had broken the curse and set us free.

Then in 1983, my second year at Oxford, studying metaphysical poetry and living in a mushroom-colored building without heat, my mother's only cousin—Gail, Pody's only child—was diagnosed with stage 4 ovarian cancer. She was forty-seven, only two years older than Pody had been when she died. The prognosis was bad. My mother described it all to me on the phone. "She woke up one morning and it was like she was eight months pregnant," my mother said, her voice trembling. Her whole abdomen filled with terrible cells. Gail—sweet, loving Gail, who loved discount shopping, who let me store my sagging couch in her basement each summer when I was an undergrad at Northwestern, whose vivid snapshots were glued right down in our own family albums among the living, not stuck up on a wall with the dead. Gail wasn't part of the past, she'd taught me how to make poached eggs and introduced me to Marshalls! She was part of the here and now.

My mother was out of her mind with grief. It's like Sylvia all over again for her, my father told us. Like posttraumatic stress.

I was twenty-three by then, and forty-seven didn't seem all that old anymore, and it clearly didn't to my mother at forty-nine, because soon after learning about Gail's diagnosis, she finally let the doctors "take everything out." She had a complete hysterectomy: her uterus and both ovaries removed. She wasn't taking any chances. Why leave anything behind to tempt the fates?

This wasn't like my mother. I knew she must be terrified.

She didn't tell any of us about the operation until it was over. I found out on the pay phone in the back of the Middle Common Room at Pembroke College, feeding octagon-shaped fifty-pence pieces into the octagon-shaped hole at the bottom of the phone. They hadn't wanted to worry us, my father explained. "And there was nothing you could do—from over there," my mother added. "It's much better telling you now it's over."

My father said the surgery had been "successful." The pathologists had gone over the tissue and it was all clean. Not a single cell awry. They'd gotten everything out of her.

"It's all about timing," he added, palpably relieved.

Timing meant my mother would survive.

Gail didn't. She rallied, relapsed, rallied again, but only briefly. It was a long, difficult struggle. She died on April 29, 1985, eleven days after her first grandson was born. They were in the same hospital, my mother told us, when she was finally able to say anything about it at all. Gail dying on one floor; her grandson born on another.

"Thank God Mom had the surgery," my sisters and I told each other.

Timing, it was becoming clear, was everything. *Timing* was different from time. Time was an abstraction, impossible to understand.

When I was little, my father took me once to the planetarium in Chicago and when I tilted my head back, trying to comprehend the artificial enormity, he whispered that everything we saw in space had already happened. It took light so long to reach us, he told me, that the stars we were admiring might already be dead.

Time, you couldn't do much about. *Timing* was different. Timing meant managing what you were allotted, making things work, taking control. Timing meant being on guard.

Timing meant we didn't define *ready* the way other people did. We always had to be ready. We were like evacuees, belongings squashed at our feet, waiting at an unknown border. There was no time to spare.

I don't remember exactly when I told Jacques all of this. Was it early on, in those wild, love-drunk early days of dating, staying up all night in his old Accord, naming constellations, lying back in each other's arms, enchanted with our different night skies and early histories? Or later, planning soberly, putting his house on the market, signing job contracts for DC? I don't remember a time when he didn't know what I know about my medical history.

I know he wasn't especially concerned. "Why worry? You can't control the future," he said.

I appreciated how calm he was, but underneath, I was afraid it meant he didn't really get it.

I tried to talk to him about heredity. About what we pass on.

Jacques shrugged. "Everyone has something," he said.

I didn't feel like I had "something," though. I felt like I had *this*. Known, assailable. Like a sharpshooter was out there, eye to the scope, waiting for me. Wherever I went, I stayed inside his compass.

Every so often the researchers at Creighton University mailed us diagrams, each woman in our family represented by a small circle. The ones who'd died from ovarian cancer had their circles colored in black. In the spring of 1985, they colored one in for Gail. The diagram looked grim, like the models of molecules we used to build in high school chemistry. Ours had way too many black circles in it—long life looked like a trait we hadn't been lucky enough to inherit.

In our twenties, my sisters and I dealt with this by staying busy. Sara was teaching elementary school in the Pacific Northwest, where she'd lived since graduation. She and Geoff, her high school boyfriend, married right out of college. Jenny was born a few years later, and then Rachel—both before Sara was thirty. Between teaching and being a mother, Sara barely had time to read the paper, let alone worry about our family history. But once she was done having children, she decided to go ahead and get the surgery over with—well ahead of schedule. Julie looked like she was on the fast track, too. She'd whizzed through law school and gotten her first job all by her midtwenties. She and Jon were both working a zillion hours a week and had already gotten married and bought a house in northern Virginia while I was still struggling through my orals.

For my part, I got through my twenties with a mixture of superstition and denial. I paid my parking tickets promptly. Finished my dissertation. If I was "good," whatever that meant, I figured the fates would leave me alone.

Just in case, I added a hefty dose of high Alpha Medicine. In graduate school I started a new phase of expert-worship: the best universities; the best residencies. Top doctors. Academic fame and fortune. I actually tried translating the Latin in the diplomas hanging on doctors' walls. Harvard—OK, that'll do—but was that a *magna* or a *magna* with highest honors? Why not a *summa*? Instead of ordinary physicals, I went to see a high-risk gynecologist at the Dana-Farber Cancer Institute. In those days, there was a whole department at the Dana-Farber dedicated to high-risk ovarian cancer, and I had ultrasounds and blood tests there twice a year. The blood test—CA-125— was new and relatively controversial—there could be false negatives as well as false positives. The test measured a tumor marker in the blood, and in theory if the numbers stayed low—under thirty-five—that was a good sign.

I didn't mind the blood work, it was the ultrasounds I dreaded. In order for the doctors to "visualize my ovaries," I needed to distend my bladder, drinking thirty-two ounces or more of water in the waiting room, and I'd sit there reading months-old issues of *Family Circle* magazine, palms sweaty, bladder aching, waiting my turn. Why are there never any windows in waiting rooms? They'd call my name— they always mispronounced it—and I'd head back into the dark, tunneled depths of radiology, my bladder swollen to bursting. Once on the table my heart would pound while the technician worked the cold wand back and forth inside of me, squinting at the monitor. Total silence. Back and forth with the wand, pressing murderously on my swollen bladder. I would lie there in misery, eyes straining to see what she saw: the gray shapes on the screen; the illegible shadows. Something would rise into view, like a gray, gibbous moon. What was that? Was it an organ, or a tumor? My heart would pound, long, slow beats: *not yet—not now—not this—not me—* It was always dead quiet in the darkened room; no expression on the technician's face. Then it would be over. I'd be free to get up, wipe the goop off myself with the blue paper gown, and tear to the bathroom before heading out to the waiting room, where a nurse, poker-faced, would ask me to fill out a questionnaire. One of the doctors at the Farber was running a clinical trial on potential links between talcum powder and ovarian cancer. You could guess his hypothesis from the order of the questions:

1. Do you use talcum powder? What brand? How often?
2. Do you smoke? How many cigarettes a day? A week?
3. Do you eat fatty foods?
4. Do you suffer from depression?
5. What does the word *risk* mean to you?

When I was finished—four "nos" and one "I'm not really sure"— I'd stuff my completed questionnaire in a wire basket along with one or two others. I didn't have much confidence the talcum powder theory was going to be proven any time soon. That was it. Six months would pass in a flash, and I'd be back again.

I lived from fear to fear.

Once in a while I'd see another patient or two in the waiting room, but none of us talked to each other or exchanged information. It was a lonely world, high-risk ovarian cancer.

I didn't say good-bye before we moved.

Instead, I headed down to Washington and left the Farber behind. I tried to act the way a thirty-year-old with a new job and a man she loved should act. Happiness was new and unfamiliar to me, like permanent good weather, and I just wanted to enjoy it. When it came time to look for doctors in DC, I skipped oncology and went straight to ob-gyns.

EVERYTHING ABOUT MY LIFE IN DC felt new. New man, new job, new house. I felt myself letting go of worry, bit by bit. I almost stopped worrying (*almost*) about cancer. For the first time in conscious memory, I stopped convincing myself each mysterious pain or bruise was the first symptom of a hideous, fatal disease. Instead of obsessing (was one of my pupils usually bigger than the other? Had that mole always been blurry at the edges?) I focused on ovulation and conception. I turned my laser beam from death to life. It was exhilarating. Being pregnant, I decided, was the opposite of having cancer. Just *thinking* about pregnancy gave me immunity.

And the best part was, I wasn't doing this alone. Julie was deep in baby planning, too. We traded information: best doctors. (The doctor we both coveted was Dr. Andrea Weiss, in Dupont Circle. But she had a long waiting list.) Basal-cell thermometers (where do you buy them and do they really work?). Stories about colleagues who got pregnant the first time they tried. Can you imagine? Getting pregnant now struck me as the world's greatest achievement. Who cared about Rhodes scholarships or Guggenheims? It was pregnant women who were geniuses. Imagine—producing life! If I couldn't be pregnant yet myself (and let me tell you, it wasn't for lack of interest), I wanted to talk about it. Not so much with Jacques, who was of course convinced things would happen "when the time was right." No discussion needed.

But with Julie, type A plus planner—*mon semblable—ma soeur!*

I VAGUELY REMEMBER HEARING SOMETHING that year about a "breast cancer gene." Was it late in 1990? Or early 1991? A friend of a friend, an oncologist at the National Cancer Institute, was talking about it at someone's house one night. I remember mentioning it to Julie, one Saturday afternoon, having coffee together in Virginia. It was all cast in the future tense—one day, they *may* be able to test women for certain kinds of breast cancer.

"I wonder what Mom would say about a test like that," I mused.

My mother had had breast cancer—a tiny, curable tumor—four years earlier. It was a freak thing—like a meteor falling out of the sky, was the way my mother described it. You worry and worry about wearing your seat belt, drive as carefully as you can, and then *wham*—a meteor comes along and smacks you in the head. (My mother, mixer of metaphors.)

Thank God, this had been a small meteor. One that let her get up, brush herself off, and go on. Back to seat belts and ordinary worries.

"Oh, Mom would hate that," Julie said. "You know how she is."

I nodded. I knew. My mother, AP History teacher and ultrarationalist, was at heart more mystic than scientist. In her mind, asking too much of the future was bad luck.

"I wonder if I'd want to know," Julie said, fiddling with her spoon. "If we had breast cancer in our family the way we have ovarian cancer. Would you want to take a test like that and find out?"

"I don't think so," I said. I didn't give it a lot of thought—it sounded like science fiction to me. Some people like speculating about things like that—my roommate in college was always trying to drag me into hypothetical quandaries at three in the morning. Like cryogenics. Would you want to be frozen right before you died so they could wake you up in a thousand years, when ninety was barely middle age? Or would it be too lonely, wandering around in a world filled with unrecognizable gadgets and people ten or more generations younger than you were?

Personally, I'm not crazy about imponderables, which is what this breast cancer test sounded like to me. Like the movie I saw years earlier when a team of people got shrunk down and injected into a human body and shot through the arteries, wide-eyed, pointing at corpuscles like awestruck tourists.

No one had to tell me I came from a cancer family. Wasn't it obvious? All you had to do was look at the pictures hanging on our upstairs wall. A blood test—what would be the point of that? Suppose it came back negative? Would I really believe it if someone told me I was home free?

Not likely. Not when I'd known about the sharpshooter since childhood. His X-ray vision, his slow, stealthy prowl.

Anyway I didn't want to talk about cancer tests. I wanted to get back to the one subject that mattered: pre-pregnancy. The most fertile times of month. Whether it was true you could really tell you were pregnant even before you missed your period. How could that be? Could the body really be so transparent? When it came to conception, I wanted all the foresight possible.

Julie was moving to another branch of the would-you-want-to-know tree. Would you want to know the baby's sex if you could tell from the ultrasound?

For Julie, that one was easy. *Definitely*. It would help when it came time to decorate and choose names.

I wasn't sure. I thought maybe not. This must be why I get the minus in my version of type A, but I actually *liked* the idea of not knowing. A stretch when everything was up for grabs.

Boy or girl? I hadn't gotten that far. I just wanted a *baby*.

"Do you ever worry," Julie asked me, still fiddling with her spoon, "about passing on the ovarian stuff? If we have daughters?"

I shook my head, not really thinking before I answered. Maybe living with Jacques was rubbing off on me. "By the time our children have to worry about this . . . ," I said, shrugging. It all seemed so far off, like a bright frontier. "By then," I said, half-believing it, "they'll have figured this whole thing out."

Julie nodded. Thirty-five years from now. Who could fathom that vast a stretch of time?

"Besides, wouldn't you still rather have your life than not?" I asked her. "Even if worse comes to worst?"

She nodded. Half a life was better than none, we'd always figured.

Lives half full, not half empty. Maybe we were optimists, too, in our own way. We circled around other topics, then zoomed back in. Who wanted to focus on doom and gloom when all of life lay before us?

All I wanted was to be pregnant. It was hard to focus on teaching, on researching time measurement in the seventeenth century.

I had an old empire-waisted Laura Ashley dress that looked like a maternity dress, and sometimes when I was alone, I'd try it on and sneak glances at myself in the mirror. I thought it looked great. Once I even wore it to Safeway.

Emily

WE COULDN'T HAVE PLANNED IT in a million years. Julie's due date: December 27. Mine: December 31. What are the odds, people would say. Of course there were jokes. "What is it, you're getting a twofer? A special family deal?" a woman in the doctor's waiting room asked when she saw Julie and me together. (We had the same doctor. Andrea Weiss, "expert" ob-gyn, top doctor in *Best of Washington* three years in a row. A friend of Lori's campaigned for us, and Dr. Weiss squeezed us both in.) We'd laugh politely, but we both knew this was too important for humor. It was a modern-day fable. *Two girls from the same (previously unlucky) family get pregnant at the same time, break their family's terrible spell, and live happily ever after.*

———

WHY DON'T POETS WRITE ABOUT pregnancy? All that spring, my second in Washington, Julie and I were transformed. Separately, together. I'd never felt anything like this. Expansive. Exquisitely sensitive to everything—smell, taste, touch. Excited, exhausted, exhilarated, nauseated, sleepy, giddy. Craving salt. Craving sleep. Dreaming of light, shadow, membrane. Bewilderingly, absurdly happy. Calling Julie constantly. For once, our timing was defiantly, spectacularly right. My mother was beside herself with excitement and planning. First she'd come to me, then to Julie. Or first to Julie, then to me. Even her maddening comparisons struck us now as funny. Who cared? Life was blessed, the rhododendrons brimming with color—magenta, fuchsia, lavender. Next came the cherry blossoms, garlanded with tourists. We moved through bloom and bracken, delirious, counting forward. How had we managed—without planning—to get pregnant, both of us, at more or less the same minute? What god smiled down on us? This one small miracle apparently lifted the spell, my parents were charming and benign, good humor reigned on our planet, schedules relaxed, warmth encircled us, released from anxiety, from high-risk gynecology, free to eat, nap, dream, grow larger.

Starting now, we told each other, our luck would be good. We'd have these babies and the old nightmares would evaporate. The babies would grow up together, sturdy and smart. We'd push strollers together in Rock Creek Park. We'd find playgroups. We'd be our own playgroup! For once, everything we didn't know seemed luminous.

Our family history was starting over. That's the thing about babies—they reset the clock.

WE'VE ALWAYS BEEN CLOSE, JULIE and I. It's funny, because we're farther apart than Sara and I in actual years. Maybe in this middle phase of life, our real age gets overwritten by our age as parents—instead of being twenty-eight or thirty-two, we become instead "mothers of toddlers" or "young women trying to have babies." I'm not sure.

I just know that spring and summer Julie and I became inseparable. We talked twice, sometimes three times a day. She'd find a sale at A Pea in the Pod and call me; I'd find an article on mercury counts in dolphin-safe tuna and call her back; we'd have the Morning Weight and See, as Julie called it, with my mother joining in for rounds of the Comparison Game on the phone every afternoon. "Julie," she'd tell me, "has already interviewed *five* pediatricians," or "Julie only gained two pounds this past month," or "Don't you think that having a fenced-in yard with actual grass might be nice, once the baby comes? Julie and Jon *love* northern Virginia. . . ." The minute the conversations with my mother ended, I'd call Julie back to do my meanest imitation of them, except for the days (of course there were days) when my mother actually got to me, and after I hung up I sulked and refused to answer Julie's calls.

But most of the time, we derided her together.

Julie and Jon drove into the city and we took long walks in Rock Creek Park, throwing sticks for Bacchus and scolding him with experimental voices when he loped too far away. After our walks, we'd order takeout and Jon and Jacques would joke about time-sharing a crib. Time-sharing a doctor. Julie was ahead of me, planning-wise. She'd picked a rug for the baby's room by May, a pediatrician by June, and by month four, just after my mother's birthday, had already chosen a name. Emily. I figured Julie needed to be ahead, since their baby was due four whole days before ours. Sometimes she'd call me just to say the name out loud, like an incantation. "Em-il-leee." She'd speed it up, slow it down, the way she used to play the Chopin prelude she labored on all through eighth grade. It was always Emily. Once, I think, it may have been Margot—then Emily again.

"What if it's a boy?" I asked. As if I didn't know. In my family, we just have girls.

"It's not a boy," she'd say, and laugh.

She kept a calendar; I kept a calendar. We pawed through little outfits at Baby Gap, honing our taste. We both liked primary colors—

hated lace and pastels. The babies were due in the same month. December, Capricorn. Patient and practical. Solstice babies, due in the month when the northern hemisphere goes dark and cold, like a closed fist. Two small sparks of light and life.

Julie usually had her appointments before me—days before, sometimes a week before—and afterward we'd compare notes, doing a postmortem on the nurses. The one with the icy hands. The one with the overbite and the compulsive questions about acid reflux. Julie took her alpha-fetal-protein test, I took mine; she Scheduled her ultrasound, I scheduled mine; like a two-step, a fox-trot, she stepped forward, I stepped back. It was July, I had goose bumps from the air-conditioning in the study, I was poring over photocopies of calendars from the sixteenth century, trying not to listen to Bacchus scratching the kitchen door, wanting out, and when the phone rang I started laughing when I saw the number on caller ID, having already talked to her twice that morning, once to hear that her boss had reassigned her to yet another dismal case, once to complain that my mother had returned the perfectly nice scarf from Nordstrom we sent for her birthday because it was "too expensive" and she'd never wear it. I was all set to hear another story about the Justice Department or those anticipated syllables—"Em . . . il . . . leee"—but it wasn't Julie, weirdly enough, it was Jon, and I was still half-laughing as I tried to change gears and make sense of what he was saying, *hospital, ultrasound*, it was all jumbled, I could barely hear him, and then it wasn't him. Julie took the phone, her voice clear as a bell. "I had my ultrasound, hon." Pause. "The baby—" Her voice broke. She was nineteen weeks pregnant, half a week in front of me. Beginning of month five. "The baby died. I have to go to the hospital."

I was trying to catch up with her. My heart began to pound, long, slow beats.

"I have to have it anyway," she said.

It was a girl. They could tell from the ultrasound.

Emily.

Jon took the phone again. Tried to fill me in. The technician had taken forever. She kept fiddling with the monitor. Finally she left to get the doctor, and then the radiologist herself came in and fiddled some more, and then, after two or three agonizing minutes, she told them: She couldn't find a heartbeat. "She thinks," Jon said brokenly, "it may have happened a week ago."

Their baby had been dead for a week, and they hadn't known. None of us had known.

I tried to work my way back through the past week, remembering what we'd been doing. A few days earlier, Saturday morning, at her kitchen table, Julie and I had been bent over pictures of nurseries in one of those articles we derided, "Making Your Spare Room Ready for Baby." Scorning the bunnies and the sheep.

I thought, *We will never go back to that again. Uneventful is over.*

We were back to grief and worry. To bodies that betrayed us. I remember how I'd been convinced being pregnant gives you immunity from grief. *What had I been thinking?*

She got back on the phone, her voice like a stranger's.

"I have to go to the hospital. Dr Weiss says I still have to go through labor."

It was like we'd changed genres—sitcom to tragedy. I called Jacques, but I was crying so hard he could barely understand what I was saying. I kept stumbling around, picking things up and putting them down again, like a parody of a woman in labor who doesn't know what to take to the hospital. Finally I stuffed something to read and a stray roll of Tums in my book bag.

Jacques met me at Columbia Hospital for Women. Not in one of the peach-and-celadon rooms we visited later with New Age music piped in, not even in Labor and Delivery, but on a surgical floor, a beige, no-nonsense hallway with closed doors where we found Julie propped up in bed wearing a hospital gown, her face white as the sheet behind her, Pitocin dripping into a line in one hand, monitors bleating. My breath felt ragged. Jacques kept rubbing my arm and telling me I had to stay calm. *Stay calm*—a funny phrase, when you think about it, since I wasn't calm in the first place. I'm never calm. We were in and out of the room, Dr. Weiss was there, stricken and grave, a sober-faced nurse with her, and they both kept telling us, *go home.* They said it would be hours before Julie gave birth. "You need to go home and rest," the nurse kept saying.

"Go home, hon," Julie said, her eyes lifeless. "*Please.*"

I looked at Jacques, and he nodded. "They need some privacy right now," he told me in the hallway. Just before we got to the main exit I grabbed on to him.

It was the most inexplicable feeling, like something inside of me the size of a stitch had just pulled taut and released. A spider unspooling its first strand of web. A match catching and holding.

"The baby," I said, my mouth opening. "I think—"

"What is it?" Jacques was ashen-faced.

I shook my head. I figured it out as I answered him, as if the words themselves gave this meaning. "I think the baby—moved."

Here, of all improbable places. And *now.*

We like to think life and death are opposites. Sometimes it's hard to fathom how close they are. Two sides of the hourglass, sand thickening at the bottom, running down to nothing from above.

Emily was born at four in the morning, nineteen weeks old. A grief counselor came. They offered Julie and Jon the chance to hold her. They made a print with her heel in cement and told them they'd found it helps to have some tangible memento of the baby to "commemorate the loss." Most of this I heard later through my mother, who arrived the next day, shell-shocked, tight-lipped, unspeakably sad, shuttling back and forth in taxis between Julie and Jon's house and ours. I found out some things right away, some things later, after Julie and Jon learned Emily had something terribly wrong—a missing chromosome at number thirteen, a condition so anathema to life she would have died at birth or just after if Julie had lasted to term.

Jacques lay next to me at night, staring up at the ceiling. "It's really mysterious, making a baby," he said. "You think you can map it all out, you can plan all of this, but you can't, really. You just can't."

I nodded in the dark. I couldn't answer.

MY MOTHER STAYED THREE DAYS. We felt awkward and uncomfortable around each other, both of us trying hard not to say the wrong thing. I called Julie over and over again, but Jon just kept saying she couldn't talk.

Julie and Jon had lost Emily. And for a while, I felt like I'd lost Julie.

In the first days after she got back from the hospital, Julie was surrounded by a sad flurry of activity. Jon was there with her. There were phone calls, flowers, people reaching out. Sara and Geoff called from Olympia. My father called between patients. Friends and colleagues sent flowers. But at the heart of it all, there was an almost unbearable silence: all the plans gone, doctors' visits canceled, the door to the baby's room closed. Jacques and I came over and tried to keep them company, but it was clear they wanted to be alone. They bought a tiny Japanese maple and planted it in their garden.

"I'll call you when I can," Julie said, barely looking at me.

Every day I stared at the phone, willing it to life, willing her to call, but, "You understand," she'd say when I tried calling her, or, "I can't, hon, I just can't." My mother, back in Michigan, called every afternoon, filling me in. She told me Julie was thinking about taking a leave of absence from work. In August, she and Jon went to Maine together to spend some time alone, away from DC. Time just to be on the beach, to be together.

They loved Maine, my mother reported, once they were back home in Virginia again. It reminded Julie of Charlevoix, the place in northern Michigan we always went on vacation in the summers. "It was such a relief for her, being away from DC," my mother added.

I held the phone away from my ear, staring at the wall.

Julie and I were going to do this together, I kept thinking. We were going to have the babies at the same time! I missed her constantly. I went to see Dr. Weiss. August, September. I got bigger. Fall came, I started teaching again. In my new course, Writing the Self in Early Modern England, we started by reading *The Return of Martin Guerre*, the story of a peasant in sixteenth-century France who leaves an unhappy marriage, joins the army, and disappears. When he comes back, his marriage is much better, the community loves him. He's a kinder, much more likeable man. But events unfold, and it turns out he isn't who he claims to be after all—he's an imposter. The real Martin Guerre died at war, and a soldier who knew him came back to the village assuming his identity. How can someone walk away from his life and someone else just take his place? How is such a thing possible?

"Didn't they know it wasn't him?" one student objected. "How could he just pretend to be someone he wasn't?"

"We don't always get to choose," I told her. "We like to think we always stays the same. That we're the same person, all our lives. But it doesn't always work that way. Some things are beyond our control."

LIFE GOES ON. WHEN YOU'RE pregnant, that fact is doubly true. I was getting bigger by the week. I could mark the passage of time by my outgrown maternity clothes—*that was August, when the blue jumper still fit. That was September, when I wore those black leggings every day.* The baby moved now and I could feel it all the time. I could see it moving when I looked in the mirror. We were getting ready. In October, Jacques and I started working on the nursery. We were moving on—we had to. But with each thing we did, each plan we made, I thought about Emily.

The tree they planted for her was less than two feet tall, with only the slightest furring of leaves. They had to stake it on all sides so the wind wouldn't blow it over. They made an appointment with a geneticist at Johns Hopkins—an expert. They were "moving forward," my mother said, and she made that sound like a good thing. Better than moving backward, I guess, but *back* was what I missed. Every morning, around the time Julie and I always talked, I tried to stay busy so I wouldn't listen for the phone to ring. My mother took it on herself to keep me up-to-date. She told me I needed to understand that Julie was "wrecked."

"It's life-changing for them," my mother said. "They're rethinking everything. Why they live where they live. Why they work where they work."

Everything.

I felt a little like Martin Guerre, pacing around in a life that no longer felt completely like mine.

IN LATE OCTOBER, JACQUES AND I started prenatal classes. We learned how to pant during labor and how to choose a focal point to stare at during contractions. Jacques tried rolling a tennis ball, hard, into the lower part of my back. We sat in a circle with people we didn't know and practiced diapering a plastic doll. "Parenthood," our teacher told us, "is a journey. As with every journey, you have to start with one small step." I couldn't believe she could say that with a straight face. I took a deep breath, passing the doll to the lobbyist on my right. When he stared at me, I realized I was holding it by its ankle.

I threw myself into teaching. In November, Lori and Dave gave Jacques and me a baby shower. Even though I knew Julie wouldn't come—she'd called, choked up, to apologize in advance for not being there—I couldn't help looking around for her, the whole time I was opening boxes with tiny outfits and ingenious baby devices. Once the doorbell rang and I looked up, hopeful. But it was only one of the twins from next door.

AFTER THANKSGIVING, JACQUES AND I went back to the hospital to take a tour of the prenatal wing.

"Has your pregnancy been uneventful?" the form asked. All I could do was check a box for Yes or No. There was no space to write about Emily.

I checked the box for Yes—*uneventful*. But I knew it wasn't true. There had been these things: This tiny lost cousin. This danger skirted, this ineluctable will to survive.

Ninth Month

THE LAST STAGE OF PREGNANCY, according to my *What to Expect* book, is a time to think and plan ahead. But you shouldn't forget to "reinforce romance." The authors recommended going out at least once a week together to do something "special (and unexpected)"— like miniature golf. Or hitting the flea market. You weren't supposed to forget your partner. "At dinner," they advised, "spend at least some time asking about his day, talking about yours, discussing the day's headlines . . ."

THIS SOUNDED LIKE GOOD ADVICE, but in our case, it wasn't happening. Jacques was working late most nights, trying to finish up a project before the baby came. He thought this was a good time to squeeze in a few extra loops to Boston. So instead of discussing the day's headlines with him or doing something unplanned or unexpected, I lay alone on the couch eating Stoned Wheat Thins and watching the Weather Channel. Between crackers, I worried.

Here were my worries, in order of intensity:

The baby wasn't growing the way it was supposed to. I had reason to worry. After Julie and Jon lost Emily, one of my tests came back outside the normal range. It was too late for an amnio, so we did what Dr. Weiss advised, which was to sit tight and try to stay calm. By my thirtieth week, there was another problem. According to the ultrasounds, the baby looked too small. Dr. Weiss, her voice taking on a new edge, told me I had what is known as "an inhospitable womb." At each visit, she measured me, frowned at the ultrasound, and clicked away with her computer mouse. *Click click click.* The baby wasn't thriving the way it should, she told us. It wasn't a crisis, but we needed to be aware of it. There were several possible reasons for this, but the question was what to do. One option would be to deliver the baby early and let an incubator finish things up.

I tried to work through the phrase "inhospitable womb." I was a Midwesterner. I used to bake my teachers cookies in middle school. I joined a sorority in college where we learned how to greet people at the door and serve chocolate fondue with the right-size napkins. How could my womb be *inhospitable*? It wasn't fair, I complained to Jacques. It was bad enough coming from a family with doomed ovaries. I didn't need an unfriendly womb on top of that.

Jacques told Dr. Weiss we would prefer to avoid the incubator option, and Dr. Weiss nodded, as if we were talking about room reservations at an overcrowded hotel. *OK, fine, we'll stick with the cramped single. Click click click.* "Also, the baby is still breech," she reminded me. "If it doesn't turn on its own—"

Worry number two. The baby, in addition to being small, was breech: right side up, instead of upside down, the position that's supposed to happen naturally by thirty weeks or so. What if the baby wouldn't turn upside down on its own and I needed a C-section and either the baby or I or *both* the baby and I hemorrhaged and died, like on an episode I'd seen once on *ER*? If it were just me who died, what would I have left behind for the baby? In the early modern period, women sometimes wrote journals to their unborn children, the likelihood of dying in childbirth was so great. Usually these journals were filled with elaborate instructions on how to lead a life of Christian devotion. I had no idea what wisdom I hoped to impart to our baby. *Be like Jacques. Live your life. Stay informed, be smart, but don't obsess. But don't be only like Jacques, not if you want time to return the rental car and still make the plane. Don't be like me or like Jacques. Be like yourself. Keep a sense of humor. Stay out of dark alleys. Brush your teeth, read good novels, use protection. Take a class in self-defense.*

It was too late. I'd left no instructions behind, only a wad of receipts and my notes on seventeenth-century timepieces. If I died, the baby would have to figure everything out on its own, without so much as a Post-it note for guidance.

Worry number three. From time to time, the baby stopped moving. Dr. Weiss claimed this happens when the baby sleeps and is perfectly normal, but I didn't believe her. Look at Jacques when he slept, he flailed like a drowning man! I didn't trust stillness, even during slumber. When the baby hadn't moved for a while, what I did was to manipulate the sides of my belly with both fists, *push push push*, just to wake it up a little. *Wake up, little one! Wake up!* Was this hospitable or inhospitable? Usually, the baby (sweet baby) kicked back in response. We were getting to know each other, this baby and I. Once or twice, though, it didn't move so much as a centimeter, despite all my knuckling, and I had to head over to Dr. Weiss's office for a glass of orange juice and a stress test. After a few of these episodes, Dr. Weiss's nurses knew me by heart—my file was thick as a phone book.

What if the baby turned out like me and not like Jacques? If it was a girl, then at least in this one way she would be like me, first and foremost. Susceptible to everything I'm susceptible to. Inhospitality. Chronic worry. Compulsive clock-watching and calendar marking. Second-guessing. Fear of heights.

What if the baby turned out like Jacques and not like me? If it was a boy, how would I know how to play with it or what to teach it? What if he was chronically late or disliked poetry or wanted to be a skydiver or a flamethrower?

Or what if the baby was like neither of us and we had nothing in common with it and had to sit around the dinner table for the next two decades wracking our brains for something to talk about?

ONE THING I DIDN'T WORRY about was whether the baby would inherit a disposition for ovarian cancer. I don't know why, but I just didn't. Maybe I just wouldn't let myself go there. Maybe it was because fundamentally I didn't think that would be a deal breaker, even if it were true. Presumably it *was* true, because it was all we knew. I'd lived thirty-two years thinking I had a very high chance of getting ovarian cancer, but I'd never once wished I hadn't been born. Yes, I worried about my health. Constantly. But even so, life—even life with risks—seemed like a much better deal than no life at all.

And of course, there was always the science fiction of the future. Good humanist that I was, I secretly believed science could do anything. Remember what Julie had said about finding that breast cancer gene?

Who knew what they'd find next?

By the time our children were old enough to worry about cancer, they could probably just go to the doctor's and get outfitted with computer chips like jewelry that lit up whenever a cell malfunctioned. *Warning! Unruly cell division at 986CR97! Maintenance required!*

I didn't worry about the baby inheriting my bad genes. But then, I'm only type A minus. What my mother would call a worrier-in-training.

THE FIRST DAY OF MY last month of being pregnant. Drizzle, fog, Washington's raw, filmy version of winter, 163.8 pounds on the kinder of our two scales. Wearing my *Glamour*-Don't wellies and Jacques's parka, I huffed up seventeen stairs to the second floor of Ignatius Hall in the middle of a stampede of students. I had a final exam to give in English 263, Writing the Self. After that, I'd be done for the semester. More than that—I had the whole next semester off, plus the summer. Eight and a half months yawning in front of me.

I've never liked finals. I like the first weeks of class, so much possibility, nobody upset yet about their grades or pigeonholed as The One Who Talks Too Much or The One Who Spilled Her Coffee on the Lacrosse Player. Endings are harder. We all want to tie everything together, but instead it comes down to this: blue books. The clock ticking. All of us worried we haven't said what we really meant.

My students filed in one by one, wearing flannel pajama pants and Hoyas sweatshirts. The room smelled of coffee and shampoo. It was too warm in the building and once the exam started they were all squirming, alternating furious bouts of writing with long pauses in which they stared out the window, faces blank. I'd given them essay questions instead of IDs—open-ended questions about self-fashioning—but there was still so much collective pressure. Every fifteen minutes, I heaved myself off the table and wrote the time on the board. My watch was just out of sync with the university bells, which gonged a few minutes after each pronouncement.

Ten forty-five. One hour and fifteen minutes left.

They looked up at me, shiny haired, smooth eyed. Monica LeGraf opened her water bottle, slurped noisily, and sighed. I crossed and uncrossed my legs, eye on the clock.

I'd never actually come right out and told them I was pregnant, assuming it was obvious. But you'd be amazed what college kids don't assume. "You're kidding!" Monica had exclaimed when she came to my office hours the week before the exam, and I told her I was going to be staying home with the baby next semester. "I didn't know—" And she'd glanced down at my spreading girth, nonplussed. Then, heartened, she grinned. "My mom's expecting, too," she confided.

One touch of pregnancy makes the whole world kin. Last year, someone had mistaken me for an undergraduate. Now, I looked like everybody's mother.

Pregnancy felt different, now the end was in sight. Time felt material in a new way. Twenty-eight days left. Twenty-seven. Twenty six. The baby was creating its own calendar and nothing we did could change it.

Everything had a new kind of finality now. My last class. My last lunch with colleagues. My last attempt to swim laps in the pool at Yates. I made plans with friends, knowing next month everything would be different.

> Essay Number 1. Choose any two characters we have studied this semester and in a well-organized, focused essay, explain how selfhood is defined in opposition to an "other" or antagonist. Think about what characters include in their self-representation as well as what they leave out.
>
> Be sure to consider what changes as well as what stays the same.

Fifteen minutes left.
What changes. What stays the same.
Ten minutes. Five minutes.
Time.

JULIE AND I HAD STARTED talking again at some point in the early fall. It took effort at first, but little by little it got better. At first we stuck to the phone, which seemed safest. Usually I called her, instead of vice versa, and I tried to gauge from the sound of her voice whether she was up for hearing from me or not. We kept things light. We didn't talk about Emily. In fact, we didn't talk about anything having to do with pregnancy, though there were things, were we back in our real previous lives, I would have loved to tell her. How distended I looked from the side. How I woke up at night with awful cramps in my feet and had to hobble out of bed gasping in pain and crouch on the cold bathroom tiles until the spasms subsided. How my colleague Valerie had given me a large cordless drill as a baby present, telling me (slightly ominously) that in time, I'd learn what it was for.

I didn't tell Julie about the inhospitality of my womb or the breechness of the baby or the multiplications of worry.

It was lonely, shoring up all the things I didn't tell her. Like I'd lost a twin and was suddenly lumbering through life alone.

Little by little, we started doing things together again. In October we met a few times at our favorite place—the café at Kramerbooks, in Dupont Circle. In November I drove out to northern Virginia to have brunch with her. The room they'd set up as a nursery was filled with packing boxes, still folded, and towers of masking-tape rolls.

"What's going on?" I asked her.

Julie shrugged. "We're putting some stuff in storage," she said evasively.

I stared her down, and she relented. "Jon wants to put the house on the market," she admitted. "The Realtor thinks we'll get a better price if it's uncluttered."

What did she mean, *he wanted to put their house on the market?* Where were they going?

They weren't definitely leaving the area, she assured me. It was just in case. Just to keep their options open. Who knew—maybe they'd move back into the city, into Cleveland Park or Chevy Chase. Maybe they'd rent for a while. Anyway, they weren't in a hurry. It would probably be ages before they figured out the next step.

I doubted that. Once Julie gets an idea, there's no stopping her. But Julie didn't want to talk about this now—that much was clear.

We dropped the subject. We talked about little things. We got together once a week or so, and talked about everything except what really mattered. Emily. How she was doing. How pregnant I was getting, what she and Jon wanted. Why she was still packing. Where they were headed.

My mother dropped the bombshell on the phone. "So," she said, in her best confiding voice. "Can you believe it? About Maine? Did you talk to Julie yet about the job?"

"What job? What about Maine?" I shot back, and instantly she was contrite, guilt-ridden, *oh no, nothing, no, she should tell you herself—I just thought, you know—*

She thought Julie would've told me already. Clearly. Because why wouldn't she?

Now I knew two terrible things: Julie and Jon were moving, and Julie had told my mother and not me.

Anyone who's ever been in a relationship triangle knows what this is like. In my family, the triangles got drawn and redrawn with all the intensity and firepower of a medieval romance. Sometimes it was with my sisters: Sara, Julie, me. Sometimes it was Sara, Julie, and my mother. But at this stage, it was my mother, Julie, and me, all pining, yearning, fury, competition, and one-upmanship. Who told what. When. Who said what, who gave what, who got what, who won what. Who had the upper hand.

All that fall, I'd felt like Julie, having lost Emily, was winning the Love War. She was tragic and suffering and my mother pored over every minute of every one of her days like a rabbi scouring the Talmud for signs of messiahhood. I, on the other hand, was bloated, pregnant, ordinary, with nothing but an inhospitable womb to evoke compassion. I knew how infantile all of this was, but I couldn't help myself.

Now, Julie and Jon were moving, and my mother knew all about it, and I knew nothing.

I fumed for days. Fine! Let her move to Portland, an ice cube of a city, hours from anything that mattered. As if I cared. We'd be *fine* here on our own, with our cordless screwdriver and our yet-to-be-purchased crib.

I didn't need my mother either, thank you very much. And I let her know that.

"Why don't I come in when you have the baby and stay for a few weeks?" she suggested one afternoon on the phone, in her most chipper, there's-no-reason-for-anyone-to-be-mad-at-anyone voice.

I evaluated her tone. Was she being dutiful? Did she really want to come, or was this perfunctory?

"That's OK, we're good," I said. Testing.

Silence. Hurt silence.

"We want to get our feet on the ground before you come out," I added, amending. Of course I wanted her! But I wanted her to *want* to come—to want *me*. In my unhappy heart, I pictured my mother crawling on her hands and knees through Julie and Jon's future Portland house, spritzing Lysol, scrubbing and readying things for them, while our baby came (feetfirst) into a lonely, alien world, bereft of family. No loving aunts and uncles waiting. No grandparents. An undersized waif, an almost orphan!

"You and Julie need to talk," Jacques said, while I crouched on the cold bathroom tiles, trying to get my foot cramps to subside. "You won't feel better until you do."

I didn't want to talk to Julie. I felt abandoned, lonely, obscenely big. I could barely see my feet when I looked down. I missed coffee, and Diet Coke, and wine, and Orbit, and sleeping more than three hours at a time, and being able to breathe. I missed my old self. I missed what Julie and I had been.

Now, the tables had turned. Julie called repeatedly, and I was the one who didn't answer. "I know Mom told you about Portland. We need to talk," she said on one of the multiple messages she left, which I listened to while drinking weak herbal tea, my eyes narrowed at the answering machine. Let her suffer. She was leaving me here alone, wasn't she? *Off to colder pastures.*

"Stop torturing yourself. Talk to her," Jacques said, while I lay on the couch knuckling the baby back into motion.

Finally, I caved in. I called her back.

She and I met in a café in Georgetown. The place was packed with students, all so healthy-looking and in such high spirits, talking up a storm, holiday shopping. I ordered chamomile tea, looking irritably at her espresso.

I held out for a few minutes, until I couldn't stand it anymore. Then I told her how I felt. How lonely, how abandoned. How guilty.

She knuckled her eyes. She couldn't really talk about Emily, she told me. Not yet. Maybe once she and Jon were pregnant again. But now—

A tear plopped down on the table.

"And *Mom*," I said, switching gears. "All I hear about from Mom is you and Jon! She can't talk about anything else. She's obsessed."

She loves you more than me, I thought idiotically, though I didn't say it.

Julie let out a long, sad sigh. "She's unbelievable," she said. "Do you know what she said to me when she came out here in July?"

I shook my head.

"I'd just gotten home from the hospital, and she walked into our kitchen and looked at me and burst into tears. And she said, 'But you're usually so good at growing things!'"

We both thought about that. Julie still had tears in her eyes, and so did I. But the image of my mother comparing Emily to a philodendron was so ludicrous, and so *like* her, that it made me start to laugh, despite myself. That was my mother all over—like pregnancy was an AP exam, and Julie had only managed to score a three.

"Only Mom," I said.

At least this broke the ice.

She should've told me about Portland weeks ago, Julie admitted, but it had all been up in the air for so long. They hadn't known for sure. They'd actually wanted to leave the area for a while, but they'd never admitted it to themselves until they lost Emily. They'd had it with the city, the traffic, the congestion. Everything cost so much, took so much effort here. At first, the idea of moving was just a fantasy— something to distract them from what had happened. Now it looked like it was really happening.

"But you love DC," I reminded her numbly, stirring and stirring my tea.

I'd picked DC because of her, remember? *She* was the family I had here. Without Julie and Jon, DC was just a place. An alphabet soup of streets. Planes buzzing low over the campus, heading else-where. Everyone heading elsewhere.

She couldn't meet my eyes.

They'd gone to Portland in August, just to get away, and they'd both loved it. It felt like being on vacation there, Julie said, but they decided to put it on the back burner, and then, out of the blue, a headhunter called Jon. A firm in Portland needed a labor lawyer. They even had some part-time work for Julie.

They'd found a house to rent in Cape Elizabeth, ten minutes from Portland, a few blocks from the ocean.

"So," Julie said. "I guess it's really happening."

"Well," I said, trying to sound happy for her. "I guess that's good."

According to my AAA chart, it is 562 miles from Washington, DC, to Portland, Maine.

"It won't happen for a while, Mellie," she said, putting her hand near mine on the table. "We still have to sell our place and find a place to live."

We called each other "Mellie"—my mother, my sisters, and

I—whenever something hard came up and we wanted to be ironic about it instead of getting emotional. It came from watching *Gone with the Wind* so often when we were growing up. Mellie, of course, is Scarlett's gentle, loving cousin, the one Ashley really loves. The one played by Olivia de Havilland, who we all thought we should really want to be, instead of Vivian Leigh, the conniving, hard-hearted heroine. The scene that kept us riveted was the one where Scarlett was pulling the wagon out of burning Savannah, and Mellie was rolling around in the back in utter agony, in labor and dying at the same time. "Hang on, Mellie! We're almost there! We're going to make it!" Scarlett kept crying.

We'd grab one another's arms, all four of us, and shriek along with her, "Hang on, Mellie! Hang *on!*" as if somehow we could keep her going, from our couch-bound, 1960s vantage.

Years later, my parents, Julie, and I took a trip together in northern Italy during the spring break of my second year at Oxford. Sara was already living out in Olympia and teaching full-time, so it was just the four of us. We met in Florence, my father rented a car, and we took a hairpin drive through the Apennine Mountains. Unbelievably narrow roads bent back and forth at right angles around the rapidly escalating heights, and if you peered out the window, like Julie did, it was a sheer drop down. Italian drivers kept barreling down at us from what appeared to be the same lane, honking furiously. My father was trying to curse back at them in Italian, and Julie, who had a miserable cold, clutched her backpack on her lap and shook all over, she was so scared. "Mellie" started then. "Hang on, Mellie," I crooned meanly, tucking my arm through hers as a truck rounded the bend in front of us, swaying dangerously. "I think I see—Tara!"

Ever since, all of us used the name at moments of risible discomfort. It was a communal nickname, Mellie, shared, with its remnants of irony.

It meant: "I know you're upset, but don't lose your sense of perspective."

Now, Julie used it—to appease me. To distract me from worrying how soon they'd be gone. And how far away they'd be.

She probably had the boxes packed already.

I couldn't be glad for them about moving. But not being glad was strangely uplifting. It leveled the field between us. It meant I didn't have to feel so guilty about the baby.

"I'll get you an ice pick as a housewarming present," I told her.

As luck would have it, they found a place easily. Someone made an offer on their house, and they made plans to move in late January or early February. Winter in Maine. Eighty-two inches of snow so far that year, and temperatures had been ranging from the low single digits to the low teens. She might really need that ice pick.

After a while, it stung less, thinking about her in Portland. Under the rational note in Julie's voice I heard something else, and I thought, *This will always be the place for her where Emily died.* That was the real problem with DC, and it was never going to change.

MOST OF MY FIRST WEEKEND post-teaching I lay on the couch, feet up (Dr. Weiss was hoping gravity might make the baby flip upside down). "You never know," I told Annie when she called and made fun of this idea. "It could work." In the seventeenth century, they might have applied leeches.

Lying on the couch, I went through blue books, reading what my students had written about Margaret Cavendish and Samuel Pepys. Everything seemed suddenly slowed down. I felt like I was being inflated with an invisible pump: Each breath I took seemed to stay inside me. If I got any bigger I might explode. How was it possible I could be this big, when according to Dr. Weiss's most recent computer clicks, the baby weighed barely five pounds? Even my little fingers were puffy.

My womb was still inhospitable, but they were willing to give us a chance. Now Dr. Weiss used a tape measure at each visit as well as ultrasounds.

Baby still breech, she noted at my last appointment.

———

SELFHOOD IS A PERFORMANCE. PEPYS appears to keep the diary for himself, but every "confession" is actually an attempt to articulate an identity for a wider audience.

BETWEEN BLUE BOOKS, I WATCHED dust motes filter through the afternoon light. Once in a while I recited things to the baby, fragments of poetry I remembered from my oral exams.

> *When to the sessions of sweet silent thought*
> *I summon up remembrance of things past—*

Or

> *The mind is its own place, and in itself*
> *Can make a hell of heaven, a heaven of hell*

I wanted to stay like this forever, in between, not one thing or another. Not one, not two. Inside of me, the baby pulsed: Every second of every minute of every hour, the baby was growing, cells multiplying, limbs lengthening—I didn't have to move an inch, lift a single finger, and so much kept happening.

The baby was good company, even though I didn't know much about it yet. Boy or girl? Its features in my last sonogram were soft and blurry, like someone caught off guard, moving before the camera snapped.

I tried not to notice he or she wasn't moving again. Knuckling it from either side, I tried to picture health. Wholeness. *Peace.*

One more knead, and the baby popped back into motion, like a giant cork.

All will be well, little one, I crooned, almost believing it. We needed no words. We breathed, we turned, we slept. Cell by cell, we grew larger.

Birthday (I)

SUNDAY EVENING, UNUSUALLY MILD FOR December. Jacques and I were in bed, talking before sleep. We'd had dinner that night at Dave and Lori's, whose baby girl was ten months old. She'd sat through almost all of dinner in her high chair, burbling at us, so solid and human-looking. Dave and Lori looked like they had life all figured out. Our "lead indicators," Jacques called them. We spent most of dinner asking for advice, and then, finding the advice overwhelming, trying to ignore it.

This was the stretch of time—between the end of the semester and my due date—I'd blocked out for getting ready for the baby. I had it written in my day planner in capital letters, with a long arrow to

show how much time I had. GET READY FOR BABY————————,
right there from December 3 to December 31.

There are lots of ways to get ready for things. My focus was on
the baby's room.

Our house was narrow and tall, and we'd decided to put the
baby in the middle room on the third floor, the one with the fan-
shaped window and distant view of the aviary. In the mornings you
could hear birdcalls, which I figured the baby would like.

The room was mostly done. We'd set up white shelves in the
closet, scrubbing the walls with Fantastik. Every few days I added
something: a small stack of towels. A Kleenex box. We had royal
blue carpeting installed, hung up blue-and-yellow borders, and fitted
in a fresh white bureau and changing table. Everything was there but
the crib, which had been on the top of my to-do list for weeks. I'd
actually found one that seemed perfect a few weeks earlier at Baby
World in northern Virginia—simple, white, pristine—but Jacques,
who likes comparison shopping, still wanted to check out a few other
possibilities.

Why couldn't we just get the one at Baby World? It was perfect.

For someone prone to criticism, I'm easily satisfied when it
comes to material objects. Many of them strike me as ideal, just the
way they are. Not Jacques. He likes the hunt.

"What's wrong with the one we saw?" I asked on Saturday, my
first weekend since the semester had ended. After hours of lying on
the couch, coaxing the baby to turn, I was ready to get out a bit.

"Oh," Jacques said, deep in the paper. "I still want to check out
a few other options."

"*What* other options?" I asked. Was he thinking maybe something that *rocked*?

I set my jaw, the way I do when I want something to happen
now and he wants to delay just for the sake of delaying.

The crib wasn't the real issue, though we ended up arguing about
it that afternoon. A new problem had inserted itself into our lives.

A job had turned up in my field in Boston.

I say this like the job found me, instead of vice versa, and in fact, this wasn't true. In September, when I did my usual quarterly scan of the Modern Language Association job list, there it was—a job in Boston. In my field. Given that I knew who was teaching seventeenth-century at every British university in Boston, this qualified as a near miracle. I called Annie immediately to read her the ad, just for a reality check. Then I applied for the job and tried to put it out of my mind. No one at Georgetown knew about my application except my chair, one of the kindest academics on earth. And he seemed to forget about it right after e-mailing the department in Boston on my behalf. That made it easier for me to stop thinking about it, too.

I'd managed to repress it pretty well, in fact, though my mother hadn't. *When are you going to hear about the job in Boston? How many other people did you say applied? What will you do if they want to interview you?* "We'll see," I kept saying. Or sometimes, less kindly, "We'll *see!*" Then that weekend, right before Jacques and I headed over to Dave and Lori's, I got a call from the chair in Boston telling me I'd been chosen for an interview. I was dumbfounded.

As a hypothetical, the job had seemed appealing. But as a reality—

Be careful what you wish for, I was thinking now. Applying for the job had made more sense in September, when I could still get up and down stairs without hanging on to the banister. The baby was due in three weeks and three days. How was I possibly going to make it to an interview in another city the week after Christmas?

They were nice, the people from Boston. They understood there was no way I could make it to the convention. But what if we set up a telephone interview next week?

My situation, the chair pointed out, was not insurmountable. Of course, if I ended up getting a callback interview . . . her voice trailed off. I knew the chances of that were slim. That wouldn't be until late January or early February, she said, and by *that* point—

"Oh, by *that* point," I agreed, matching her low chuckle. I could certainly make my way to Boston by *then*. If, of course—

Late January seemed as far off as the moon.

I was mulling all this over, Sunday night in bed.

All weekend, Jacques kept finding ways to sneak in the virtues of Boston, and it was starting to grate on me. What happened to "wait and see"? Where was this newfound desire to plan coming from? I found myself shooting back all the advantages of the District. Short winters! Friendly people! It wasn't just Boston versus DC, I realized now, shifting uncomfortably. It wasn't even the prospect of the job— it was everything. The more I thought about our dinner with Dave and Lori, the worse I felt. Lori seemed so sure of herself, so experienced. What was I going to do? I had no idea what babies ate or how to get them in or out of their various pieces of equipment or what you did when you spent time alone with them. Sara and Julie were the ones who'd babysat during high school—I'd taken a job selling handbags at B. Siegel instead. Before Christmas, all sorts of nice middle-aged men would come in and open the bags up and look inside them, bemused, and after a lot of deliberations, they'd say, *OK, I'll take this one*, and I'd ring them up and gift wrap, and then, the day after Christmas, the women themselves would come and wait in line to return them. "Things just fall *right* to the bottom of this!" one cried, shaking the bag at me like I was the harebrained designer. What a waste of time. I could've been learning to diaper and soothe.

I had no idea what to do with a baby. I had a vague plan to work on my book while the baby slept next to me, but I got the sense from Lori that might not be realistic.

"You're really planning to work from home?" Lori had asked. She's a prize-winning reporter; their ten-month-old was on a schedule; they had a great nanny. But Lori didn't even try to work from home. Too many distractions, she said, not meeting my eye.

"Are you going to have help?" she asked, when I mentioned my writing plans.

Trust me, I've never been a hero when it comes to doing things on my own. I use full service in the gas station. I get things fixed at the dry cleaners. If I get a flat tire, I call AAA. I'm happy to delegate any and all tasks, it's just that taking care of the baby hadn't quite registered yet as a task. I stammered something: "We'll play it by ear," with a "flexible schedule" and "work from home" and another Jacques-ism or two thrown in for good measure. When I wasn't looking, Lori and Dave exchanged the knowing glances of people who have been to the Dark Continent and barely survived.

Now I was thinking this over. "We may have to reconsider the nanny issue," I said, and right as I said it, I became aware that something wet was whooshing out of me in unbelievable quantities. All over my side of the bed. It was like a bathtub had been unplugged. What on earth—?

I began shaking Jacques's arm. As I did, I guessed what had happened—my water had broken. But—it wasn't time yet! I still had more than three weeks left!

Twenty-four days, as a matter of fact. The due date was right there in my day planner—six days after Christmas. In ink.

For once, I wasn't ready. Truly not ready. I hadn't packed yet. I wasn't done grading blue books. We didn't even have the crib!

This was the last inhospitable act of my inhospitable womb. It was like ushering a guest to the door while dessert was being served.

Sorry to rush you, little one. But it looks like it's time to get going.

I'M SURE EVERY PERSON'S EXPERIENCE of labor is different. For us, it started by arguing over where to park the car. "How long do you think we'll be?" Jacques asked, squinting up at the parking rates at the entrance to the hospital lot. I shrugged. I hadn't had a single contraction yet. That might mean days. On the other hand, Dr. Weiss was meeting us. We were being taken care of. "Go for the short-term lot," I advised. Ignoring me, Jacques headed to 24 Hours or More, carefully trolling each level for the optimal spot.

Jacques wasn't the only one taking his time. The people in Labor and Delivery were all moving in slow motion. One woman behind the desk was on an interminable phone call, her back to us. "I know! I know!" she kept saying, her shoulders shaking with suppressed mirth. Another was sleepily riffling through paperwork. Yawn, riffle, yawn. After what seemed like forever, she jackknifed a clipboard in my direction.

Paperwork, paperwork, paperwork. So many forms to fill out. Mother's maiden name. Mother's social security number—"social," as it was cozily abbreviated by the woman at the desk through another yawn. State of birth? Date of birth? Allergies? Next of kin? Primary care physician? Ob-gyn? I signed and stamped and addressed and authorized, wondering why this never happens in the movies. Finally Dr. Weiss came in, snapping on a natty little blue jacket with OR efficiency.

Dr. Weiss, at least, was ready for action. "So," she said when she saw us. "What have you two decided?" No preliminaries, not even a hello.

The baby was still breech, and Dr. Weiss wanted to know how I felt about trying "version." "Turning the baby gently while we monitor all its vital signs in the hope that we can maneuver the baby into position" was how the process was described, which two months later we learned Blue Cross considered elective and charged us for. A thousand dollars a minute, and I didn't even enjoy it.

Dr. Weiss warned me version wasn't easy, but I was game. I had that little thrill I'd gotten when I signed up for Honors Latin in graduate school instead of the one for people who can't learn languages. We moved into one of the brand-new birthing rooms, and I lay on the table while Dr. Weiss got things ready. As she connected me to the monitor, it occurred to me Honors Latin hadn't gone that well.

It's impossible to describe what version felt like. "Breathe and relax," Dr. Weiss instructed me—easier said than done—as she and the nurse proceeded to grab onto my belly and twist with all their might.

It was like having my head rotated a hundred and eighty degrees. I screamed. This seemed like the kind of thing that might have happened in the sixteenth century, in a dark back room of the Tower. Dr. Weiss glanced at the nurse, frowned. "Again!" she instructed. The second time, knowing what to expect, my entire body tensed before they could get near me. *Version unsuccessful*, Dr. Weiss scrawled on the form the insurance company duplicated and returned to me two months later with Payment Due attached.

I'd failed version. Our options were narrowing—water broken, baby breech. We needed a C-section, Dr. Weiss announced.

A C-section. That was real surgery. Weeks of recovery. I grabbed Jacques's hand as they prepared me for a spinal and mouthed the phrase that had long been linked in my mind with this possibility: *baby nurse*.

Dave and Lori had had one. Her name was Annette, and she was a model of starched decorum, shooing away pesky visitors while swiftly scooping up gifts and casseroles, imposing only so often to bring their baby in, spanking clean, to nurse. She stayed for three weeks, and I wanted her.

"Don't worry about that now," Jacques murmured, looking down at me with tender eyes. "We'll figure that out later."

Later. A core word in Jacques's philosophy. I was about to explain why *later* wouldn't work this time when the orderlies came and wheeled me into the OR. Everyone flew into action. They hung up a sheet to separate my lower half from my shoulders and head and pinned my arms to my sides, which I hated, but they explained it kept "the field" sanitary. At least I was conscious and there was no pain. This wasn't how I'd imagined childbirth, but there was something sweetly egalitarian about the fact that Jacques—he looked good in scrubs, he should've been a doctor—could hold my hand and we could both approach the whole thing from the same vantage. We were partners in all of this—what a good omen! Of course, as I reconsidered, we weren't *literally* in the same position—I was actually lying on the table, my belly swabbed with Betadine, and Jacques was standing in scrubs and a mask next to my head—but still. We *felt* close.

One thing nobody ever mentions is how long it takes to actually reach the baby during a C-section. Twenty minutes. Thirty minutes. What were they doing? How much was there to get through down there? I had gained forty-five pounds, was that the problem? We talked, we paused, we waited, it was awfully quiet, and finally there was this funny tugging sensation, like my belly was a suitcase and someone was trying to pull out the rolled-up pair of pants way underneath all the other stuff—tug, tug, tug—and then Dr. Weiss said, in this marveling Addison-from-*Private-Practice* kind of voice—"Well! You have a beautiful baby girl!"

A girl.

Jacques and I stared at each other, trying to assimilate this.

Sacha, we said to each other in unison, trying it out. Her birth certificate name would be Alexandra, but Sacha was her real name—the name we knew her by the minute we saw her. The Russian diminutive for a name our grandfathers shared.

Maybe it was partly the hormones and the euphoria of delivery. Maybe it was the perfection of Sacha's tiny body, her little fingers and toes, her wide, alert eyes. The agony of months of worry evaporated, and holding her, I felt something close to grace.

She was healthy. She was perfect, perfect, perfect. And she was *here*.

I kept saying her name. Whispering it, crooning it. Sacha. Sacha-la. Sachabelle. Bellie. Belle. Named, she was immediately nicknamed, as if there were no degree of closeness close enough for this one noun. No one name special enough. Each layer of nicknaming made her more completely and identifiably *her*.

She'd inherit the best of both of us, I assured her. Jacques's optimism, his keen ethics, his sense of the possible. His parents' warmth. My parents' humor. My love of detail and discipline.

Alexandra was a big name for someone so small. Sacha, on the other hand, fit right from the start.

OUR WEEK AT COLUMBIA HOSPITAL for Women was the week of big babies. Ten pounds. Nine pounds eleven ounces. Eleven pounds nine ounces. Big baby, big baby, big baby, and then there was Sacha: five pounds six ounces, curled up like a shrimp, red faced, scowling, insanely bright lights in this place, can't a baby get some *rest*? I scrutinized her with the anxious eyes of a soccer mom whose child has been left all season on the bench. "Yours is so tiny," the woman outside the nursery said sympathetically, like I'd drawn the short stick on a desert island. "She's *early*," I said, ready to defend her to the death; early, ahead of herself, on the ball—not like those chunky, laggard babies! Premature. *Pre.* Ahead of herself! Two days old and already there was competition. What is it about having a child that is so instantly and profoundly comparative? I couldn't help it, I was already eyeing the other babies and worrying about their disproportionate strength and acumen. Already comparing Apgar scores as I trolled up and down the hallways tethered to my IV pole. Sacha was so tiny, so ruddy, so crustacean-like. But the splaying of those miniscule fingers put me in a trance, she was dazzling, the others were bruisers and ours a pearl!

She wasn't due for another three weeks and already I'd thought and felt half the things I'd always sworn were beneath contempt.

I loved my five days in the hospital. There was a system in place. The babies were lined up in Lucite boxes on small wheeled carts in the nursery, swaddled in waffle-weave blankets with an air about them of utter calm. I had a crank on my bed, up, down, in between, and meals that arrived with shrink-wrapped condiments, everything the same soothing shade of taupe, and a buzzer to push for more Percocet, and in one pile at my left I had the last of my blue books to grade, and baby catalogues with pages folded down, things I'd never even known

existed—baby-wipe warmers! Nostril suctioners!—and the phone
numbers of three baby-nurse agencies, and on the other side intermit-
tently Sacha herself arrived, tucked up by the nurses into nursing
position A.

Ah, nursing.

There was a whole science to it. There was a hotline you could
call for help—the La Leche League—and within twenty-four hours
I discovered nothing I'd learned before was as important or as gut-
wrenchingly hard.

Nursing seemed to take at least four hands, if not six. First, there
was the positioning of the breast (block-hard, enormous, so painful
that the whoosh of the hospital gown against it caused agony). Then
the unclamping of Sacha's groping mouth. *Grope, clamp. Grope, clamp.*
Chomping at the air like a desperate thing. The holding of Sacha, so
tiny, so unable to hold any part of herself airborne on her own. The
excruciating pain of her chomping mouth. Nothing came out of me,
I was sweating, Jessie—my favorite nurse, seven AM to three PM shift—
was sweating, Sacha was sweating; we switched positions, named them
(the underhand, the overhand, the underdoggy, the overdoggy); we
tried chemical heating pads, ice packs, massage; by day three my breasts
filled the entire bed, the entire room, the chomping and stapling hurt
so much tears sprang to my eyes at the very sight of Sacha, mitered in
her onesie. Why was there so much combat in this very first act? I was
ready to give up, ready to do anything but this, ready to sign on for a
wet nurse, bring us bottles, we are starving! Then suddenly, on day
three and a half, in the middle of the night, wincing against the sweet
sting of her clenching jaw, milk spewed out of me, hot, sweet, sticky.
And this was all we did anymore. We were a remarkable pair, a perfect
duo of supply and demand. I filled up the minute I saw her; I heard
her cry and milk spilled down the front of my hospital gown. We fit
together beautifully, I was all breast and she was all mouth.

Instead of postpartum depression, I felt a kind of euphoria. I
called my parents, Julie, Sara, my in-laws in South Africa, I called

Annie. I was tenderhearted and exhilarated by the newness of it all, Sacha's fingernails with their perfect plum translucence, her miniature perfection. The whole world glowing in each tiny eye. Each visitor, each flower, each present was dazzling to me. I peeled the petals off the mauve roses sent by my in-laws and glued them one by one into Baby's First Book given to us by our neighbors; I recorded headlines from the day of her birth (SOVIET UNION DISSOLVES); I noted the weather (fifty-three degrees, rainy).

On the second day, there was a knock on the door. I was expecting our pediatrician. "Come in," I called, holding Sacha and gazing tenderly at her tiny face.

It wasn't the pediatrician. It was Julie, holding the biggest stuffed bear I'd ever seen.

"Hey, Mellie," she said.

Tears sprang to my eyes—hormones, joy—and then to hers, and we both sobbed, and we tried to hug each other without squashing Sacha between us, and she told me how sorry she was that she hadn't been there for me these past few months, and we cried together about Emily, and I told her I was happy for them about Portland, honestly, I really was, I'd been selfish before, but now— We hung on to each other and kept crying until Sacha was sopping wet. Sacha was a mitzvah, a charm, a catalyst, things would be OK, Julie would be OK, they were "trying" again, she told me, blowing her nose. She rubbed Sacha like a talisman. "Wish us luck, little one," she whispered.

The bear took up the whole corner. I named him Pepys, and even though he had slightly creepy eyes, I loved him.

MY PARENTS ARRIVED FROM DETROIT just as we were being told by an obstetrical resident that Sacha had jaundice and might not be able to come home with us right away. The resident delivered this news with perfect calm. It was not uncommon with babies born "a bit early," he told us. He explained this like he thought it would cheer me up. He didn't look much older than my undergraduates.

Right in the middle of this, my mother came in without knocking, holding a pink flowering begonia in front of her like a shield.

I tried to pull myself up into a sitting position, squinting at the resident. I had negotiated this visit with my parents—I hadn't wanted them to come until we were home, settled, and knew enough about what we were doing that I wouldn't feel completely self-conscious and awkward. They wanted to come *right away*. The compromise was, they won. They were staying with Julie and Jon, and we agreed they'd *just* come to the hospital, say hello, and meet the baby. They'd come back for another (short) visit the next day, then go back to Detroit. They'd be back for a "real" visit over Christmas, in a few weeks.

Short as their visit was, I wanted it to go well. At the very least, I wanted to have washed my hair, to be nursing without visible pain, to be giving off an aura of maternal calm. This wasn't how I'd planned for them to see me: I had dried breast milk all over me, my hair was unbrushed, and I had a blistering headache.

But for once, I couldn't focus on what they thought. I was too busy trying to understand what the resident was telling us.

"It's just a matter of days, maybe a week," he said, as if he were talking about a library book that needed to be held back behind the counter for rebinding. Sacha needed light therapy, and the standard procedure was to stretch her out in a special nursery and beam a light at her. A bilirubin light, it's called. I pictured a butterfly drying on a rack.

My father leapt on this. Breaking medical issues around my father is like throwing raw meat to a wolf. He started barraging the resident with questions and throwing around medical jargon before Jacques and I could even respond.

Jacques, hero of the hour, took my father gently aside. "No worries, Dale," he said, not looking yet at me. "We'll get good advice and figure this out."

I waited for my mother to leap in with plans of her own, advice, suggestions.

Another surprise: a new side of my mother came out. She didn't say a word about jaundice. Instead, she set the begonia down, out of the way, came over to pat me on the shoulder a little—she was never big on hugging—and leaned in to scoop Sacha out of the Lucite bassinette beside me.

"Hello, Sachabelle," she said, apparently immune to the chatter of the resident behind us. She seemed completely unfazed, eyes only for Sacha.

She nudged me over a little with her hip, sank down onto the bed next to me, and proceeded to reintroduce me to the perfection of Sacha's face. "Look," she said admiringly, "at those eyelashes! Look at those dimples! Look—" Sacha was grabbing tightly onto my mother's pinky, her fingers squeezing tightly. "Look how *strong* she is!"

Temporarily, I stopped trying to read the signs the resident must be giving to suggest which option was better: leaving Sacha in the hospital for three days of light treatment, or bringing her home and hooking her up to what he called a "bilirubin blanket." Over my mother's shoulder, I got caught up in readmiring Sacha. I had to admit she looked good. The jaundice made her look a little suntanned, like she'd just been to the beach. My panic subsided. I heard, tacitly or not, the subliminal message in my mother's voice: *She's going to be fine. I'm a mother, I know about things like this, and you have nothing to worry about.*

Another surprise: Jacques was already speaking up. "We'll bring her home," he told the resident, without a shred of hesitation. No "later," no "one step at a time," no "let's wait and see." I looked at him, considering. He had a whole new sound in his voice.

It was really something, this parenthood business. It was changing all of us, and Sacha had only been around for four days.

———

WHEN IT WAS TIME TO leave the hospital, I was in tears. It was like leaving summer camp, I wanted everyone's autograph, I wanted to stay forever. What would happen to our little Lucite box? Where would our system go? Every part of my body seemed to be leaking. Jessie, my favorite nurse, brought a stack of forms to sign with my breakfast tray and she and I hugged, rocking back and forth, while I reminded her she was the one who taught us the underdoggie, she was the one who brought me prunes when I couldn't go to the bathroom, she was the one who gave Sacha her first bath. Why couldn't she leave the hospital and come home with us? Sacha needed us both, two mothers!

I reminded her I knew pretty much nothing about babies.

Sacha was swaddled in three waffle-weave blankets stamped CO-LUMBIA HOSPITAL FOR WOMEN, most of the N rubbed off. Her face looked wizened and pathetically grave. Jacques was trying to get the car (24 Hours or More) out of hock. I rode downstairs in a wheelchair, holding Sacha on my lap—barely five pounds now, her newborn diaper big as a kilt on her, and outside a winter gale was raging.

What kind of world were we bringing her into?

"Just take her home and love her," Jessie said.

And we did.

Help (I)

⟨≈≈≈⟩

COMING HOME FROM THE HOSPITAL, I wanted my mother. I wanted
her to be standing outside our back door, arms stretched out, ready to
take Sacha from me. I wanted her to be in the kitchen, whipping up
something fragrant and soothing for dinner. I wanted her to be everywhere, putting things away, getting things settled.

Instead—just like I'd insisted—she and my father were back in
Detroit, waiting anxiously for us to call and say it was OK for them
to come back.

There were six steps up to the brick porch outside our kitchen.
I winched myself up the iron railing like it was a tow lift, my abdomen
torched with pain. Jacques was behind me, holding Sacha in the car

seat that detached and became a carrier. It took four hands just to get her inside the door.

Inside, our house overwhelmed me. Bacchus, leaping forward with unrestrained joy. The twins from next door had been walking him, but he still had a week's worth of pent-up energy to share. Stacks of unopened mail on the table. How were we going to manage on our own? The dining room table was piled with baby equipment: monitors, diapers, changing pads, cotton balls. I looked around, disoriented. I hadn't planned on feeling so tired.

"I know it's probably hard to climb stairs," Jacques said, looking like he'd just won the lottery, "but I have something to show you up in Sacha's room. Can you make it?"

I took a deep breath. There were thirty-seven stairs between me and the third floor. But I could see from Jacques's face this was important.

We took our time. Bacchus went first, tail flicking like a metronome. Then Jacques, holding Sacha. Then me, tugging on the banister, trying to hide each wince. "I'm fine!" I huffed disingenuously, as I fell farther and farther behind.

Finally, we made it to the top floor. I inched my way along the corridor, while Jacques nudged open the door to Sacha's room.

I let my breath out, half in pain, half in wonder.

My parents had only been in DC for two days, but while my mother was here and I was in the hospital, she and Jacques had whirled into action, taking over my incomplete to-do list. Everything was ready. They'd set up the changing table, complete with its stack of wipes. They'd arranged miniature onesies in tiny piles on the fresh white shelves.

My eye roved approvingly. Then I turned and saw it. The crib from Baby World. White, simple, perfect—just the one I'd coveted. It was all set up, with a note hanging from it tied with an enormous pink ribbon. *"Welcome home, Mellie and Sacha-la. Love, Bomma and Boppa."*

They'd driven out to Virginia with Jacques to get it. While I was in the hospital learning how to breastfeed, Jacques had assembled the crib, using the cordless screwdriver Valerie had given us, and my mother had arranged the bedding: waterproof sheet first, soft flannel next, an adroitly folded cotton diaper where Sacha's face would lie, all starched and sweet-smelling and cocoonlike. I stood against the door jamb, still panting a little, and looked around at the room with its rocking glider for nursing and the blue-and-yellow border and the fan-shaped window, and I looked back at the crib, and I burst into tears. Bacchus, panting decorously beneath the rocker, watched me with soft wet eyes.

"Your mom wanted to get the crib," Jacques said apologetically. "I felt bad, having to put you off like that. But she wanted to surprise you."

I thought about how convinced I'd been that she didn't care, that she didn't want to be out here with us. And all the while, she'd been crib shopping long distance.

Now I wanted to call her and tell her I'd changed my mind. *Come back! Come and help us! Move in, stay forever!*

But we'd made a plan, they'd bought their tickets to come back over Christmas, and I tried my hardest to be brave when I called her later, raving about Sacha's room. Thanking her for the crib.

"Are you guys all right?" she asked. "You're sure you don't want me to come out sooner and help for a little while?"

I was sure, I told her. I swallowed, hard. Hopefully the days between now and Christmas would fly by.

HELP WAS ALL I THOUGHT about now. Time was suddenly carved in two: time with help, and time without.

Julie came over and helped, but she had to get back to the Justice Department. She was working overtime, trying to save money before she and Jon moved. Lori was busy working on a story, our neighbors were busy, Annie was busy, the world was going on and people were living their lives, and we came home and it suddenly felt like every minute of every day had become a challenge.

We needed help. We needed a baby nurse, I explained to Jacques, for so many reasons. Because I'd had a C-section, and because we were brand-new parents and didn't know how to do anything, like making the bassinette comfortable, or cutting Sacha's nails, or washing Sacha's hair, or diagnosing or curing diaper rash, or figuring out how the baby monitor worked, or deciding whether the used-up chemical heating pads counted as toxic or could be thrown out with ordinary trash. Not to mention cooking dinner while holding Sacha, talking on the phone while holding Sacha, holding Sacha while she was crying, keeping Sacha from crying interminably every day from three o'clock until midnight, or figuring out how to sleep in two-hour increments. On our own, we couldn't tell the difference between normal cries and cries that meant something was wrong.

We tried to get Annette, the baby nurse who had helped Dave and Lori, but she was booked through the first week of May. But there was Clara, the agency told us. A friend of Annette's. Every bit as experienced, if not more so. And she was available just a few days after we got home from the hospital.

Available was a plus. "Good," I said. "Clara sounds good."

She could come at the end of the week. In the meantime, Sacha needed everything.

Twice a day the Bilirubin Lady came and monitored Sacha's jaundice. For this to work, we both needed to hold her. I took one end, Jacques took the other. The Bilirubin Lady was actually a visiting nurse, and we were indebted to her, because if not for her and the bilirubin blanket, Sacha would still be in the hospital. Each time she came, she took a small lancet from her medical kit and stabbed Sacha's heel with it until it welled with blood. One vermillion bead swelled bigger and bigger, dropped away into the Bilirubin Lady's test tube, and got stoppered up and taken away. As the lancet plunged in, we all sucked in our breath—Jacques, me, Sacha—until Sacha trumpeted hers out in an ear-splitting, world-ending howl.

Her cries shattered me. They were so primeval, and to hold her while she shuddered, to offer treacherous assurances—*it's over, all over, she's finished, look, you're fine, fine*—these were the first lies I told her, because I knew she'd be back, the Bilirubin Lady. Twice a day, every day for a week. After the Bilirubin Lady was done with her ministrations, I scooped Sacha back into my arms, furious and spitting, a small knot of misery. Every part of her curled up with shrieking: her fingers, her tiny legs, and I tried to smooth her back into forgiving us.

We set up triage units around the house: one downstairs, one up—little care stations, with stacks of products in various states of half-openedness: baby wipes, ointment, teetering piles of diapers so small they looked like sanitary napkins. We needed to be near electric outlets in order to plug in the bilirubin blanket, which encircled Sacha with turquoise light, healing her underdeveloped liver. This limited us in terms of mobility. We found if we bumped her heavy pram up and down over the threshold between the living room and the kitchen in time with Billie Holiday, Sacha's wheezy, early-evening cries spluttered into silence, and she fell, if not asleep, at least into a trance that mimicked sleep. That, in a way, was help.

We found two or three positions that let us hold Sacha and talk on the phone at the same time, and this was critical because the phone was a lifeline for us, marooned as we were in this world of swabbing and wiping. This, too, was help.

But there were so many moments of confusion. Where would Sacha go if Jacques wasn't there and I needed to go to the bathroom (something which, in and of itself, demanded help at this phase)? I had dreams I'd left Sacha somewhere: on the kitchen counter, in the back of the car. On the top step going down to the basement, like a half-finished book.

Right from the start, I was nervous. I didn't want to be—I

wanted to be one of those nonchalant, all-knowing mothers you see from time to time and admire. Instead, I was frazzled and compulsive, sweating all the small things. This could be partly because I wasn't sleeping. I slept in fitful twenty-minute bouts, afraid Sacha was with me or that she wasn't. I had a recurring, half-waking nightmare that she was in bed with us, or that Bacchus was in bed with us, or that they were both in bed with us, and one night I grabbed on to something warm and alive and thought: my God! It's true, Sacha's in bed with us, if I roll over I'll crush her, and I grabbed hold of her, terrified, but what I was hanging on to was only Jacques's leg.

We made calls, we took calls, and in between we waited for Clara.

One of the calls, Monday afternoon at three o'clock, came from the search committee in Boston.

I'd completely forgotten about the telephone interview until that morning. And even having looked over some notes for an hour, it was hard to get myself into decent interview form. I was so sleep deprived I could barely remember what day it was, let alone how people measured time in the seventeenth century. I had to look at my notes to remember things I used to know by heart.

John Donne, I reminded myself, handing Sacha off to Jacques, who was poised and ready. *George Herbert. Thomas Thompion. Tempo. The invention of the pendulum.*

The earliest watches date from the late fifteenth century, though they weren't called "watches" then. Not until later. Horologia, or clocks. Some were ornamental. Some hung from ball gowns; one anecdote describes a timepiece dangling from a great lady's ear.

Things I knew broke off and ran through my head. Answers to things I hadn't been asked.

The interview committee consisted of four professors from the English department. They were on speakerphone, which they weren't used to, and after some introductions and good-humored joking about the situation, everyone introduced themselves. Two of the professors were named Paul, which made the whole thing trickier.

I drew a dial on the back of a piece of paper, writing in names at different points of the clock—one Paul at three o'clock, another at noon. Elizabeth at six, Mary at nine. They asked about my research. I was starting, I told them, with hourglasses, tracing what happened when timepieces became more mechanically advanced in the seventeenth century. I was especially interested in the ways in which time changed how people lived and worked. Wearing timepieces, for instance—called "watches" in this period for the first time—made people feel more compelled by time, more driven by it. I mentioned the ball gowns, the earrings. Bringing mechanical clocks inside the home later in the century did the same thing. Clocks on mantelpieces. Clocks in bedrooms. As we talked, I found myself relaxing, and soon the conversation felt natural enough that I could even start to tell the two Pauls apart.

"How did it go?" Jacques asked when, just at three thirty, we'd said round-robin good-byes and I had hung up the phone.

It worried me that he looked so eager. I didn't want to disappoint him. Did he really want this job to happen? I could barely make it from one room to the next at this point. The thought of taking a new job in another city—even a city I knew and loved—confounded me.

"How did it go?" my parents echoed, when they called later to check on us. "OK," I said. I could tell my mother was holding her breath, biting something back. Curiosity, maybe. Or advice.

EVERYONE HAD ADVICE FOR US. New babies seem to attract advice like Bacchus hair on velvet. During our first few days at home from the hospital, waiting for Clara to arrive, we listened to all the advice, trying to sort it into branches, like a great tree of knowledge.

My mother and I talked several times a day now, and she had advice about everything except jaundice. I had to admit I had questions for her. Sacha's room had looked so perfect when she arranged it, but now the edges of things were beginning to curl up. My own attempts to re-create the crib's perfect linens turned out frowsy and homemade. How did I reach the farthest corner? Every time I got one part smooth, the rest sprang loose. Everything new was losing its patina.

We were glad when Clara came because she diverted us from the advice. But once she showed up, we needed as much advice about Clara as we did about Sacha.

Clara was a large woman carrying a large, hard-sided suitcase, more Old Golly than Mary Poppins. She pronounced her words carefully when she spoke, as if she came both from another country and another century, though in fact she was merely from Virginia. Clara was nothing like Annette. Instead of sprightly grace, she exhibited a certain fixed stodginess, and a lazy eye that rolled opportunistically toward the TV. She asked Jacques to carry her bag up to her room, looking critically at our narrow staircase. Jacques grappled with the suitcase, his face turning red. The suitcase was going up to the guest room on the third floor, conveniently next to Sacha's little nursery. Our idea was that Clara would wake when Sacha cried, change her, and bring her down to our bedroom; with a gentle tap she'd wake me—me, and not Jacques, who was planning, now that Clara was here, to hightail it back to the office first thing in the morning, and therefore needed sleep.

Needed sleep! Who-needs-sleep-more had become the competition du jour, replacing whose-week-is-harder or wait-and-see versus let's-go. Who-needs-sleep-more could get mean. We negotiated, then upped the stakes. We debated. We argued. We alternated between low-pitched, reasonable voices and mounting hurt and anger. Which is harder to do on little or no sleep: ride a bicycle to Foggy Bottom and write computer code, or guide a jaundiced infant and sulky Labrador through another day? When we tied, it was grim. Clara, we were convinced, would solve this problem. We both needed sleep! Jacques had his data to analyze, I had my blue books to grade, we both had the house to take care of, the increasingly sullen dog, and of course Sacha, who woke so effervescent and alert in her bilirubin blanket. Clara was a baby nurse, Clara would help.

Clara was not a city person, she told us, and because she was slightly deaf in one ear, she'd been advised by her doctor to wear noise-canceling headphones when she wasn't, as she put it with a delicate cough into an old-fashioned handkerchief, "on duty." Upstairs, she unpacked a neoprene eyeshade the size of a black sports bra. Jacques and I exchanged glances. What were the off-duty hours for a baby nurse? The agency hadn't mentioned this detail.

Clara was happy to offer advice. What we needed, she told us, was a system. Her eye fell with displeasure on the battery-powered baby swing Annie had sent while I was still in the hospital. *Up to one thousand hours!* the swing proclaimed whimsically on its uppermost bar. The idea was that the baby went in the swing, you pushed the ON button, the baby whirred rhythmically back and forth, and presto! Hands free for dinner.

According to *What to Expect the Baby's First Year*, it isn't good to become dependent on the swing. Thirty minutes is the maximum time period advised, the authors advised in cheerful, slightly accusing italics. It's best to interact with Baby while she swings. Swooping in and cuddling are encouraged. *Be wary*, was the underlying message. *Do not love the swing.*

We couldn't help it—we loved the swing. When Sacha was in the swing I felt almost like my old self again—upright, conscious, both hands free.

Clara remarked with a faint cough that she was not inclined to believe the swing was altogether *good* for the baby—

I thought Clara might want to swoop in and cuddle. Or try one of those clapping games.

"She's useless," Jacques whispered, low voiced, in the kitchen. "Does she expect us to *wait* on her?"

"Remember," I said, "we mostly got her for the nights."

Nights were enemy territory. Nights began around three in the afternoon when Jacques and I started arguing about whether or not to wake Sacha from her nap and when to feed her next. We were both believers in strategy, Jacques and I. The question was, which strategy would work? I thought if Sacha got nice and tired, she'd sleep better at night. Jacques thought if she got overtired she wouldn't sleep at all. We took turns peering down at Sacha during this last nap of the afternoon. Sacha was a crystal orb in which our future lay. Our future was eight hours long. What would make her restful?

It turns out it is pretty much impossible to wake a sleeping baby. All day Sacha slept, sodden, curled on her side in her oversized terrycloth onesie, fingers mitted in their cotton rolls. She breathed the long deep breaths of unshakeable slumber. I woke her to nurse and she sucked, eyes fluttering behind closed, translucent lids. She was in another world, dreaming of shadow, of membrane and capillary, swimming in sleep like a minnow, amphibious and untouchable, crisscrossing from one form of life to another.

Then it was evening, and cell by cell she came to life, a flutter, a wince, a grimace, a small batlike shriek, she rattled into crying like something inside her had broken. *Cry cry cry*, inconsolable and shuddering, spasmodic, mouth clenched in agony, all cramp, unable to suck, to be soothed, a caricature of crying, and we began our long choreography: Sacha over Jacques's shoulder, Sacha swinging on her belly on my arms, Sacha on my lap while I rubbed her back, she was not a baby but a cry, she was a radio station we couldn't change, a shore that forbade landing or retreat. It was eight and then nine and then ten o'clock. There was the changing and rechanging of diapers, the unpeeling of hot, wet terrycloth, the stringent ointment on abraded skin, Bacchus cringing and accusing in the corner, the long slow crawl toward night.

We tried to induce rest. We played Vivaldi's *Four Seasons* (classical music soothes the brain cells!). No tea for the breastfeeding mother. The breastfeeding mother lay on the sofa with a chemical heating pad on one breast and a blue book on the other. Analyses of self-construction dulled and stupefied the breastfeeding mother, causing her to nod off. This kind of nodding off was not allowed, we had a careful schedule of naps, assigned and unassigned, the breastfeeding mother was pilfering unapproved sleep units, but so much for that, Sacha was squirming, awake, clenching and unclenching her mitted fists, it was nighttime, Sacha was determined to be up. *The mind is its own place*, as Milton wrote; in Sacha's case, the mind made its own time. Or as Milton said elsewhere: *What hath night to do with sleep?*

At eight we were stoic, at nine we were apprehensive, at ten we were anxious, at eleven we were wiped out and no longer speaking to each other. I'd hoist myself up the stairs, crawl into bed, and fall asleep within seconds. I barely knew when Jacques came to bed, but there we were, sleeping together! This was utter joy, this was ecstasy, but the next thing we knew it was the middle of the night—two? Three? And we heard crying, a thin, high-pitched wail that cut into our consciousness like a knife. Sacha was crying, but where was Clara?

Clara, it turned out, was a sound sleeper. Who knew what she had tamped into the labyrinths of her large, city-phobic ears.

We lay awake, rigid, waiting for our system to kick in.

Nothing—no Clara. Only *cry cry cry* from our desperate daughter.

"Fuck," Jacques said to the ceiling. He lumbered out of bed, hauling himself off to the nursery, thwacking the door of the guest room on his way up and his way down. Not a peep from Clara. In the morning we were foulmouthed and foul-tempered. There was a thin film on everything, the newspaper lay unread in its plastic skin, Bacchus glowered from the corner, only Sacha, her aquamarine bilirubin blanket aglow, was cheerful, snuggled, sweetly dreaming on her tiny back.

BY THE SECOND NIGHT, WE had a new system. The idea, we explained patiently to Clara, was for her to take over one feeding in the middle of the night. A "relief feeding," my mother called it when we discussed this at length on the phone, designed so Jacques and I could get some rest. Thankfully, Sacha was happy to take a bottle, and we had one all set up, the formula ready. All Clara had to do was wake when Sacha woke, give her the bottle, and let us sleep.

The trick was how to wake Clara. We used a broom—handle end, not the straw—to tap with four sharp raps on our ceiling, which happened to be the subfloor of the guest room. Jacques sang out sharp little oaths with each tap. *TAP* (fuck). *TAP* (fuck). Sacha howled miserably, I couldn't bear it. *Help*, I whispered miserably into the pillow. *We—need—help—*

By the third night, while Clara slept, Jacques inched his way up along the banister, anger glinting in his eyes. He came back down with Sacha and lay next to me, waiting rigidly, eyes fixed on the ceiling while I nursed.

By the fourth morning, dour and unyielding, Clara was packed and ready to leave, unfazed by our short list of "reasons for dismissal" required by the agency.

Sacha was almost three weeks old, and we were officially on our own.

First Christmas

⬯⬯⬯

TECHNICALLY, CHRISTMAS ISN'T OUR HOLIDAY. On my side of the family, we're assimilated Jews, both sides from Eastern Europe, but we celebrate Christmas anyway. We got the tradition from my mother, who got it from Sylvia.

Sylvia and Pody got Christmas at school. They got school from Meyer, their father, who wanted them to belong to this glorious new world he'd gotten by happenstance. Meyer had run away from the tsar's army at fourteen, sailed alone to America, and eventually made his way to Chicago, following an older boy from the boat who knew someone with a leather factory on the near North Side. It was the usual story: Meyer worked his way up, learning just enough English to get by. Eventually he was running the company. He was an earnest man who loved simple and ordinary things—the wetness of city streets in the morning before the first motorcars appeared, the click of the shutter on his camera. The smell of rubber. The crackle of newspaper in his hand. From the papers, English words spelled out disasters he and his family had been spared. Spanish flu. The Great War. He sounded out the unfamiliar words, piecing together the stories, and with each catastrophe avoided, felt a deeper sense of gratitude. The world whirled over their heads like a tornado, while he and his family stayed safe at its windless eye. At the factory Meyer was tough-minded, fearless, but at home, he padded about in his old slippers, mousy and bemused. What to do? So noisy! Words whizzing past like bullets! And the girls, much as he adored them, with their strange tempers, their slamming doors, their moods that hung in the hallways like storm clouds.

Meyer's wife, Bea, was the one with clout. She'd been born in Chicago, and he deferred to her on all matters of consequence. She knew about America. She knew where the sofa should stand and what cut of brisket to serve at dinner. She knew everything about the girls, their mercurial moods, their intricate after-school lessons. She wanted them out of the public schools—who knew what went on there, so many rough boys?—so once Meyer started making money, Sylvia and Pody were sent down the hill to St. Theresa's Catholic Academy for Girls. It was clear that nobody bothered to translate *Catholic* for Meyer, who still went to synagogue every Saturday morning. But Meyer liked the school's ornate front gates and its emphasis on calisthenics. And the girls were happy there. Sylvia, two grades ahead of Pody and a natural mimic, soaked it all in: what kind of coat to wear to keep out the biting cold, how to sweep your hair back, how to roll your trolley money in your socks. Before long Sylvia was listening to ragtime, rouging her cheeks, and dashing off after school to shop with her classmates. December rolled around, and the school prepared for Christmas with a kind of frenzy. Sylvia and Pody learned hymns about Baby Jesus and the manger and "We Three Kings," and they took part in the December pageant, each begging to play the part of Mary. Mary had been Jewish, hadn't she? Then Christmas itself arrived. Watching her friends gather around decorated trees, opening lavish parcels on December 25, Sylvia stamped her perfect foot and told Meyer that she and Pody were being gypped. And Meyer, who ruled the factory with nerves of steel, dissolved in the face of Sylvia's rage. So Christmas was imported into their near-North-Side home along with American slang and flapper costumes. Year by year the Yiddish faded and the ornament collection grew, and Meyer, watching his honey-haired daughters dash out the door in matching raccoon coats and pearls, barely glancing back at him, wondered proudly—and a little sadly—what dream it was he'd garnered.

Sylvia's Christmases: Beautiful boxes festooned with curling ribbon. A white wire tree. Ornaments made of glass with smaller ornaments inside them. Silver tinsel that shivered when the front door opened or closed.

When my father and mother got married, my mother brought Christmas with her, adding her own idiosyncratic touches. Christmas gave her license for excess. At other times, shopping was complicated for my mother. It could go one way or another. She liked novelty, collecting and arranging—but she also liked things to be neat, spare, the scantest possible version of themselves. Her unpredictable asceticism threatened our trips to the mall. Enough was enough, too much was too much, but the distinction all depended on her mood. There we'd be, the three of us, trying things on in Saks, excited, upbeat, in and out of one another's dressing rooms, cheering one another on, admiring, and she'd be outside, exuberant, part of it all, when suddenly her mood would change: the skirt that on the rack seemed "classic" was suddenly pronounced "too expensive," the sweaters too low or too tight, the whole enterprise questioned. We'd leave with bags full, or with nothing. Who could read her? She was an enigma.

But not at Christmas. Christmas was for plenty.

At Christmas, we were spared discernment. We had boxes of

presents, ingeniously wrapped, and bulging stockings. A tree weighed down with ornaments. Huge meals. Morning Cookies (the recipe gleaned from *Seventeen* magazine) made with bacon and raisins for a pre-breakfast snack. Broccoli with red sauce at dinner. Our Christmases stood for every kind of plentitude, and long before Sacha was born, I dreamed of re-creating this sense that at least on this one day, every wish could be granted.

Here was another way Jacques and I were different. Jacques grew up in South Africa, the youngest of four children born to a Jewish mother and Christian father in a time and place when any kind of intermarriage was deeply suspect. Christmas—religious holidays in general—was downplayed. His family lived simply, and in any case, it was a midsummer's holiday in the southern hemisphere, and with four children, institutionalizing plenty was hardly wise. That's how Jacques remembers it. In fact, having compared photographs of our parallel Christmases circa 1965 or 1966, it's striking how similar the two scenes look, at least to me: What I remembered as never-ending bounty appears, to the unschooled eye, all but identical to the scene Jacques recalled as conscientious parsimony.

That didn't matter. The point was that in the here and now, I wanted to fill things up—the fridge, the house, the space under the tree—and Jacques wanted to keep things spare. I wanted things to be perfect, and for me, perfection meant bounty. Things—lots of things. Over the past few months, I'd carefully selected presents for Sacha, even before I knew who she was—eleven gifts, each adorably wrapped. An infant stim-mobile to rotate over her changing table. A teething ring. A clown puzzle with brightly colored plastic rings. Miniature blue jeans from Baby Gap. A stuffed ark with a dozen tiny stuffed animals inside. A pat mat. A splat mat. A squeezie toy for her car seat. A soft blanket that looked lovingly hand-knitted, though admittedly, given the price, it was probably made by machine in central Europe. In the evenings I grouped the presents in clusters under the tree and tried to keep Bacchus from chewing them. Bacchus had his own pile (don't neglect the dog!). I considered the scene with pleasure, but Jacques looked anxious every time he surveyed the bounty. Is this really what we want to teach her? Unable to identify, let alone fight for the aura I was trying to create, I defended the eleven presents on their own terms. So useful! On sale! Would've bought it anyway! "Who," Jacques asked, looking at me, "is going to *open* all these things?"

I looked at Bacchus's pile. I hadn't thought that far ahead.

Then my parents came and brought their own version of plenty. A yellow freezer bag filled with food, precooked and frozen: bagels from the good deli; the red-and-green broccoli; two casseroles; a batch of Morning Cookies. Three suitcases, two filled with clothes, the third with presents. Two shipping cartons full of baby clothes reimported from Sara. Jazz CDs from my father. Whiskey! A carton of wine! And not just things, but energy: their exuberance, their voices, my father's music wafting down from the bathroom, my mother's cries of excitement. They were witnesses; our lives were transformed by them into something meaningful, something that mattered.

I couldn't get over watching my mother with Sacha—she knew exactly what she was doing, she was so casual, matter-of-fact, warm, offhand, just the way I wanted to be, how did she know how to *do* all of this? I wanted a transfusion, I wanted to pour her knowledge into me, I wanted to know how to fold a cloth diaper and use it to make a clean place for Sacha to lay her face, how to swaddle with three taut folds, how to hold Sacha's ankles in one deft hand and wipe her with the other, how to tuck the phone under my chin while I rocked her, how to slide Sacha into some magical crook in my arms or on my hip while I did a million other things, all casual, easy, and this was astonishing to me, because much as I may have admired certain things about my mother before—her discipline, her tenacity, her organization—I'd never wanted to do what she did, none of it had ever held any interest for me, but now—I was besotted, she was my hero! We ignored Jacques's grumbling about too many presents (Scrooge!) and my mother gave me the recipe for the red-and-green broccoli (so easy—so

1950s—who knew something with bouillon and cheddar cheese and canned mushroom soup could even be edible?). We talked in a way we'd never talked before, like members of a secret club of two, I was interested in everything she had to say, I was listening, she was listening, it was magic.

Until, of course, it wasn't. Day One, we were all fresh, happy to see each other, tactful, supportive, overlooking foibles, generous, filled with good intentions. Day Two was still good. But Day Three (Christmas) we all woke up out of sorts. My parents were staying in the guest room next to Sacha, recently occupied by Clara, and when asked, they mentioned they hadn't slept well. Totally offhand, just a little comment, nothing to do with our bed or the traffic on Cathedral Avenue or the four times we'd been up with Sacha, whose wails no doubt pierced the walls like air raid signals.

They hadn't slept well? I tried not to glower at them. Who had?

What was this, Canyon Ranch? Weren't they here to help?

Oh, and by the way. My father just thought he should let us know the outlet in the upstairs bathroom was on the fritz. And the towel bar was coming a little loose—not an emergency, but if we had a screwdriver handy—

Jacques got out the cordless screwdriver. I flashed back to Valerie in my department hallway. A woman, I thought, with foresight.

Over breakfast, my mother started dropping hints. Sara, she began—apropos of nothing—had started cooking waffles from scratch this winter, using organic wheat flour from her local co-op. If she froze them ahead, she could just pop them in the toaster for Jenny and Rachel on busy school mornings.

Busy school mornings. That sounded so Norman Rockwell to me, even without the waffles. I shifted Sacha from one breast to the other, irritable, as my mother's eye panned to the box of cornflakes on our kitchen counter. Expired.

As usual, she thought it was her job to catch us up on one another.

Sara had started substitute teaching at Jenny's elementary school so she could teach where Jenny learned. "She's so *involved*," my mother added.

"That's good," I said, tight-lipped.

I missed Sara. She lived so far away—six hours of flying, plus a two-hour drive. We hadn't seen each other since last Thanksgiving. Now that I was a new mother myself, I would've loved to reconnect with her. I was sure she had a million stories about taking care of newborns. But as always, my mother's attempts to make us feel connected backfired. She'd tell each of us more and more great things about the others until we felt like we'd been pent up for years together on a desert island.

"Sara is a *wonderful* mother," my mother concluded brightly, by which point I didn't want to talk to anyone in my family for the rest of the day.

Julie and Jon were coming over later for dinner. My mother tried to stay off the topic of Maine, and Emily, and the move, but she kept veering back, like a compass needle tugged north.

"Have you seen the pictures yet?" she asked me. Meaning the pictures Julie and Jon had taken on their last trip to Maine, house hunting. Sweet Victorian cottages a stone's throw from the bay. Yes, I'd seen them. Wrap-around porches, weather vanes. You could practically smell the sea.

"It's a great place, isn't it," she mused, helping herself to more coffee. "A perfect place to start a family—when they're ready, of course," she added quickly. "When the time is right."

"Mmmmm," I said, looking longingly at her cup. Nursing, I was still stuck with herbal tea.

"The fresh air," my mother added, deep in thought. "And the sense of community. I think a smaller town—"

I shifted around, trying to signal (body language) that I didn't really want to talk about the advantages of Maine. Sacha started to whimper.

"Oh, by the way," my mother added. "Did you notice there were some shifty-looking men hanging out in your alley the other day? Have you and Jacques thought about putting an alarm system in, now, with Sacha—?"

Yes, we'd thought about it. Or actually *I'd* thought about it, but Jacques wanted to mull it over. Comparison shop. How did my mother know how to zero in on the one thing we'd been arguing about?

Sacha started crying now in earnest, and I tried nursing her again, this time on the other side. Nothing worked. Her cries got more frantic.

My mother (who'd bottle-fed all three of us) wondered if I held Sacha the *other* way, with my arm bent a little, whether it might be easier. Had we thought about giving her a bottle during the day? The earlier mood of plentitude was fading. I heaved myself up, Sacha dangling and squirming in my arms, and tried to find her pacifier on the counter. My mother's stacks of thawing dishes were in the way. Our house was jam-packed, no surfaces anywhere, why was there so much *stuff* everywhere? Why was Jacques always right?

My mother meant well—she just thought out loud. Sara's dentist had told her pacifiers hurt the baby's upper palate—what did our pediatrician say? Didn't I want to sterilize that pacifier after it fell on the floor?

After breakfast I caught her looking warily around our living room. She loved the way we'd set it up—*for now*, she told me.

I blinked at her.

"It won't be long," my mother predicted, "before she's crawling, and then—"

Sacha was barely three weeks old, and my mother already saw her as an almost-toddler, aimed for disaster. At the moment, I just wanted Sacha to stop crying. I wasn't in the mood for fast-forward. Why couldn't we just relax and deal with where we were right now, without jumping ahead a year?

My response was to withdraw, a kind of emotional pleading the fifth, and all the while I was thinking that what my mother and I were, the ways we nudged and irritated each other, managed to be insensitive to each other's sensitive spots and blurt out tactless things without caring—none of this had *anything* to do with Sacha and me, with the ways in which Sacha and I were connected, the way her cheek felt against mine. Sacha and I were different, would always be different, we were a separate species, there was no way my mother could ever have held me like this, I could never have been this small, she could never have bathed me or fed me or worried about me like this. I wanted to let my mother know this somehow—*you and I are different, this baby-and-me thing is different, it's earth-shattering—*

Of course, I couldn't say any of this, for all the obvious reasons, so instead we kept bumping into each other in small spaces all day (Sacha's closet, the third-floor bathroom), arguing about which part of Sacha's ear should be cleaned and how, and how many months we could possibly get out of the three-to-six-month-size outfit Lori and Dave had given us, and why I should actually exchange it for a bigger size, and why it would be *really hard* to go back to work next fall, before Sacha was even a year old, and what Sara had done, and what Julie was planning to do, and finally the only thing I felt filled with was rage.

THEN IT WAS CHRISTMAS DINNER and Julie and Jon came and we were almost our old selves again, with a few changes (Sacha swooping in her swing), and everyone but me drank lots of red wine and my father got sentimental and proposed a toast about family and then, clearing his throat, reminded us an important milestone was coming up.

I didn't know what he meant. I looked over at Julie, and she looked puzzled, too.

"*Dale,*" my mother said, in that voice she used when she was annoyed with him, and then I remembered.

Of course. February would make five years since my mother had found the lump in her breast. Five years was the big milestone. It meant she was safe—like reaching home free in tag.

I felt bad, having forgotten this was coming up. But she'd done so well we all just let it go, little by little. Life had filled in around the original fear, like water rushing around a boulder.

Besides, so much had happened over the past five years, it felt more like decades. I tried to remember back to where all of us had been.

Five years earlier, I hadn't even known Jacques. Julie had still been finishing law school, interviewing for jobs. Sara was pregnant with Rachel, her second daughter.

It was 1986, a year after Gail died. I was in graduate school, in that grueling period leading up to oral exams, and I remember I was in my tiny apartment in Eliot House when my parents called. Both of them together on the line, which should've been my first clue something was wrong. What they told me didn't make sense at first. A lump in her breast? It all seemed so baffling, like somebody else's bad news.

Nobody in our family had ever had breast cancer, except for one great-aunt who'd recovered and died decades later from Alzheimer's. We didn't have breast cancer in our family. We had *ovarian* cancer. Was it serious? Invasive? "No," my parents said in unison, "not serious, not invasive." Sara called me and I called Julie and Julie called my parents, and we went around in circles, confused, worried, trying to figure it all out.

Thankfully, the tumor turned out to be contained. And tiny—stage 1. They'd found it early, there was no lymph involvement. Her chance of complete cure was 95 percent. She reported all of this from Dr. Kempf, the gynecologist she'd been seeing for twenty years. Her favorite doctor. He was very reassuring. "If you're going to get cancer," he told her, "this is the kind to get."

While my mother weighed treatment options, Sara, Julie, and I checked in with one another, trying to gauge how worried we should be. In our family, the word "cancer" clanged like a five-alarm bell. On the other hand, lots of women had breast cancer and did well. We all knew survivors—mothers of friends, colleagues, celebrities. This wasn't the kind of cancer that had haunted us since childhood. In some dim, superstitious way, we all concurred: this was the trade-off. This was what medical sleuthing and foresight had bought her: the chance to be dealt this (much better) card. Obviously, it wasn't great having cancer. But better this kind—so much better this kind!—than what Sylvia and Pody had. What Gail had. Given what we knew, what we'd grown up dreading, *tiny* and *curable* sounded good.

My father still had questions. He called someone he knew at the Mayo Clinic to ask whether my mother should get a second opinion. He didn't like the fact that her tumor was nonestrogen receptive—that meant it could be harder to treat. Should they fly out for a consult?

My sisters and I were exasperated with him. What did that even mean, "nonestrogen receptive"? Couldn't he focus on "tiny" and "curable," like everyone else? *Ninety-five percent curable*, Dr. Kempf had said. Wasn't 95 percent ever good enough in this family?

In the end, they didn't fly out for a second opinion. My mother hated the idea. In any case, the doctor at Mayo approved the treatment plan laid out by Dr. Kempf. It looked like my mother had lucked out. Instead of getting horrible, stage 4 ovarian cancer like Sylvia, Pody, and Gail, she'd made it through her forties safe and sound. Now, at fifty-three, she'd gotten something—but not a fatal something. A tiny and curable something instead.

The pathology after her lumpectomy reassured everyone, even my father. She wouldn't need chemotherapy or more surgery. Wouldn't need an oncologist. She could keep seeing Dr. Kempf, which was a huge relief—my mother loved him. They spent each visit comparing cruise itineraries and grandchildren's report cards. Dr. Kempf had been on a Baltic cruise one year, and to the Scandinavian fjords the next. My mother and father were saving up to take the same ship on a cruise of the South China Sea. They saw eye-to-eye, my mother and Dr. Kempf. For six weeks, she drove herself to radiation every day on her way to teach at Country Day. She was there when the clinic opened at seven so she could be at school by eight thirty, for AP History first period. Nobody knew she was having treatment, not even her department chair. That was one of my mother's conditions: We weren't allowed to tell anyone she had cancer. No one! She was fine, and that's how she wanted people to treat her. Other than feeling a little tired—like she was coming down with the flu—radiation was easy, she told us.

She did well through it all. Well enough, in fact, that she made it to Julie's graduation from law school in June without missing a beat. Before we knew it, she was all better, and—just the way she'd wanted—nobody knew. Nobody, that is, but us.

Now, four years and ten months since her diagnosis, she was safe. She was here, eyes sparkling, playing the Comparison Game, and I felt badly for having been annoyed with her all day. It was Christmas, after all. Wasn't this what plenty was? All of us here together?

BEFORE I KNEW IT, DAYS later, the visit was over, my parents were packed and ready to leave, the guest room bare, I was crying, Sacha was crying, even Jacques was crying; they'd given us so much, taught us so much, done so much for us, and now they were leaving and it would just be the three of us again. The cab came, their bags went in the trunk, they were hugging us, calling out things they'd forgotten to tell us, waving, and we stood in the alley waving back till our arms ached. Then they were gone. I stepped back into our house and thought, *This is it, the emptiness I'm always trying so hard to fill up.*

And our first Christmas with Sacha was over.

For some reason, standing outside and watching them go, I remembered the last of the Sylvia stories: my mother's first week home for the summer after freshman year, back in their tiny apartment in Lincoln Park, Sylvia wrapped in an afghan on the couch, her abdomen filled with fluid. She was forty-three. Her cancer was inoperable: They'd opened her up, looked inside, and closed her up again. "How long does she have?" my mother asked one of the doctors, the way people asked in those days. And back then, the doctors answered. *Two or three months. Maybe the summer, if we're lucky.*

July Fourth, my mother's nineteenth birthday, there was a lop-sided cake on the table in the kitchen that Jennie had baked, but Sylvia was too sick to get up. She sang "Happy Birthday" from the couch while my mother sat at the table alone, leaning forward over the candles, trying to get her breath. Fresh out of wishes.

That was the last of the Sylvia stories. The one my mother almost never told.

Going Back (I)

JANUARY. THE GROUND WAS FROZEN, gift wrap trailing from trash barrels in the ice-slicked alley, the sky gunmetal gray. For the first time in conscious memory I wasn't going back to school after the winter break. I was home, the holidays over, the house quiet as a tomb. After the buzz and tumult of the last few weeks, the stillness was deafening. The Bilirubin Lady had packed up her lancets and left us, liberating Sacha from her glowing aquamarine blanket. No baby nurse, no babysitters, my parents gone, all the presents unwrapped and put away.

It was Monday, seven thirty in the morning. Jacques was officially back at work.

He'd be gone a whole work day, followed by a Boston day—

seven AM till nine PM, if the planes were on time. A fortune of hours away.

I hadn't expected this to bother me so much. We'd been over it all—Jacques actually *wanted* to be involved with Sacha as much as possible, it was part of the plan, he's a New Model man, a doer of dishes, a walker of dogs, a rememberer of big and small kindnesses. But that morning, watching him tug his clothes on like a fireman on high alert, all warm and steamy from the shower, humming a little, hurrying, brushing his hair, pulled as if by magnetic force toward the world outside, I hated how eagerly he was thinking about a day full of things that had nothing to do with Sacha or me. Coffee, breakfast, grabbing the paper, he was dashing around so freely, so unperturbed by each of Sacha's almost cries. Before we knew it, he was gone, one last kiss and *poof*, he was out the door, and Sacha and I were on our own.

Alone with Sacha, I'd left clock time behind, plunged back into something older and more organic—closer, maybe, to the medieval way of time reckoning, living by seasons and rounds of the day. Or even further back, time reckoned by cataclysm and upheaval. We lived together now in Sacha Time, where a minute could last anywhere from a nanosecond to a millennium.

Time slowed to a crawl. It was eight o'clock in the morning and I paced and fretted and worried about Sacha and looked at the clock and somehow it was still eight o'clock, as if we were stuck here, the two of us, immobile, while the rest of the world rushed on without us.

Being alone with Sacha made me nervous. What if something happened to her? What if she started choking? I pored over the pictures of the Baby Heimlich in *What to Expect Your Baby's First Year*, certain I'd never get my fists in the right position if something went down her windpipe and got stuck. I knew she was months away from being able to get hold of a nut or a bead, but I worried in advance. What if I tripped, carrying her downstairs? "Nothing will happen," Jacques said wearily when I called him at the office to be sure he was there, on constant alert. But I barely heard him. I was too busy scrutinizing Sacha, sleeping or awake. All the energy I used to pour into worrying about my own body now went into worrying about hers. Did she always make that whistling sound when she breathed? How long had she had that little rash? Was it normal for a baby to cry so much?

Annie called to check in, and I described the blister on Sacha's lip for her in intricate detail. A few minutes of this, and she told me someone was on call waiting and she had to go.

Late afternoon and early evening were hardest. Sacha got more irritable and harder to console as the day wore on.

"Maybe it's colic," Julie said helpfully.

I didn't think it was colic. I'd been reading up, and this wasn't consistent enough. "She just gets exhausted, I think. Too much of the day builds up in her."

"I remember that," my mother said, when I tried to describe this to her on the phone. "We used to call it 'the witching hour'—the time when you just couldn't calm down." She thought about this, from the distance of a generation. "You, more than Sara or Julie," she added. "They were both a cinch."

Of course. Here we were, back to the genetic lottery: Sacha had inherited this unease from me. Who could tell what else she'd gotten? I'd been studying other people's babies and I was discovering Sacha was not a particularly mellow baby.

"Don't compare," our pediatrician said cheerfully, and I tried not to, but the other babies in the waiting room all looked so rosy and unperturbed.

Sacha was not, I was finding, easily settled. She was sensitive to stimuli: bright lights, clapping, high-pitched voices. If she heard a sudden noise, her eyes would widen and her jaw would quiver and a cry would come from her like a stuck alarm—a public emergency, *stop this!* kind of cry. My mother was right, afternoon into evening was the hardest, Sacha seemed to collect all the experiences of the day—the crackle of newspaper, Bacchus's barking and scratching, the blare of a siren, and it would gather and gather in her, until by late afternoon she was inconsolable.

I tried my best not to compare or worry. We survived three of Jacques's Boston Days. His first week of work morphed into the second, and little by little, Sacha Time felt less bewildering. Like jet lag, I started to get used to it. My initial panic softened to a state of restless attentiveness. We nursed, and napped, and toured, and slept, and the sink filled with cups and bowls and gunky spoons, and bit by bit Sacha's face rounded a little, the sharp pins of her elbows and ankles filled out and softened. She wasn't mellower, necessarily, but we were getting used to each other, she and I. Either I was getting less anxious or more accustomed to her, and somehow we found our way.

Every morning Julie called, and every morning and every afternoon my mother called, and on weekends Sara called, and my father called, and once in a while Annie called, and in between I put Sacha in her Snugli and walked to the zoo, and we looked at the flamingos preening on their skinny legs and the birds circling in their netting and little by little, I got bolder. I started to expand our excursions—we took the Metro down to the Mall, we drove to Georgetown to meet my colleagues. When it warmed up a little in the afternoons, I walked her round and round our tiny garden. Some days Julie stopped in on her way to or from running last-minute errands—she was cutting her hours back now, getting ready to move—and soon Sacha was a month old, and then she was five weeks old, and then six weeks old, and before I knew it, it was the end of January, and Julie and Jon called to tell us that they'd scheduled Mayflower to come on Saturday and pack up all their furniture and boxes and get ready for their long drive north. They wanted us to come over Saturday morning so they could give us the food they couldn't take with them. And, of course, to say good-bye.

THE DAY BEFORE MAYFLOWER CAME, I got a phone call. I was sitting in the kitchen watching Sacha, who was strapped in her baby carrier watching the pale slivers of sunlight move across the kitchen table. I listened to the phone and thought, *The phone is ringing. Someone needs to answer it.* On the fifth ring, the one who answered it (was there anyone else?) was me.

"H'lo," I said into the phone, in my suspicious, I-*know*-you're-a-telemarketer voice. The phone is always an intrusion. If I wanted to talk, wouldn't I have called?

It was the chair of the English department from Boston.

We had a bad connection, she was clearing her throat, and I was distracted, watching Sacha's eyelids flickering, down down down *up*, down down down . . . *up*, trying to gauge whether she was drifting off to sleep, allowing me to keep talking or—more likely—about to snap alert and scream.

"—really enjoyed your telephone interview," the chair was saying, adding that she realized the circumstances were unusual, but now that MLA was over and the committee had met—there was a whole world out there of people going back, people meeting and making decisions while I was sitting here surrounded by gunky spoons—they'd voted, and they wanted me to come to campus for a real visit. A chance to really talk, the chair concluded. Several "reals" and "reallys" wove their way through our conversation, as if she could see straight into the unreality of my new world.

Would that be possible to arrange in the next few weeks? A visit to Boston? It would be for two days: meetings with different groups in the department, deans, and a dinner with the committee; and the next day, a presentation to the department. I'd need to give a half-hour talk, and there'd be another half hour for questions and answers.

My answer flew out right away. Yes, I wanted to come.

By late afternoon, every member of my family knew about the on-campus visit and had called to congratulate me. It was clear from the general euphoria my family had already skipped over a few steps—such as my actually getting the job. Or agreeing to take it, if I did.

Julie was overjoyed. If we moved to Boston, we'd only be two hours away from Cape Elizabeth!

"I am *not* picking my next job based on where *you're* living, Mellie," I said sharply, though I'd already checked the distance from Boston to Portland. 104 miles.

My mother had her own agenda. She'd started pricing airfares from Detroit to DC on Northwest, convinced Jacques would need her help while I was away.

"Of course I'm coming," she said, even as Jacques started frantically waving his arms at me in protest from across the kitchen. "There's no way you're taking that baby on a plane!" Did I know that a single sneeze could hang in place in an airplane cabin for up to seventy minutes?

She'd help Jacques out here in DC, while I was gone. She could even do a little cooking for us while she was there. Freeze some dinners. I remembered the stacks of thawing dishes on the counter over the holidays.

"Let her come," I said to Jacques, after I'd hung up. "She'll feel useful. She can help with Sacha. It'll be good, you'll have company."

"I don't need help," Jacques said. "Honestly. We'll be fine here on our own."

There were big questions looming (was this the right job opportunity, the right time?) and there were logistical questions (should we let my mother come? how could I leave Sacha for almost two full days when I was breastfeeding?). Jacques and I focused on logistics.

"Let's just take this one step at a time," Jacques said, which really meant *please tell your mother to cancel her plane reservations*.

"OK," I said, which really meant *I'll ask Julie what she thinks*.

"OH, JUST LET HER COME," Julie said the next morning, while I made her pose in front of the Mayflower van. I snapped half a dozen pictures of her holding Sacha in front of the last tower of boxes, all marked FRAGILE—DO NOT DROP. "It'll make her feel involved. And with Mom, it's always better that way."

Julie looked different to me, her skin rosy and her mood unusually good for someone about to drive fourteen hours behind a moving van. She twirled Sacha around, playfully pretending to sit her down on top of the highest box and laughing at my distress.

"What's with you?" I grumbled, taking Sacha back from her. I could only go so far when it came to feigning enthusiasm for this move. Their house looked so forlorn, squatting behind its blue-and-yellow SOLD sign. There was nothing left inside but old phone books and a pile of takeout menus. "You're in good spirits," I observed. "Happy to be escaping the big bad city?"

She grinned, thought for a second, then grabbed my arm, clearly unable to keep quiet another minute. "I'm *pregnant*, Mellie," she whispered.

I started. "You're *what*? Why didn't you tell me? *When?*"

"I'm already eleven weeks," she said. Jon and Jacques were peering at the map together, plotting the best route, and she filled me in out of earshot. The baby was due August 2. They'd done a new kind of test very early—something called chorionic villus sampling, or CVS—and this time, everything was OK. No chromosomes out of place.

"It's a girl," she told me, eyes shining.

Of course it was.

"And Mom knows already," she confessed, not quite meeting my eye.

Of course she did.

I hugged her and she hugged me back and we both burst into tears, Sacha—as usual—squashed between us, and Julie squeezed Sacha's foot in its loose pink sock. "Don't get anything on that outfit, Sacha-la," she teased her, smoothing down the front of Sacha's fleece coat. "Keep it nice and clean for your little cousin-to-be."

"Hey," Jon said, coming out of the garage with a lone rake. "We have to get going, Jules. At this rate we won't make it to Maine till next weekend."

My family doesn't do good-byes well. Julie and I looked awkwardly at each other, then away. "Well," I said, clearing my throat, and she echoed me, and we patted each other nervously on the shoulders and finally gave in and hugged each other again, and I cried a little more. So did she.

"Take care of your mom," Julie said, sniffling on Sacha's sleeve. "You hear me?" She didn't look at me, just at Sacha, whose eyes were big and ponderous. "I need her to come and help me with your cousin-to-be this summer. Don't let her stress out about the job in Boston, OK?"

Jacques and I watched as the movers put the last boxes in the van. We took a few more pictures. That was it. They got in their respective cars. In the end, we got their rake, a carton of Jon's lactose-free milk, and a few knobby carrots.

We watched till all we could see was the empty street.

"OK," Jacques said at last. "We should go."

"Wait," I said, when Jacques cleared his throat and leaned in to scoop Sacha from me.

I headed around the house, immaculate as always, to the backyard. For late January, it was warm, almost fifty degrees. The air smelled faintly of mud.

Emily's tree was still staked to the ground on all sides. One of the strips of cloth used to wrap the trunk had come loose. No buds yet, but the branches looked strong.

"Good-bye, little tree," I said. "Grow well."

The Interview

FOR THE NEXT FEW WEEKS, while Sacha napped, I alternated between working on my job talk and worrying about going to Boston.

"I can't believe I'm leaving her," I told Annie when she called to
see how things were going. "The books say if you miss too many feedings in a row, the baby may never nurse again."

"Forget the books," Annie said. This, from the Ivy League.

"I don't know what I should give my talk on, either," I told her.
It felt like ages since I'd thought about anything other than bilirubin
levels and Baby Heimlichs. When I went up to my study and flipped
through what I'd written about early modern time, it seemed unfamiliar, like somebody else's project. The manuscript had three sections:

the first, on timepieces; the second, on calendars; and the third on temporal narratives—histories, chronologies, and horoscopes.

"It's February," I pointed out. "Maybe I should talk about the history of Lent. About how people came to associate the month with giving things up, with punishing themselves."

"That sounds cheerful," Annie said.

I was actually warming to the idea. February has always been an in-between month. The Romans didn't have a name for it; it was a lawless period, between winter and spring. A temporal wilderness, full of weather.

In the Old Celtic calendar, they thought the last day of January divided winter from spring. The night between the two months was called Brigid's Night—Brigid, one of the most beloved of all Celtic goddesses, was associated with fire, fertility, household arts, and poetry. Pregnant women prayed to her to guide them to a safe delivery. On February 1, people lit candles to summon Brigid, hoping to scare away the darkest part of winter.

"Now all we have is Groundhog's Day," Annie commented.

She didn't sound convinced.

"Talk about something from the first part. The stuff on watches and early clocks," she suggested. Annie collects vintage watches. Her favorite part of my manuscript was the description of a gift Queen Elizabeth had received from a foreign official: a tiny gold watch-ring that she wore on her little finger. It had an ingenious alarm: A pointer popped out and scratched the queen's finger to signal the hour had changed.

I trusted Annie. She'd been writing grant proposals over winter break, sharpening her mind while I was learning to swaddle.

"OK," I said. "I'll talk about timepieces."

While Sacha rocked in her carrier, I sifted through slides. Slides of watches shaped like death's heads. A watch of Mary Queen of Scots carved with Latin mottos from Horace, warning that time is fleeting. *Flesh is but grass.* A seventeenth-century French enameled watch from

Blois, painted with a woman baring large round breasts, an hour hand cradled in her cleavage. An hourglass set inside a frieze in which a bronze Eve offered an apple to a bronze Adam. *Taste, and time begins.*

Hourglass figures, women. Bodies swelling out, then in, then out again. Holding within them the promise and penalty of generation. Next, and next, and next, and next: children and grandchildren and great-grandchildren and great-great-grandchildren, time running through their bodies like so many grains of sand.

Breast, cleavage, hand, hour.

I looked at Sacha, who looked back at me, and suddenly it hit me, here in our living room miles from the Folger or the Library of Congress, that part of what these early timepieces were doing was borrowing metaphors from the body. Borrowing them, and giving them back again.

Why do we talk about the *hands* of a clock? Or its *face*? Don't we turn timepieces into symbols of our own bodies—holding time, measuring time, signaling time's progress and decay?

After an afternoon of reading and thinking, I decided to give my talk on second hands.

Until late in the seventeenth century, mechanical clocks only had single hands, what we call "hour hands," fashioned out of hammered metal. Late in the century, after the mechanisms improved and clocks could measure smaller increments of time reliably, watchmakers began adding second or "minute" hands. At first these new timepieces were called "physicians' watches," because they were often used to measure the rate of a patient's pulse.

It was imprecise at first, this counting of heartbeats. In fact, one professor of medicine in Padua told his students to practice by getting training in conductor's tempo. People still believed the body set the standard, rather than the instrument that measured it.

Then all of this changed. There's a well-known story about Galileo, bored in church, working out his theory of the pendulum's motion by watching a lamp up near the pulpit swinging back and forth on a cord. At first, Galileo tested his theory by measuring the number of oscillations against his own heartbeat, assuming his pulse could provide the standard. Later, he flipped this around, realizing it was the pendulum that offered the reliable measure and not his heartbeat after all. This marked a major change in thinking: From this point, clocks began to provide the standard against which the body was measured, and the human pulse came to be recognized as erratic, susceptible to endless variations.

What interested me most was the in-between period, while all of this was still in flux, when bodies and clocks became briefly (and closely) elided. There's a great story about a servant of Pepys panicking when he heard a small clock chiming in his master's bedroom—he thought the clock was alive. As clocks got decorated with human characters and faces, described in increasingly human terms ("grandfather clock," for instance), people paradoxically began to see themselves in mechanistic terms. Were their bodies *working*? Were their hearts beating out time the way they should, or failing, winding down? Donne once tried to tell how sick he was by measuring his own pulse: "One hand asks the other by the pulse . . . how it does."

Two hands. One the physician, one the patient. One hand probing, measuring; the other quickening and slowing with fever, hunger, passion; the patient hoping the disease would pass, for now, and he might live. In Donne's case, at least at this point, he did. He survived whatever awful thing he had—probably typhus—and went on to write twenty-three *Devotions*—one short of the number of hours in the day—all written in the present tense, as if in the very instant of facing death.

There was no such thing in the seventeenth century as a "survivor story." People didn't think it was possible to triumph over disease back then. Instead, disease was seen as a constant and unshakable enemy, the body terrifyingly vulnerable. Rather than triumphing by the end of the *Devotions*, Donne ends with a fresh bout of terror, dreading what he sees as inevitable relapse.

Awful, in many ways. Not many modern readers like this side of Donne—he seems so anxious, so gloomy. But there's another aspect to this. Terror frees Donne from the necessity of "triumph." It wasn't, in the seventeenth century, a question of winning or losing, because people didn't think they got to choose. All they could do was try to understand. One hand gauging how the other was doing: a kind of early modern self-exam.

SOMETIMES, WITH SACHA, I FOUND myself thinking about the big questions. How we measure and understand time. Why we dread disease as much as we do. What we pass on from one generation to the next. Why we choose places only to leave them. I looked at Sacha's crib, the blue-and-yellow border in her bedroom, the hovering presence of Pepys, the huge stuffed bear from Julie, with his peculiar, watchful eyes. This, I murmured to Sacha, walking her slowly back and forth in her room, is home. Why would we ever want to leave?

With Jacques, I talked about breast milk.

The plan was I'd take the first flight to Boston on Thursday morning, stay overnight, be back on campus the next day, and come home on the last flight Friday evening. We counted up the hours, divided by feedings, and I got to work.

I loved storing milk. I made neat little bottles, labeling each with a Sharpie, lining them up in the freezer in glowing rows. It reminded me of those scenes in *Little House in the Big Woods* when Laura and Mary helped Ma prepare for winter, gathering in the squash and the pumpkins, hanging the herbs in the attic, stacking away the smoked meat for the cold days ahead. While Sacha nursed, I pumped, and before I knew it I was stepping up production, making a surplus, and while I expressed and bottled, Jacques and I laid out the plan. My mother was coming Wednesday and staying until Saturday, giving us a "buffer day" on either side of my trip. She'd take care of Sacha during the day, and Jacques would ride his bike back and forth to check on them, and before they knew it, I'd be back.

The more bottles I made, the less I had to think about leaving Sacha. How would it feel to be in another state, eight hundred miles away? It was like one of those story problems from sixth-grade math. *If a plane flies four hundred miles an hour and a baby is only nine weeks old and her mother is going four hundred and forty miles away and is only able to express thirty bottles of milk, will her baby even remember her when she gets home?*

WHEN THE DAY CAME (SLEET; windy gusts up to forty miles an hour) I felt like I was masquerading—stuffing myself into my work coat, riffling through files in my briefcase, snuffling sorrowfully over the pajama'd roll that was Sacha. Would she know me when I came back? Would she nurse again after so many straight feedings from a bottle?

The taxi came, and I followed Jacques's route to the letter. The Parkway to National. Terminal B. Long lines at ticketing, at security. The cold, muffled air of the plane. Ice pellets on the windows. When I was home with Sacha, watching Jacques disappear and waiting for him to come home, this orbit always looked so glamorous, the chance to order a cup of hot coffee and hold it in both hands. Uninterrupted time on the plane to read the newspaper, close my eyes. Doing it myself, it just felt lonely.

I HAD ONE LONGING FOR this visit, and that was for an uninterrupted night of sleep. Guiltily, I'd fantasized about this ever since I agreed to come. I pictured the night beginning luxuriously early, maybe around nine, and slipping through the expansive darkness like a long, quiet train: the billowing fields of ten o'clock and eleven; the gray tunnel of midnight; the smoky mountains of one and two and three o'clock giving way to the golden plains of early morning. If nothing else, these two days away would be worth it just for one solid, solitary night of sleep.

The hotel chosen by the university, set over a four-lane highway,

had an unspecified historical theme: plush velvet ropes, period paintings. There were antique weapons in display cases and the front entrance was guarded by a man in a Beefeater costume. I signed in, got
my room key, and rode the elevator up to the seventh floor. Room
712: small and beige, almost entirely filled by a queen-sized bed with
a butterfly-shaped stain on the coverlet. A white paper sash proved the
toilet hadn't been used since the cleaners had been in. A radiator rattled, I called the department chair to check in, confirmed my schedule, and halfway through the phone call realized my breasts were
beginning to ache. Almost four hours since I'd left home, and somewhere, hundreds of miles away, I pictured a thawed bottle of breast
milk nudging its way into Sacha's eager mouth. My breasts swelled,
hard as bricks.

Thursday afternoon was spent in back-to-back meetings with
administrators (dean, provost, dean), punctuated by frantic trips to
the bathroom where I closed the stall behind me, sweating and nauseated, wrenched open the buttons of my blouse, leaned over, and emptied breast milk into the toilet. My guide, a cheerful grad student
working on Dickens, probably thought I was bulimic—I tried my
hardest not to groan with relief as milk spewed out of me (wasted!)
into the sewers of Boston. By the time dinner came, I barely cared
what happened, I only wanted to be back home, clutching Sacha.
Who knew being a mother could be so physical, so much more intense than any other kind of desire?

Except, that is, the desire for sleep. Dinner, small talk, dessert,
by eight thirty I started making the small fidgety motions of a person
who has done her part and really needs to go back to the hotel, Beef-
eaters and all.

The small talk went on. Who wanted coffee? I tried not to look
aghast as various people agreed that was a good idea.

It was almost ten o'clock before I was in bed at last, staring grate-
fully up through the reflected light of the highway at the acoustic
ceiling tiles, wondering why my breasts felt disturbingly normal (was

I drying up?) or whether it had been rude to yawn when one of the department members suggested drinks after coffee (what did they think this was, a *party?*). I was embarrassed by the luxuriousness of this moment, the not-until-seven-AM of it all. It was like infidelity: I was cheating on Jacques alone in this Beefeater-themed hotel, and I rolled over and closed my eyes and waited for waves of sleep to wash over me. I curled to the right and then to the left, missing Sacha, missing Jacques, guilty that all this was *mine*, this whole empire of sleep, and rolled over again, what was that *noise* out there, was that really just the Mass Pike buzzing like that, *don't notice it, go to sleep*, one more roll, another, was that little red light on the alarm going to glow like that all night? The sheets had a clammy slipperiness to them, the buzz intensified, I sat up and glared at the alarm clock, 10:47, and suddenly I was rigid with wakefulness.

It was eleven, then eleven thirty, then midnight, and I couldn't sleep. I rearranged the pillows. I adjusted the blinds, turned the alarm clock to the wall, tried more covers, then fewer covers, snatched a pillow from the closet, and finally sat straight up, staring balefully out the window at the Mass Pike. Cars were streaming in four feverish lanes, headlights boring into the night, a dull roar below me. The noise, I decided. It was the noise. Who in their right mind built a hotel on a highway? I dimly remembered my Lonely Planet guidebook recommending earplugs for times like this, but I didn't have any—just nursing pads, cotton discs the size of makeup sponges. It was after one AM by now, my continent of sleep precipitously eroded, but I still had six hours left! I folded up the breast pads, origami-style, wedging one in each ear. Back to the pillow rearranging, the Kama Sutra of sleeplessness, the underdoggy, the overdoggy, the knee tuck, the back dive, the swan. It was one thirty and two and finally I was in tears, breast pads shredding in my fingers as I called the Beefeater on duty at the front desk and begged—*demanded*—a quieter room. I could hear him tapping away at his computer. *Tap tap tap*, quiet room, quiet room, was there a keyword to search for this? Did they put people in noisy rooms first just to see if they noticed? "Ma'am," he said nasally—when did I stop being Miss and start being Ma'am? Did having a baby do that?—"We have a room on the fourteenth floor but that room *also* has the highway, and then of course there's the elevator nearby . . ." There was no point changing rooms now. It was two thirty, then three, this was the hour when Sacha would be waking up, rubbing her fists across her lips that way she did when she was hungry, like she was playing a harmonica, looking for me, and there'd only be eight bottles of milk left by morning, and somehow, between three and four, I must have finally drifted off, because the next thing I knew the alarm was ringing—no, it was the phone, the *phone*, it was Jacques, was something wrong? Was it Sacha?—and I was grabbing the receiver, gasping his name, it was six thirty and he was so sorry he'd woken me. He wanted to wish me luck. He wanted to make sure I was OK. He wanted to tell me Sacha was awake. "And guess what," he said adoringly. "You'll never believe it. Last night, she slept through the night for the first time."

The House with the
Green Shag Carpet

IT'S FUNNY HOW OFTEN PEOPLE refer to place when what they're really thinking about is time. "Remember Charlevoix?" my sisters and I sometimes asked one another. Charlevoix is the lakeside town in northern Michigan where we went on vacation every year until Sara went to college and we began to go our separate ways as a family. We hadn't been back in almost fifteen years. My mother, angling for a reunion, was trying to get all three of our families to join them there next Labor Day weekend.

"When?" Jacques asked, nonplussed.

"You have to plan early to get so many people together," I

said defensively, not wanting to hear my mother and her calendar lampooned.

Charlevoix. I loved the idea of going back there with Sacha. When I thought about Charlevoix now, I imagined the fossilized time of summer childhood: a white beach, a bucket of Petoskey stones, the low horn of the *Beaver Islander*—all associated for me with a time when we were young, intact, our parents in good spirits, summer flapping in front of us like a white sail.

We talk about things being "far off," "distant," and that winter, thinking about moving back to Boston, I realized that what I was picturing wasn't a change in geography, but a move back in time. "Boston" to me didn't really mean a new department or a new neighborhood, but Harvard Square, circa 1989: my favorite café on JFK Street, which used to be called Boylston Street (and before that— before my time—something else); running the bridges with Annie along the Charles; browsing on my hands and knees through shelves in secondhand bookstores. It was 1989 I was picturing more than Harvard Square, which had already gone through several separate waves of construction since we'd moved away. In 1989, there were no cell phones, or Internet cafés, and in every last area of my life, from romance to work, I'd been floating in an ether of anxious potential.

I used to read science fiction as a break from Donne and Milton, and there was one point that always got to people when they speculated about time travel. They called it the "grandmother question." Suppose you could go back in time, two generations. You showed up in an earlier era, wore different clothes, spoke differently. You did various things, met people, life happened—and along the way you happened (completely by coincidence) to meet your own grandmother. Suppose one thing led to another, and you were the sort of person who did this kind of thing and you got in a terrible fight with her—maybe there was an antique revolver involved—and you ended up killing her. Then what? What would happen to your own mother—or to you? Could either of you still be born?

One group, sci-fi determinists, claimed to have the answer. If you went back in time and met your own grandmother, they reasoned, you could only act in predetermined ways. You wouldn't be *able* to kill her—something would stop you at the last minute.

I had a different question: What if you could actually *help* your grandmother? What if you could keep her from dying young? Say, for instance, you could go back to the 1940s, take a train to Chicago, over to the near North Side, and let's say it was a nice day, maybe in May, and you could go to the hat shop where Sylvia was learning to curl ribbon with a knife, and you just strolled to the counter with a beautiful hat you were thinking about buying, one of those hats you just can't find in the late twentieth century, not even on eBay, and right before she reached over to wrap it up for you, you grabbed her hand—small, warm—and you pressed it, hard, and got her to look up at you. The two of you staring at each other, gazes locked. And you said, "Sylvia, I know this sounds insane, but listen. Listen! I know you're feeling great right now, I know you're a single mother, you've got a beautiful daughter, you've got other things on your mind, you're not thinking about your ovaries, you love to go dancing, you have a closet full of dresses, but Sylvia, listen—"

What if you could *save* your own grandmother? What then?

It wouldn't wreck the future. Your mother could still have her life. And you could have yours. Only better, in hundreds of ways.

Rewind, play backward. The ground opens up, the coffin lifts upward, the lid opens, Sylvia sits up, brushes her hair back, drowsy, a little stiff, starts to climb out, looking around her, confused. "Where am I?" Now you can play the tape again. Forward, but repaired. My mother turns nineteen, Sylvia is healthy, ruddy, they have dinner, Sylvia bakes the cake herself, they sing together at the table. My mother, able to be nineteen the way most girls are nineteen, rolls her eyes when Sylvia gets sentimental about how grown-up she's getting. Afterward the two of them curl up on the couch together and make plans. They have nothing but time, sometimes they quarrel over insignificant things, make up, laugh, quarrel again. The pictures in our upstairs hallway change in a blink. Look: There Sylvia is, arm linked through my mother's, and my mother has her mouth open wide, laughing. Forward, forward. Sylvia fussing over Sara's bassinette. Lifting me from a swing. Oh, and there's Pody with her. She looks older, my mother says fondly, with that isn't-it-amazing-how-old-we're-all-getting warmth in her voice. It's wonderful how much older everyone looks. There's a third act to the play, and a fourth. Gail is there, too. She and my mother say how glad they are to have each other, since neither of them has a sister. They all come to Michigan for Thanksgiving. We have to get more chairs, the table is so crowded! The cups fill to the brim, winking a little under the chandelier.

We don't worry much, as a family. Not in this version: Family 2.0. Why sweat the small stuff, when you have your whole life in front of you?

In the real version—1.0—we worried all the time. About our bodies. About bad weather, terrorists, freak accidents. We called each other, asked how things were going. It was like we were always waiting. "For the other shoe to drop," my mother said, and even though I didn't know exactly what that phrase meant, I got the implication. We were waiting for the next worry—as if we'd know it when it came.

THREE DAYS AFTER I GOT back from Boston, I got a call from the department chair offering me the job. Between appointments with the pediatrician, and Sacha's first and second set of shots, and long phone calls with Annie and my sisters and my mother, and long nights up with Jacques, making lists of pros and cons and tearing them up and insisting we should just go with our gut, we decided I should take the job. Sad as I was about leaving Georgetown, it seemed like the best choice for us now as a family, and suddenly it was like we were rewinding the tape, taking things off shelves and putting them in boxes, emptying the fridge, recorking the champagne. We put our town house on the market, and soon there were always people over we didn't know, opening up cupboards, inspecting the surfaces of things. With each visit, I'd put Sacha in her Snugli and walk up and down the steps in front of or behind the Realtors, defending the narrow stairwell, the distant nursery, the burn mark on our exposed brick wall.

The agents were unimpressed. The market was in a slump, and people with children—the bull's-eye of home seekers—wanted detached houses. With garages. And yards.

Nobody had a nice thing to say about our third-floor nursery.

Then, just as suddenly, a couple in their fifties (children grown) came to look at the house, came back twice with an architect, and within days had made an offer. Not a stunning offer, but acceptable. They had all kinds of plans to "open things up" and knock out walls, and the agents thought it was a miracle. We signed the purchase and sales agreement and before we knew it, our house was on its way to belonging to someone else.

One Saturday Jacques helped me cut the royal blue carpet out of Sacha's room with an X-Acto knife and roll it up to take with us. We also took some leftover blue-and-yellow border. I would've taken the exposed brick wall if we could.

March was a month of good-byes. We said good-bye to neighbors. To Dave and Lori. I said good-bye to the people in my department, to former students, to Dr. Weiss, to Dr. Lennox. We packed boxes. I started out with a great attitude and a neat outlay of supplies—fresh cardboard cartons, sharp scissors, boxing tape, permanent markers. This move, I told myself, was a chance for revision. In our new life I'd pare things down to mere essentials, everything would have its place. I stacked books neatly in boxes by author and subject. *Shakespeare. Seventeenth-Century Biography*. I still had no idea where any of these things would end up. Every Tuesday and Thursday when Jacques flew up to Boston, he looked at places for us to rent. All I could picture was my old apartment in Eliot House, with its green door opening onto the parking bay. Or Jacques's little house with the pear tree.

"Back," I said to Sacha, who pursed her lips in what I thought was an approximation of the letter *B*. "We're going back."

Through all of this, we packed, and then one Tuesday Jacques called, excited, and told me he'd found a place to rent. Admittedly, it was in the suburbs and not in Cambridge, but it was an actual house—detached, not even a town house—with three bedrooms, a fenced yard for Bacchus, and most importantly, no lead paint. That was a big deal. In Boston, landlords weren't allowed to rent to anyone with children under the age of five if there was lead paint on the walls or trim. That law had knocked almost every place Jacques had looked at so far out of the running.

"Which suburb?" I asked. I knew Arlington a little.

"Newton," he said, after a pause.

We'd made a pact, Jacques and I. Not Newton. Not that there was anything wrong with Newton—it's pretty, full of trees, safe—but it seemed to both of us to epitomize suburban living, a leap forward into middle age. We weren't there yet.

"Don't worry," Jacques said. "It's just for a few months." The plan was we'd settle in, using the rental as base camp. We'd find something permanent soon enough.

He brought a picture home, which I taped up on our fridge, like a focal point.

"Well," I said judiciously, leaning in for a closer look. "It's not that bad."

"It has shag carpet on the first floor," Jacques mentioned, as I centered the picture between the ice maker and the door handle. He frowned, inspecting the picture. "Kind of mint green shag, if you can picture that."

FROM THE OUTSIDE, THE HOUSE with the Green Shag Carpet looked like a child's drawing of a house, a white box with shutters. We arrived late-week, late-March, during an early spring snow squall. Moving north, we seemed to have set ourselves back almost two months in terms of weather—it was like leaving the world of color and going back to black and white.

The house stood behind a neat front lawn in a row of other houses, closed up and immaculate, each with its own plastic can marked YARD WASTE. No people outside anywhere. Inside, each room was a perfect square. Every room on the first floor except the kitchen was carpeted in thick green shag—not a color I'd ever seen before, but one that my mother later nicknamed Donnagel Green, after the kind of medicine she made us take when we had diarrhea as children.

We only unpacked what we needed right away, stacking the rest of our boxes (*Shakespeare, Comedies; Ski Hats, Long Underwear*) in a side porch. Annie sent us an oven mitt in the shape of the Liberty Bell, which I hung up in the kitchen. This, Jacques reminded me as we trailed from room to mint green room, was just a place to park ourselves while we looked for something permanent. We wouldn't be here long.

"What's it like?" Annie asked, when I called to thank her for the oven mitt. In six years of grad school, she'd never been to Newton.

I tried to describe it.

The House with the Green Shag Carpet—eight miles from Cambridge, walking distance to no more than an Exxon station and a Star Market—was a distinctly middle-age house, with its wall-to-wall shag, attached garage, and swirly stucco ceilings. This was a house that smacked of trips to the hardware store, of Lysol and wind chimes, of mildew and old socks. The house had more space than we needed or wanted, and most of it we left closed up and unexplored: cedar closets for storing winter woolens, a mudroom, and the garage, where we found coils of rubber hoses and a pyramid of Ice Melt pellets. Mostly we huddled in two or three rooms, like campers avoiding the fringes of an unfriendly forest.

Unattractive as we were as potential tenants, given the lead laws and Bacchus, I knew the house was a windfall. It was for sale, which meant Realtors might intrude on us "once in a while" to show it, but—Jacques loved this part—it was a tenancy-at-will, which meant all we had to do was give a month's notice when we wanted to leave. Of course, as I pointed out, that worked both ways. The owners (relocated to the edge of a golf course in the Carolinas) only had to give *us* a month's notice if the house sold, lending a certain urgency to our house hunting.

Jacques didn't mind. He liked the pressure. It made the whole thing a kind of race!

Except, he reminded me, that didn't mean we should relax our standards. Jacques was still smarting from the hit we'd taken selling our house in DC, and he kept emphasizing this was a time for patience. For comparison shopping. In his mind, there was no rush. We were planning to settle here permanently, and Jacques wanted what he called the "Forever House"—a place we'd settle down in until the distant day someone came to roll us off to assisted living. Personally, I was hoping a house might show up a little closer to this end of our lives than that one. March gave way to April, and I could feel the months left for nesting and decorating dwindling at an alarming rate. I wanted time over the summer to plan my courses for the fall, time to line up a babysitter. I wanted to find the Forever House *now*.

I tried to throw myself into the hunt. A house would come on the market, we'd pack ourselves up, get Sacha ready, look over the listing sheet or replay the message from Sandi, our broker, and convince ourselves this one would be it. In the abstract, each house sounded perfect. But inevitably, there'd be a problem. The house would be on a main road, or in ruins, or the size of a shoebox, or way too expensive, or all of these things at once, and we'd come back, glum and irritable, and the green shag would be waiting for us, scratchy, ugly, not even ours to change.

Maybe it was moving back to Boston with so little warning, finding myself in a place both known and unfamiliar. All I know is that the House with the Green Shag saddened me. Each room felt lonely in a different way. The basement was the worst, with its old remnants of family fun: a box of dented Ping-Pong balls, a banner from someone else's high school days.

I had no interest in playing in the playroom or dining in the dining room or living in the living room. I wasn't myself. I didn't feel like driving up to Maine to see Julie, or joining playgroups, or getting myself a new library card and taking Sacha to Story Time. One of my new colleagues called, wanting to meet for lunch, but I didn't have a babysitter and didn't feel like bringing Sacha, who'd been irritable and off-schedule since we moved, so I just declined. Instead, I called my mother from the phone in the kitchen, our borrowed table cluttered with baby cereal and real estate listings. I made fun of the house and when my mother laughed, I felt better.

I was annoyed with myself for missing DC. When I was in DC, hadn't I sometimes wished we were back in Boston?

"The carpet," my mother reminded me, "is always greener on the other side of the house."

IS IT POSSIBLE TO GET delayed postpartum depression? I missed everyone that spring. I missed Jacques, who—back to a regular schedule—had traded in his bicycle and telecommuting for regular hours, five days a week, except in his world, *regular* meant long, intense hours, six days a week. I missed our DC neighbors, and the zoo, and my colleagues at Georgetown. I missed Julie, who sounded manic and slightly out of focus when we talked, working extra hours to put money away before the baby came, interviewing pediatricians, making a million plans. She and Jon loved their rental house—it was a Victorian with a view of the bay, and she was fixing up the baby's room on weekends, dying for us to come up, and instead of being helpful and sisterly, I felt exhausted and even (despicably enough) a little jealous. Why couldn't *we* find an adorable cottage we both loved? Why were Jacques and I getting crankier and crankier with each other, erupting into predictable arguments about whose turn it was to bathe

Sacha or walk Bacchus or who got to sleep ten minutes later or sneak off to run an errand?

This wasn't us. It wasn't the *us* I wanted, anyway.

I called Annie. I tried explaining all of this to her, but she didn't really want to hear about it. She'd just renewed a lease on a walk-up in a bad part of West Philly, had fallen behind on her car payments, and didn't particularly care what color our carpet was. "Remember what it was like before you married a captain of industry?" she asked me.

"He's not a captain of industry," I said, irritated. It was clear Annie wasn't in the mood to lend a sympathetic ear. As far as she was concerned, I had a semester off and was squandering it. "What do you *do* all day?" she asked me once, sounding mystified.

Remembering that, I felt doubly slighted now. What I really wanted to tell Annie was how lonely I felt, how baffling it was spending so much time alone with a baby. But I couldn't seem to find the right words. It sounded like I was complaining, and I didn't mean to complain. I loved being home with Sacha, it was just—

I tried telling her about our next-door neighbor, a pert woman with a knowing eye. She had three basketball-playing sons, and I thought I could make Annie laugh, complaining about the sound of heavy panting outside the window every evening.

I could tell she was tuning out.

When I took Sacha to Harvard Square in her Snugli, we walked past places where Annie and I used to hang out and I felt like I was on Mars. Same places, different people. In some instances, different places. They kept closing the old cafés and putting in banks and office supply stores.

"It's like I'm dealing with ghosts," I told Annie.

"I found a dead man on my front stoop this morning," Annie told me. "At least your ghosts are only metaphors."

"MAYBE," MY MOTHER SAID EXPERIMENTALLY, one afternoon on the phone, "you need to get out a little more. Meet people."

This, from a woman who only opened the door for the exterminator. My mother loved it when *we* showed up. Everyone else was an intrusion.

ACTUALLY, I'VE NEVER MINDED BEING alone. Academics are bred for it: You work alone in the library, reading things written hundreds of years ago. You write alone. You grade papers alone. There are brief interludes of too-much-togetherness—department meetings; students bunched up outside of your office, waiting for help with papers or letters of recommendation. Sometimes when you're teaching, you dream about the chance to be alone again.

But this was different.

For one thing, I wasn't exactly alone. I was with Sacha, and Sacha made it hard to do any of the things I liked doing when I was alone. Reading in general was out, since Sacha saw paper, like most things, as something to be torn up or sucked on. Writing was also out: She was an inveterate grabber of pens, a smasher of keyboards. When it came to housework or organizing, especially folding laundry, Sacha was herself an unfolder, a puller-outer, a creator of domestic disruption. Not to mention that she generated laundry and waste by the bushel.

I usually waited to call my mother till the hardest part of the day, the hour after the nap, the hour when Sacha was at her crankiest, smelling of sour milk, her cheek creased from the wrinkle in the flannel crib sheet, smacking crossly at my ear.

I was coming to depend on these talks.

My mother was like the authors of *What to Expect*, upbeat, sure of herself, only ironic, and the advice was tailored just for me. She was funny, honest, optimistic. She remembered things I'd done when I was a baby and things she'd done wrong and offered subtle and unspoken encouragement that one day, Sacha would be grown, solvent, able to talk on the phone and hold a spoon without dropping it. She admitted to making mistakes and reminded me I'd survived them.

Best of all, she admitted she'd been bored and lonely half the time when we were little.

"It'll get better," she promised. "You'll see. You'll meet some nice people with babies, and it will get better."

Mostly, so far, the people we met were Realtors. We met them one of two ways: Either they'd come over to pick us up, Sacha and me, to look at a house that had just come on the market or had been on, languishing, and had just changed price; or we met them because they were coming to the Green Shag for a "showing."

Here is something I learned: Even though we were the same people in both situations—the same slightly colicky four-and-a-half-month-old baby, silky light brown curls, thoughtful eyes, saloon-man's belly laugh—the same new mother (me) in my stretchy black pants (still a ways to go before I tried anything that zipped)—even though! We were *not* the same people when the Realtors came to us as we were when we went to them. In the first instance, we were "the tenants." That is how we were introduced, if we got introduced at all. When you're a tenant, nobody adds colorful details about your profession (Renaissance English) or where you're from (DC, actually) or fills in delightful details about your baby (just over four months, isn't she precocious?). As tenants, your job is just to answer the door and evaporate, suggesting to prospective buyers nothing but the ease with which you can be erased from the scene they're about to witness. So we had no names, no identities, and there was no particular interest in the nap schedule of "the baby," whose room—just to the left upstairs, the one with that *lovely* blue carpet—*must* be seen, it gets *such* good light, waking poor Sacha if she'd managed to sleep through the doorbell or the thunder of Bacchus's responsive bark.

The irony was, we were looking at more or less identically priced houses in Cambridge, and when we were the buyers, the Realtors—friends or partners of the very people we'd seen that morning—were totally different: all curiosity and attention, eager to learn our likes and dislikes, our slightest prejudices about curbside parking and downstairs bathrooms. When we were the buyers, they were so caring! Jacques's piano became a fascinating challenge to puzzle out in each of the pint-size living rooms we navigated ("parlors," they called them). "Could the piano go *here*?" one agent wondered, flattening herself against a coat closet in a tiny foyer.

Sacha saw each house with us. Her eyes widened as we climbed narrow staircases flocked in Victorian paper, or ducked our heads under the low ceilings of euphemistically named "third floors." She nodded off in her Snugli as we opened and closed ancient medicine cabinets, where antibiotics from the Cold War crumbled in dead vials, peered into dim nooks advertised as kitchens, or sidled down rotting staircases into basements glowing with stalactites of mold.

In the afternoons, my mother called and I described each house for her in faithful detail. She nicknamed them for me. The house with the leaky roof and the neon-bright kitchen on Anawan Road got recast as "An Nah Want It." The house with the fault line in the foundation became the "Crack House." The house where I tripped on the basement steps was dubbed the "Mouse House," after I admitted that under a garment rack stuffed with musty, 1950s dresses we'd seen the sad, sideways curl of a long-dead tail.

My mother loved anatomizing houses. She was good, too—good enough to eliminate or promote a place long distance, armed with penetrating questions (no first floor closet? What do you mean, no sink?). Sight unseen, she could suggest a corner of a front hall could become that much-needed bathroom. Her ingenuity astonished me. Couldn't you put a bedroom addition over the garage? Couldn't you knock down the wall and make that room big enough for the piano? *Couldn't* in her lexicon meant *could*, and her sense of what was possible was unceasingly capacious. For Jacques and me, a house was *wysiwyg*: "what you see is what you get." No bathrooms, no closets, no room for the piano, forget it. My mother felt differently. Things could be "opened up" or renovated or repositioned, and eventually I began to realize we were talking about more here than mere stucco and glass.

She must have known, more than I did, that I was a little depressed that spring, moving back to Boston; that with Julie gone, missing Annie, between jobs, waiting, not knowing exactly what I was waiting for, I felt lost. Here I was, a mother myself now, my diplomas framed and propped up in the makeshift study Jacques and I shared. I had everything I'd ever wanted, and I still needed my mother to reassure me it would all work out. That *couldn't* could still mean *could*.

For a long time, when I was little, she was my mother, and I needed her. Then I grew up and she was still my mother and I loved her, but I didn't need her anymore—or at least, I didn't *want* to need her. Then I was busy and working, and I missed her sometimes and other times, didn't. And now, almost thirty-three, I was discovering her again, and needing her again, and actually *wanting* to need her. It was as if having a baby and becoming a mother somehow made the lights snap on and I was figuring it all out. Or at least this piece of it. So this is what it's all about, this mother-daughter thing! Somebody to complain to who actually laughed about the next-door neighbor, and didn't try to get off the phone.

WHILE SHE RENOVATED FOR US long distance, my mother was packing for her trip out to see Sara and the girls. It was April break, and she and my father were taking them up to Vancouver Island and Lake Louise. They'd be gone ten days.

Ten whole days without talking to her. Oh, she could try to call us from the road, but she'd be with Sara and the girls, and it would be different. I could imagine the breathless, I-can't-really-talk-now sound in her voice. "Don't worry," my mother said, as if reading my mind. "I'm coming out to see you in May. I'm spending Mother's Day with you, remember?" My mother was convinced if she didn't see Sacha every few months, Sacha would forget who she was. Babies have short memories, and my mother was determined to update her imprint on a regular basis.

I couldn't wait for her to come. Probably yet another sign I was losing it.

My mother, for her part, loved being needed. "See, Mellie," she teased. "You become a mother, and guess what? All of a sudden, your own mother comes in handy."

Later, walking Sacha to the park past the empty swings, I thought about that remark.

What about her? Who'd been there for my mother when she'd had Sara? And then, two years later, when she'd had me?

In every baby picture we have, my mother is alone. Lifting up Sara, laughing. Pushing me on a swing. Digging in the sand with Julie in Charlevoix. Of course, my father must have been there, taking the pictures. But a lot of the time, it must have felt like that for her. Time alone with us. Time missing Sylvia.

I USED TO THINK OF Sylvia's death as a single event: September 1953. She died the second week of what should have been my mother's sophomore year of college, except my mother, knowing how sick she was, had taken the fall term off. The father had been out of the picture the whole time, and all the details were left to her. She was nineteen. With my father's help, she organized a small funeral in Chicago, and two months later she and my father got married in one of the function rooms at the Drake Hotel. My mother wore a calf-length, pale blue dress and a pearl bracelet. She looked so ethereal in the photographs in the wedding album: a little like Audrey Hepburn, slender necked, with a wistful, unfocused smile. We loved looking at those pictures. We'd sit on the couch in the living room and my mother would turn the pages carefully for us, so we wouldn't get fingerprints on the photos. We pored over the pictures of the three-tiered cake, the corsages.

We anatomized every last detail of my mother's dress, her hair, her white gloves. But even as children, we could tell there was something off in those pictures. A stilted, melancholy air.

"Why didn't you wear a real wedding dress? A long, white one?" Julie asked once.

My mother looked vague. "Oh . . . ," she said, offhand. You could tell she was thinking about the best answer. "I didn't really want that. My mother had just died." She shrugged, remembering. "I was still in mourning. I wasn't really in the mood for a big traditional wedding."

We couldn't fathom that. Julie's favorite doll came out of the box already wearing a wedding dress, complete with a veil and white pointy shoes. The dress seemed glued to her. The bride doll wore it all the time, even when we used her as a prop in Reptile Rodeo out on our driveway with our neighbors' pet lizards.

Julie patted my mother on her arm, concerned. No wedding dress? None of us could grasp the gravity of such an error.

There were so many things we never asked. Who helped her find the dress she did wear, the pretty blue one? Who helped her pick out the fancy cake, with the icing beads and the real flowers?

We saw some of what was missing. The white dress, the veil. But we didn't see the biggest absence in the picture: the emptiness next to my mother where Sylvia should have been.

Self-Exam

MIDNIGHT, EARLY MAY. JACQUES WAS working in the study we shared. Sacha was asleep, and I was sitting up in bed, reading a monograph on early modern horoscopes. I've always been a night owl. I love that stretch of night when everyone else is asleep, the whole world is quiet, and for once, you can actually think. It's the time of day cut loose from logistics, schedules, planning.

The word *horoscope* literally means "to watch the hour." In theory, if you study the hour when you were born, something will be revealed both about your character and about events to come. Auspicious and inauspicious days. I lay back, thinking about what it meant to see ahead. What if you really could see the future, if the hour you were born told you something that mattered? Would that be a good thing? I'm not much of a horoscope person, although I've always liked the descriptions of Taurus—earthbound, stubborn. Fond of security and luxury fabrics.

In my own way, I've always been an hour watcher. Back then, I loved trying to imagine where we'd be in ten months or ten years. It was the closest I could get to time travel. What would Sacha be like when she was almost ten? Would we ever find a house? Would I like my new department?

When would we have another baby?

Even now, knowing we had our hands full, I was starting to dream about a second child. I couldn't imagine Sacha growing up without a sister or brother. May, my birthday month, pushed the hands forward to another position on the clock. I was turning thirty-three. Another step closer to thirty-five, my looming deadline. At the back of my mind, I'd been trying to forget about our family history. I hadn't been back to the Farber yet. I needed to make an appointment, needed to start mapping out what came next.

Maybe once we'd found a house . . . Once I'd settled into teaching . . .

Sacha was too young—only five months old. I was still nursing. But I didn't want to wait forever, either. If we wanted to have another baby before I turned thirty-five . . .

I started counting backward again. In order to have a baby next summer—

I hadn't realized how tired I was. I still had my old nursing bra on and I needed to take a shower, but I felt like I couldn't move. I was reaching up to shuck the bra off, moving slowly, when my finger grazed my breast and I felt something. *That's weird*, I thought.

My finger went back, zeroed right in. If my breast was a clock, what I was feeling was at two o'clock, near the nipple. A small hard lump.

A cold feeling spread through my stomach. I felt literally sick— the room spun. *No way*. There was no way this was possible.

I sat straight up, flicked on the overhead light. I took both hands and pressed experimentally on my breast, probing, trying to stay calm. There. Right in the same spot—small, about the size of a pea. A definite lump.

I lay back down, shaken, eyes on the ceiling. It's probably nothing, I told myself, all the while thinking, *Something! It's something!*

It was punishment for greed, I told myself, a terrible taste in my mouth. For trying to plan a second baby. Why couldn't I be happy with what we had? Why did I have to tempt the gods by always wanting more?

I knew my breasts by heart. My sisters and I had grown up in the era when girls' locker rooms were plastered with laminated drawings demonstrating how to examine yourself once a month. Usually the instructions showed a cartoon-drawn, circular breast made up of different colored rings, like the targets we shot at in archery at summer camp. Red, yellow, blue. You were supposed to examine yourself in the shower or lying back on your bed, inching your fingers carefully around each section. I could have told you at any given day what each part of each breast felt like. Even nursing, I knew every little change. This lump was utterly unknown: an enemy invader.

I pushed aside my book, hauled myself out of bed, and padded into the next room, looking for Jacques. He was sitting at the desk in his boxer shorts, intent on a stack of papers. My heart was pounding.

When I'm really worried, I don't go in for small talk. "Can you feel this?" I asked him, grabbing his hand and pushing his index finger in the direction of the lump.

He was in the middle of looking over a deferred tax form. This wasn't what he'd expected, 12:20 on a Sunday night.

Jacques knows me. He let me guide his finger around until I zeroed in on the right place. I could see his face change expression as he registered it under his finger. "There?" he asked, pushing a little. It didn't hurt, exactly. It just felt funny.

I nodded, my mouth dry. "What do you think it is?" I demanded. Expecting him to answer. I'm not sure why what he said mattered so much to me: Jacques can take a computer apart and put it together again, but he doesn't know the first thing about anything medical. He deliberately avoids reading articles about diseases. Don't look for trouble, is the approach he favors, and the odds are, trouble will stay away.

"I'm sure it's some kind of breastfeeding thing," he said. "Doesn't that happen when you're nursing? With all those hormones?"

"Then why hasn't it happened before?" I shot back accusingly. I wanted him to reassure me, but I was ready to attack any reassurance he offered. "I've been nursing for five months!"

"I wouldn't worry," Jacques said, turning back to the tax form. "But if it bothers you, why not have somebody check it out?"

I stared at him. He sounded so rational, but the minute he suggested that I "check it out," I started picturing worst-case scenarios: biopsies, bad news, toxic regimens. Cancer everywhere.

He hadn't reassured me at all. He'd told me I needed to have this checked out! The message was clear: He was worried. I was in trouble.

I thought about my mother's tumor, and my mouth went dry.

Inauspicious day. My personal terror alert shot from high to very high. I didn't sleep much that night. I kept tossing and turning, trying not to jab my finger back in the general direction of the lump, which by five AM I was sure had gotten bigger. I was damp and sweaty and miserable, furious with myself for being so panicky, but unable to stop worrying, and by the time Sacha started whimpering from the next room, I was a mess.

I spent all Monday morning calling around, trying to find a doctor who could see me. I called my old doctor in the high-risk ovarian group—I was late making an appointment to see him, the gods were punishing me!—but his nurse said he had left the practice, and I should call back another time to make an appointment with one of his partners. Panicked, I called Annie, who knew me well enough to drop what she was doing and get out her Rolodex. By that afternoon I'd gotten an appointment with her sister DeeDee's gynecologist, a lovely, slightly faded older woman, Dr. Millis, who ushered me into her office with a no-nonsense air. I brought Sacha with me in her carrier, and Dr. Millis made a funny, clucking sound at her, the way older women sometimes do when they want to show how much they remember about being around babies. I lay back on the examining table, gown on, bra off, and she slipped the gown apart, probing. Her hands were cold and methodical. "Yes, I see," she said after a moment, pressing the lump firmly. She pushed at it for a long moment, frowning. "When did you say you first noticed this?"

When did I say. She sounded faintly accusing.

"Yesterday," I said. "Actually, last night."

"You didn't waste any time coming in," she commented, still feeling. I was on my back, arms behind my head, staring up at the ceiling. She was palpating my breast, gauging, assessing. Two hands: one, the physician's. One, the disease.

"OK," she told me. "You can sit up, put your gown back on."

She looked at me, then over at Sacha. "I think," she said slowly, "that what we're feeling is most likely a cyst, very common in nursing mothers. But—"

My heart sank. *But. This is it, this is it.* I gripped the sides of the table.

"—given, as you've told me, that your mother has had breast cancer, and given that we're in Boston, with the best of the best available to us, I'd like to have my colleague Dr. Henneker have a look at you. He's a surgical oncologist at the Brigham, and he'll be able to suggest what he thinks makes most sense. Either we do a biopsy, or we watch and wait." She pushed her glasses up, matter-of-fact. "He'll be the best judge. Stop at the checkout desk on your way out," she added, with a last wink for Sacha. "They'll get you set up to see him." She scribbled something unintelligible on a slip of paper and handed it to me.

I tried not to fall apart as I got dressed, picking up Sacha's carrier. My mind was racing. Biopsy. She said "biopsy," right? And *oncologist*. She definitely said "oncologist." Sacha was smacking at the toys dangling from the handle of her carrier. She was making the little syllable sounds I loved. I was already ten steps ahead of Dr. Millis, imagining myself sick, hairless, dying, abandoning Sacha and Jacques. No chance for a second baby. No future left. I barely remember getting out to the parking garage, finding my car, snapping Sacha's carrier into its frame in the backseat, driving home.

When Annie called, I actually burst into tears.

"It's going to be fine," she said with complete conviction, and I remembered why I loved her. "Trust me. You'll be there with your ugly shag for a long, long time."

I could barely eat dinner that night. I couldn't sleep.

"The doctor said," Jacques reminded me, "it's probably nothing. Probably just a cyst. Right?"

I ignored him. I got out my old *Merck Manual*, the one I used to look things up whenever I felt anything out of the ordinary. The book was tatty from overuse. Several pages were dog-eared: *Brain, tumors in. Esophagus, cancer of. Melanoma. Uterine cancer.* Some pages were coming loose from overuse. "Don't get ahead of yourself," Jacques admonished me. He hated it when the *Merck Manual* came out.

He hadn't seen the look Dr. Millis had given me. The way she wrote so quickly, so gravely on her little pad.

Exasperated, Jacques rolled over, getting into his I-need-to-go-to-sleep-and-you're-driving-me-insane position. I had no intention of sleeping yet. I turned on my bedside lamp and opened the *Merck Manual* to the index. With one finger, I rolled down to the entry for *Breasts. Cancer of. Cysts in. Cancer of* came first, and had a much longer entry.

———

I SAW DR. HENNEKER ON Thursday. The fact he was willing to squeeze me in with so little notice made me certain I was in trouble. Maybe that was what Dr. Millis had written on the slip of paper—*See her immediately! Something is very wrong here!* Jacques canceled an afternoon of meetings to come with me, which made me worry even more. Jacques never cancels meetings. Dr. Millis had probably called him already, I told myself. *Be sure to come with her. It looks bad—*

We walked through the oncology floor at the Brigham, Jacques holding Sacha. I literally felt like I couldn't breathe.

"Here we go," Jacques said, holding open a door to a large waiting area. Inside there were mauve-and-beige couches and tall rubber plants, and we sat and waited for what seemed like forever before a nurse called us. Then all three of us went in. I changed into the blue and white cotton gown, and we waited together.

Dr. Henneker was small and wiry, older than I expected. He knocked on the door and came in at the same time, without waiting for me to say "Come in." "What do we have here?" he boomed, looking straight at Sacha, who looked nervously back at him. I was sitting on the table, my arms full of goose bumps. He winked at me, like we were all in on some kind of joke. "Dad," he said to Jacques—was he kidding?—"why don't you wait outside with Baby while we take a look here."

Jacques took Sacha back out to the rubber plants, leaving me alone.

Dr. Henneker was quicker examining me than Dr. Millis had been. His fingers went right for the lump. "This?" he asked, and I nodded, holding my breath. He seemed completely unconcerned. "Breastfeeding?" he asked. I nodded. He gave me a look like I'd gotten the answer right on an oral exam. "This," he said, after about twelve more seconds of probing, "is what we call a galactocele. That's a small cyst filled with breast milk. You may notice it gets a little larger," he added, "but it's nothing to worry about." He smiled at me. "In three or four months, or whenever you're done nursing, come back in and we'll check on it. But I can give you a ninety-nine percent assurance that it will either be half the size or completely gone by then."

I stared up at him, relief flooding through me like adrenaline. It was like he'd released me from a death sentence. I wanted to throw my arms around him and weep.

"Better get going," he said, giving me a pat on the shoulder. "I hear somebody out there making a fuss. I think you're needed in the waiting room."

Baby and Dad. Waiting for me.

The look on Jacques's face when I told him everything was fine was hard to decipher.

He was quiet all the way out to the car.

He didn't say, "I told you so," on the drive home. He was pale, thoughtful. Sacha had fallen asleep in the back, and he was focused on the road. Rush hour seems to start earlier in Boston every day.

"Listen," he said finally. "I'm really glad it's good news, Ame." *Ame* is my private family nickname. It almost never gets used, and when it does, it's usually at a time of stress. Like now. "But this anxiety of yours—"

I fiddled with the strap of the diaper bag. "I can't help it. It's how I grew up," I mumbled. I was close to tears—half relief, half shame.

Jacques was shaking his head. "It's just, the second there's anything—a lump, a rash—you think it's cancer. You go from nothing to the worst thing possible, zero to sixty all at once. I don't think it's healthy."

I stared ahead, not saying anything. I didn't want to worry. Did he think I *wanted* to be like this? Jacques thought you should wait and worry only when an expert told you to. Otherwise, until then, why not just live your life? Why not—strange as it sounds—enjoy what-ever time you had?

That sounded perfectly reasonable. In theory, at least. But in practice, I couldn't do it. It would be like opening your eyes at midnight, everything pitch-black, and have someone explain to you—calmly, rationally—that it was really bright as day. You just had to open your eyes and look.

"Maybe," Jacques said simply, "you should talk about this with someone."

I didn't say anything. I didn't want to go tell a stranger, not even a very intelligent one trained as a therapist, how I felt about my body. How much of the time I worried something was wrong with me. Worrying was just part of who I was. It was what I knew. *I worry, therefore I am.*

Before Sacha was born, I'd assumed my anxiety was mixed up with wanting to have a baby—quick, before I ran out of time. But now here I was, almost thirty-three, Sacha was healthy, almost five months old, and whatever I'd felt in my breast was only a galactocele (probably) and nothing more. There was a 99 percent chance it was nothing. For the moment, at least, my panic was beginning to fade. This particular panic, anyway. But not completely, and not for long. Like Donne at the end of the twenty-third Meditation, I knew something else would spring up. I was haunted by Sylvia, Pody, Gail. I felt like they were out there, trying to reach me. Trying to tell me something.

I wanted more. Another baby. A chance to watch things unfold. A whole life, not just half.

It's a funny thing, fear. How it follows you, changes shape, adapts to each new place and situation. Like furniture, which you carry around and set up in one house after another. It may look a little different in its new place, but it's still the same stuff.

THE WHOLE NEXT WEEK I was flooded with energy and relief. Contrite, I booked an appointment for a checkup at the Farber. The doctor who'd been running the study on talcum powder had moved to another hospital, but I saw a new doctor named Dr. Muto who I really liked—young, compassionate. I had an ultrasound and a CA125, and everything looked good. I set up a dentist appointment. I vowed to be careful of my health, but not obsessive. I'd be optimistic and unafraid!

I CALLED ANNIE TO THANK her for getting me in to see Dr. Millis. She couldn't talk long—she was deep in the middle of writing a conference paper—but I was in a good mood and didn't feel slighted. I had plans, too, I reminded myself. One afternoon I met colleagues from my department. Sacha and I started going to Story Time at the library. Best of all: My mother was coming for Mother's Day.

I threw myself into getting ready for her. Just because we had ugly shag didn't mean I couldn't spruce things up. I cut daffodils from the front garden and arranged them on the dresser in the third bedroom upstairs. I tidied furiously, positioning Sacha up in her favorite new device: a seat on stretchy cords that we clipped to the door frame, allowing her to bounce up and down on her own two feet, burbling and approving my efforts.

Sacha was five months old.

Five. I'd always liked that number: the compact unit it made, its rhyming perfection (Alive! Strive! Thrive!).

Five fingers to a hand.

That Sacha turned five months old in the fifth month of the year made it even better.

Here is a hand. Here are five fingers. One hand checks to see how the other hand is doing.

Getting ready for my mother's arrival, I renewed our house-hunting efforts. I was freshly optimistic. How hard could this be? A friend from graduate school had moved to Afghanistan with CNN. Another was in China. Annie's grant proposal had been accepted. People manage! "It's not rocket science," I told Jacques—something I say when I'm feeling determined, or self-critical, or both.

We could do this. We could find a house.

Jacques claimed to have only one criterion: The house had to have "a useable backyard." In fact, once he actually saw a place, a long list of other requirements came back to him. But in the abstract, the yard was what got emphasized. It had to be on the *exact same level* as the back door. He wanted to be able to open up the back door and step right outside, the way you could at his parents' house in Johannesburg. "Déjà garden," as Julie said when I told her about this. In Cambridge, for whatever reason, this particular combination of house and yard was proving hard to find.

"In your price range," Sandi added pointedly.

"Maybe," I said one night, not long after our visit to Dr. Henneker, "we should branch out a little. Look in Brookline and Newton as well as Cambridge."

I was the one who'd been fixated on Cambridge, but I was starting to think having a place to park and good schools might be more important than being near Harvard Square. Not to mention finding that elusive "useable backyard."

"OK with me," Jacques said, deep in the paper. "Either one— Brookline or Newton."

The Forever House was as good as ours.

I called Sandi to share our newfound flexibility, but she didn't sound as pleased as I'd expected.

"Newton's also pricey," she warned. "There isn't much on the market right now. And so many other people are looking in your price range—"

She always made that sound bad: *your price range*.

She typed furiously on her computer. "Wait a minute! Found something!"

I was jubilant. You *see*? I said to the silent, witnessing gods.

"Three bedrooms . . . good street . . . 'useable backyard'. . . and it's the right price range . . ." She was starting to sound excited. "I wonder why—"

"Oh," she said. Her voice fell.

"What is it?" I demanded. What gem was she keeping from us?

"It's your house," she said with a sigh. "The one you're renting."
The House with the Green Shag.

Maybe Newton wasn't the answer to all our problems, but I wasn't deterred. My mother was coming. It was spring. The lump in my breast was only a galactocele. I might have health anxieties, but I was determined to choose happiness—even if it came with shag.

"BOMMA IS COMING," I CROONED to Sacha, inspecting made-ahead dinner options in Whole Foods. I picked Chicken Selection Number Two, Lemon Piccata. With a little parsley sprinkled on top, I thought it would look homemade. "Bah," Sacha said back, with a look that could've meant anything.

My mother hadn't visited us yet in Boston. The last time she'd seen Sacha was when she came to help Jacques back in DC. She hadn't seen me since Christmas, and I couldn't help thinking, as I brushed my hair and put some makeup on, that I'd improved, looks-wise. Supposedly the last ten pounds of baby weight would come off the minute I stopped nursing. From the side, especially if I sucked my breath in, I looked almost like my old self.

And Sacha! Sacha was of course unrecognizable. So grown-up! And to hear the little sounds she'd started making! I couldn't wait to show my mother how far we'd come.

My mother got to our house late Friday afternoon, climbing out of the cab, exuberant, as if it were still Christmas and she'd never really left. She scooped Sacha up, and in exchange, I took her familiar rubberized Travel Tote, packed to the gills with baked things and frozen miniature bagels from "the good deli" in Birmingham. "They're great for teething," my mother informed me, giving Sacha's foot a knowing squeeze. Sacha made a sound like a burble, patting my mother on either cheek. How, I wondered, do babies *know*? Sacha went to my mother with such instinctive ease. In Whole Foods, when the woman at the cash register tried to touch her arm, she'd screamed.

"Of course she knows me," my mother said, staring deep into Sacha's eyes. "What do you think? We're strangers?"

There was so much to show my mother. The shag. Sacha's hanging bouncer. Our stacks of boxes. Our backyard, thawed out now but still marshy, so when you walked across it, you left footprints. I took Sacha and carried her from room to room, my mother behind me, exclaiming, noticing, and I had that visceral sense that now she was here, things mattered. It was like my mother connected the dots and made a picture emerge. Through her approving eyes, what we had here looked worthwhile.

I kept up a running stream of patter, aware even as I was going on that I was overdoing it, she couldn't get a word in edgewise. Why was it so important for me to show her every last detail?

"Mellie," my mother said at last, after I'd started to show her the listing sheets Sandi had given us—houses we'd looked at and drooled over, but couldn't afford, or houses we'd looked at and hated—"do you have any tea? I'd love a cup, if you do."

I was abashed. What kind of a host was I? I went through the choices: Lemon Zinger. Oolong. In the end, she wanted plain old Lipton's: weak, with lemon. But by the time I'd made it, she'd changed her mind. Maybe a nap was a better idea, she said.

She was a little tired, she admitted. She'd been overdoing it—the trip out to the Northwest, grading all her students' research papers.

"And you know how when you're tired, little things hurt more?" she said.

Her side had been bothering her. Every now and then she probed it with her finger, a frown crossing her face.

"I think I pulled something, putting my bag in the overhead bin on the flight today," she told me when I caught her examining herself later, T-shirt shucked up, in the small mirror over Sacha's changing table.

"What do you mean? Can I get you an Advil?"

Usually, my mom didn't like taking anything for pain, but, yes, she said she'd take some Advil. Two, she added, as I rummaged around in the kitchen cabinet for something other than infant teething drops.

IN BOSTON, SPRING IS CAPRICIOUS. It's cold, raw, damp, it feels like it's never going to get warm, and then suddenly heat blows in from nowhere, and you're still pale and pouchy and wearing your winter coat and your boots and the mercury shoots from fifty-seven to eighty in a single day. The lilacs burst from buds to full color in a matter of hours, and dazed flies loop on dizzy orbits.

Saturday morning was hot and humid. Our house was still in winter lockdown, Ice Melt bags instead of potted pansies at the door.

Jacques and I flew into action, pushing up storm windows, rolling sagging porch furniture out from the garage. Jacques had his shorts on, a butterfly of sunburn flaring across his nose. My mother sat at the kitchen table stirring her coffee, watching us. She wasn't herself.

I suggested taking Sacha for a walk, but my mother wanted to wait until the most recent dose of Advil kicked in. At lunch I caught her probing her side again with her index finger, like the Caravaggio portrait where Saint Thomas slips his finger into Jesus' open wound. Only my mother was both the probe and the wound.

Two hands. One hand sees how the other is doing.

"Are you OK, Mom?" I asked her.

Her face was clenched and inward-looking, what my sisters and I called her "reading" face. She didn't answer.

"Is your side still bothering you?" I asked, but she shook her head, reaching past me for Sacha.

After lunch we took a walk after all, up to the private school at the corner where the girls played lacrosse. Later, we drove around and I showed her some nearby houses we'd looked at and rejected, and she seemed like herself again, making fun of them, propping me up, noticing all the clever things Sacha was doing that nobody else seemed to see.

I'm glad you're here, I wanted to tell her.

But I didn't. We didn't really say things like that, my mother and I. Instead, I made her tea—iced, today, and she actually drank it— and we sat outside and fanned ourselves and fanned Sacha and looked out over the steamy backyard and talked about Julie and Jon's baby and the Fourth of July and the plans for Charlevoix.

Before I knew, it was Sunday, Mother's Day. Typical for our family, we spent half of it at the airport. I think I must have hugged her too hard at the departure gate, though, because when I pulled back, she winced.

Planning was our thing. We talked about what was coming next like we could see it all before us: shimmering, like a bright planet coming into view.

Turning Over

At six months, your baby may be able to turn over on her own.

Turn over: to examine or review. To prepare, as in turning over a garden, or a new leaf.

To change position. To start over.

Halfway through the year, time turns, the days get longer. One evening in late May I was outside walking with Sacha in her stroller, Bacchus panting alongside, and I realized it was past seven and it wasn't dark yet, and I was almost stupefied by the wealth of it—the lengthening light, the smell of barbecue, and the soft whirr of sprinklers, the sense of things opening. In a month it would be the solstice, and there'd be the subtlest of turns, *from now on the days will get shorter, ever so slightly*, a faint shadow under the brightest burden of flower, the realization that it couldn't last, light and warmth would gather to a zenith, reaching that point only to begin, second by second, to drop away.

FOR WEEKS, SACHA HAD BEEN trying to turn over. This task dominated her world now. She'd forget about it for a while, playing with a toy or laughing at Bacchus, but the minute I laid her down she'd remember, her face tightening with concentration, arms sticking out on either side, rocking back and forth on her belly.

Just a month ago it had been enough for her to lie on her back and swat at the dangling toys we hung above her, or on her stomach— either was fine! Now, whatever position we put her in was wrong, because it wasn't the other one. She flailed like a terrapin, hostage to gravity.

"It's like she's possessed," I told Julie. "She wants to do this so badly!"

"I can relate," Julie said. "I feel pretty much the same way these days. I can barely turn over anymore in bed." Julie was due in just over two months, and you could tell it was getting harder for her to move around. She had that short out-of-breath sound women get when they're very pregnant, and she moved awkwardly, as if in slow motion.

MEMORIAL DAY WEEKEND WE HEADED up to Maine on Friday afternoon. I'd persuaded Jacques to take half the day off so we could leave early and beat the traffic, get a first taste of summer. It was great to be up here—we could smell the sea. I loved the feel of Julie and Jon's house on Laurel Street. You could see a sliver of Casco Bay from some of the rooms, and the house was airy and sweet-smelling. I was upstairs in their second-floor family room, helping Julie sort through the stacks of infant clothes we'd brought up for them. While Julie and

I sorted, Sacha lay on her blue blanket, struggling to propel herself from one side to the other.

I held up one of my favorite baby outfits. Blue-and-white terrycloth, printed with airplanes. "The Pilots," my mother called it—a hand-me-down from Jenny to Rachel to us, and now to Julie. Sacha had worn this one over and over again her first few weeks. I wanted to conjure it all back up: those early, baffling days. Clara. The baby swing from Annie.

But Julie had something else on her mind.

"Listen," she said. "Has Mom said anything to you about her back?"

"Her back? I know her side has been bothering her," I said slowly. A jolt of fear ran through me, like a current. "She didn't mention anything about her *back*."

"I guess it started hurting a while ago. She saw an orthopedist last week," Julie said. "They think it might be osteoporosis—Dad said she may be getting little compression fractures in her vertebrae."

"Huh," I said, thinking this through. She hadn't said a word to me about her back being sore—only her side. But then, with a rush of guilt, I remembered I hadn't let her get much airtime. I'd been the one doing most of the talking.

My mother's favorite aunt had osteoporosis. She'd ended up with a hump on her back and stooped so badly she needed a cane. We knew that condition could be compounded by having a hysterectomy. No more estrogen meant my mother's bones could weaken as she got older. "Is it serious?" I asked. And then—"Dad's not worried, is he?"

"No," Julie said. "I don't think he is."

That settled it. My father was the canary in the coal mine of worry. If he wasn't concerned, everything must be OK.

"It's just—" Julie hesitated. "She just hasn't been sounding like herself, that's all. And she didn't call me yesterday, even though she knew I was seeing my doctor."

We met each other's eyes. That didn't make sense. My mother might miss a day—even a few days—of phone calls, especially around this time of year, with all those final papers to grade. But she wouldn't miss checking in after one of Julie's appointments. She tracked Julie like a bloodhound every time she knew one was scheduled.

"Anyway, I tried her this morning, but there wasn't any answer." Julie was struggling to get up. "You try next, OK? You can use the phone in here. I'm going to go get dinner started."

I tried twice, once just after Julie went downstairs, and again about half an hour later. Both times I just got my parents' answering machine. Was it possible they'd gone away for the long weekend? But they would have told us! Anyway, my parents weren't the types for spur-of-the-moment trips. I was getting worried. Sacha was napping and I was still up in the family room. I could hear Julie downstairs, putting silverware on the table out on the screened porch. I left a message for my parents. Then, on a whim, I called Sara.

"You know, it's funny," Sara said, when I got hold of her. "I talked to Mom the day before yesterday, and she didn't sound great."

"Why? What did she say?" I asked, twisting the phone cord around one finger.

"Oh, just the same stuff she's been saying. How her back's been hurting, but she's sure it's osteoporosis. And she said she was having some kind of scan done, but she didn't want to talk about it."

I looked out the window. Bright blue bay, white curtains. A smell in the air of summer coming, of the sea.

We promised we'd call each other once we tracked her down. In the meantime, Sacha napped, and Julie and I talked about plans, the way we always did. Getting ready for the baby. Where the crib should go.

One thing that amazes me about babies is how transparent they are. Whatever they're feeling, you see it right away: Frustration. Fear. Mirth. Always on the sensitive side, Sacha's face registered every one of her emotions. A loud noise, an unknown dog, a crash of thunder all prompted in her expression a depth of terror that made me ache for her. On the other hand, the simplest things could elicit joy. Jon playing spider games on her bare feet with his fingers. Julie making puppets for her by slipping socks over each hand. How do we learn to hide what we feel as we grow older? Watching Julie and Jon playing with Sacha after she woke from her nap, you'd never read in either of their faces what this past year had held for them. Emily. The move to Maine. Excitement and nerves about becoming parents.

WE WERE UPSTAIRS IN THEIR family room. Jacques, Jon, Julie, Sacha, and I. I stretched out Sacha's blanket on the floor and laid her down on it.

Right away, Sacha got to work, shutting us all out as she concentrated furiously on trying to get her muscles to do her bidding. Julie eased herself down on the floor and stretched out on her side, ungainly, egging her on. "Roll, Sacha-la, roll," she crooned. Jon cheered each time she almost made it.

Then Julie had an idea. She picked up one of Sacha's toys—a small, stuffed clown with rattles for feet—and brought it close to her face.

"Look, Sachabelle, look!" she said, flicking the clown a little for Sacha as if she were a matador and Sacha, the bull. Sacha, stuck on her stomach on the blanket, stared wonderingly up at her. You could tell she wanted desperately to turn over, but couldn't. Sacha gazed up at the clown, and Julie snapped it suddenly to the other side so Sacha had to turn her head the other way to see it. Back and forth, back and forth, and suddenly, without warning, delighting in the game, Sacha turned sharply to the left and kept turning until she'd rolled completely over.

There was silence, then a whoof of surprised, exhaled breath. Sacha stared up at all of us with a look on her face of astonishment, like, *what just happened?* Then she cracked a huge smile. Julie applauded. "Good job, Sacha! Look what *you* can do!"

Sacha made her happiest sound: half chortle, half snort.

She wanted to do it again and again. Jon bent over her to capture it on video camera. "She looks like one of those kids practicing 'Stop, Drop and Roll' during a fire drill," Julie said, laughing. I could've watched them forever.

Instead, Jacques and Jon stayed upstairs with her, and I went downstairs to help get dinner ready. Julie tried calling my mother again, but there was still no answer. Later we ate out on the screened porch, and after a while Sacha got fussy and Jacques took her upstairs and got her settled, and Julie and Jon and I stayed out on the porch, watching the sky darken and the fireflies come out.

In a few more weeks it would be the solstice—longest day, shortest night.

Everything felt still, as if the world were holding its breath. Out in the bay the waves lapped the shore. It felt like we were almost perfectly balanced under the huge dome of sky, the scattered pebble-white stars just becoming visible.

It was almost nine, late for the phone to ring. Four long rings, before Jon got it. I had a funny feeling, watching him cross the kitchen, picking up the receiver. It was like in a movie when the background music changes key, major to minor.

He covered the receiver with one hand.

It was my mother, he told us. She wanted to know if Julie and I were both there.

"She wants to talk to both of you," he said, looking puzzled. "She says she has something she needs to tell you."

JACQUES HAS ALWAYS SAID THAT bad news travels fast, and this seemed true, because by the end of that night we'd all talked: my mother and I, my father and I, Julie and each of them; Sara and all of us; Jacques and my mother, Jacques and my father; Jon and both my parents. My mother was trying to be matter-of-fact, but I could hear her voice cracking. She sounded so scared.

She kept going over what had happened: The pain wouldn't stop, and she'd seen two different back doctors. The first suspected it was osteoporosis; the second thought she might have a degenerative problem with her disk, but when he reviewed her history he said just to be on the safe side, because of the breast cancer, he thought it made sense to have a bone scan done.

The safe side. I remembered my father's toast at Christmas, her five-year anniversary coming up, the sense that she was almost home free.

Where was the safe side now?

She'd had the bone scan yesterday. Thursday. It had taken most of the day—first, they had to inject her with radioactive dye, which took hours to be effective. My father insisted on getting the results right away, and the radiologists did their best to rush them. Dr. Kempf met them late Thursday afternoon to read them the report. The news wasn't good. "Poor Dr. Kempf," my mother said sadly. "You should've seen his face, Mellie."

The dye lit up where the tumors were. My father called them "metastases."

All of this had happened yesterday, a whole day ago, and we hadn't known. I tried to picture what we'd been doing—driving up to Maine, joking around with Julie and Jon. Watching Sacha turn over. Why did they wait to tell us? My mother seemed to read my mind. "Dr. Kempf got me an appointment with a new doctor—an oncologist," she said. "His name is Dr. Brenner. We didn't want to tell you until we'd heard what he had to say. We saw him late this afternoon—he squeezed me in at the end of the day," she added. My mother had that everyone-is-being-so-nice-to-me tone in her voice. I guessed it was the old superstition kicking in: She thought if she were appreciative, a good sport, thanked everyone a million times, maybe then—just maybe—

My parents had gone out to dinner afterward, to talk strategy. They called Sara first, then us.

I pictured them coming into the house through the garage, putting their things down. Looking at each other. My father heading slowly toward the family room, where the telephone was. My mother on the kitchen extension.

Here's what Dr. Brenner had told them: The cancer had spread to her bone. It was "advanced." He wanted her to start treatment right away.

It all made sense now, her rib pain, her back pain. "We knew it could spread," my mother reminded me. "Remember what Dr. Kempf said?"

LLBB, Lung Liver Brain Bone, that was the acronym Dr. Kempf had taught her five years earlier.

"But," I said, my voice wobbling, "it's been five years." What happened to tiny? To 95 percent curable?

My finger flew, instinctively, to the place where my lump had been. By now, it was almost gone. My throat was dry as sandpaper.

"It can happen," my mother said. "I guess all it takes is one microscopic little cell, jumping off into the bloodstream. Dr. Kempf said it's possible," she added, her voice catching a little, "that it's been going on for a while. Maybe a year. Maybe longer." She cleared her throat. "Sometimes it happens right away, at the very start. But they just don't know."

Anger took over. Why hadn't they found this earlier? What had Dr. Kempf been doing all these years, joking with her about cruise ships and grandchildren? She should've gone to Mayo, I thought, my stomach in knots. We should've listened to my father. Where was all our Alpha Medicine when it really mattered? Where was our obsession with "experts" when we needed it most?

We'd let this happen. We'd forgotten to worry, or maybe we were sick of worrying, battle worn. We wasted worry in the wrong places so it was all used up when we needed it. We let our guard down, sent the troops home, and now—

This was supposed to be the *good* kind of cancer. This was

supposed to be the kind to want! We were supposed to be glad she'd gotten this, instead of the awful cancer, the Sylvia and Pody and Gail killer. But we'd been duped. This was the Trojan Horse of Cancers, rolling into the city all affable and benign—here I am, a gift for you, you've been spared, no warriors here—and so we flung open the gates, welcomed it, *Come in, OK, thank you,* closed the gates again. And then one night, while we were all sleeping, the horse opened up, out sprang the warriors, thousands of them, no, millions, springing out on whisper-light feet, racing through the citadel with their spears of pain—

Did we think we were an ordinary family, that we could just take our 95 percent and be OK?

Not L, not L, not B, but B. Bone. Scaffold, frame. Bone of our bone.

I was holding the phone so hard my hand was sweating.

"Nothing," I said to her, my voice breaking, "can happen to you." I said it low and hard, half incantation, half command. In that tone of voice she used with us when we were little and she'd really had it. *Girls.*

Do you hear me?

My mother started to cry. She passed the phone to my father, who tried to keep his voice inside the clipped medical range of solid facts. Reporting what needed to be reported. I came away with only phrases—*the nuclear medicine department of Rougemont.* Injections of radioisotopic dyes. The room where she waited while the scan was being done. The films, meeting with Dr. Brenner. Treatment protocols.

My father kept emphasizing that this wasn't bone cancer but breast cancer, which had spread to the bone. He said this several times. Was that better? Apparently it was, in terms of prognosis. "So we know what we're up against," he said, and I nodded, but of course he couldn't see me. He cleared his throat, said something I couldn't quite hear, and gave the phone back to my mother. She was in control again.

"Dr. Brenner says I could be OK with this thing for a long, long time," she began, and I waited for the rest, guessing there would be a lot of this ahead of us, the Dr. Brenner-says, the quoting and citing. We were all so steeped in the culture of experts and he was our leader now. My mother seemed to trust him—I could hear the relief in her voice as she said his name—"*Dr. Brenner says* he has patients who are able to live with this for years. *Many* years," she added, her voice finding a bit of its buoyancy again.

"This is *not* a death sentence, Mellie," she added firmly. She explained they were going to start first with a drug called Megace, not toxic, almost no side effects, a kind of man-made progesterone that was especially effective with metastatic breast cancer. Megace was a tumor shrinker, and Dr. Brenner said many of his patients got a good response from it and didn't have to graduate to anything stronger—not for a long time.

The longer the Megace worked, the better the long-range outcome.

How would we know it was working?

"Well," she said, thinking this over. "The symptoms will get better."

"Symptoms?" I asked. Wasn't this invisible, this thing? Didn't you need radioactive dye to see it?

"The pain will get better," she said. "And that will be good, because the pain—" She hesitated. My mother hated complaining. The pain was bad. There was a chance—a good chance—*Dr. Brenner thought* she could have a positive outcome in a matter of weeks.

My father must have thought she was being too optimistic at this point because a minute later he came back on the line and explained that the cancer was not just in her back—though it *was* there, that was why she was in so much pain when she walked—I remembered walking up to the school with her over Mother's Day now with a pang—but also in her hips, her ribs, her neck. His voice cracked again. Had my mother moved out of earshot for a moment? She must have. His voice sounded different.

"Ame," he said. His voice was very low. "It's *everywhere*."

Trying to get control, he translated that into medicalese: The metastases, he told me, were "advanced."

For once, "advanced" wasn't what we wanted. What an irony for our type A bunch. We wanted a remedial cancer, a held-back-again kind, not this overachiever variety. No AP Metastases, please. We'll take your ordinary, run-of-the-mill C plus.

I hated the word *advanced*. All my life, that's what it had come down to. Sitting at the dinner table, talking about which language class to take. Of course, take the advanced one! We pushed and pushed. I'd already started doing the same thing with Sacha and she didn't even have words yet. I had an alphabet book of relatives I'd made her. *Look, Sachabelle. This is the letter* A.

A, for Aunt Julie and Aunt Sara. For Amy (me).

A could be for other things, too. Things not in the book, but hanging over it. For AP History, my mother's subject. For the best grade. For getting ahead. For advanced. Horrible, horrible—*advanced*.

On the other hand, maybe we needed *advanced* now more than ever. Maybe my mother could take this AP personality of hers and turn it on the Megace, full force. What if she aced Megace? What if she were the best of the best? Dr. Brenner's star student, the Rhodes scholar of Megace?

There was a pause. I could hear other voices (distantly) on our line. We must have gotten crossed with another call—a man and a woman, with southern accents. I wondered what they were talking about. Maybe they had news to share, too. Better news.

On our line, we were running out of things to say. None of us wanted to hang up yet, though, so we talked about talking: how hard it was to be far apart right now, how late it was, how hard this must be for us to hear, hearing and hearing, how we'd be all right, how she'd be all right. We went over dates, times, numbers, when we could come in, what days would work. When she'd be seeing Dr. Brenner again. Each fact was like a pin, tacking us to something real.

We all wanted to come in now, right away, this week. Sara was going to look into rescheduling things at home. Maybe she could extend her visit around the Fourth, make it longer; the girls could come out later with Geoff. We'd talk again, figure it out. It was easier for Julie and me to come in sooner. We didn't want to wait for her birthday to see her—that was more than a month away.

My father came back on the phone. He must've overheard the plans kicking in. "Listen," he said, his voice low again. "Keep your powder dry here, OK?" A military term from my very nonmilitary father. Meaning "hold tight." Get ready for battle.

"There's going to be plenty of times we'll need you to come in," he added.

Save your energy, in other words. The hard part hadn't started yet.

PART II

Lying is done with words, and also with silence.

Adrienne Rich, *On Lies, Secrets, and Silence*

Two Calendars

CALENDARS HAVE THEIR OWN HISTORIES. Ours, for instance, got completely overhauled in the 1580s. Pope Gregory dropped eleven days in order to realign man time and star time, resetting the year to start in January instead of March. One by one, most European countries went along with the changes, but England (and a few other Protestant countries) held out. For the next century and a half, England kept the old calendar, cut off from the rest of Europe by eleven days. If you traveled, like lots of merchants did, you needed to keep two calendars in your head at once. A little like flying to Tokyo from Boston, except that instead of moving forward fourteen hours, you had to move back eleven days. And then forward again.

Pope Gregory's calendar was on my mind that summer, because

once we learned my mother was sick, we lived in two calendars at once. In Calendar One, life went on. It was June. Realtors came over with prospective buyers; Sandi came, we looked at houses; I went over to my new department to fill out paperwork; I got names of child-care agencies from Annie's sister. Summer settled in, hot and dull. In the late afternoons, the sky turned the color of a bruise, thunder rattled the house, and Sacha, six months now, scuttled across the shag like a beetle, tried to pull herself up on things, and fell back down again with a surprised grunt.

Sara, Julie, and I strategized, trying to map out visits home. Sara was reorganizing summer plans so she could come out and stay for several weeks, from late June to mid-July. Living so far away, one longer stay made sense for her. Julie and I were already scheduled to fly in for the Fourth of July. But when we heard the news, we decided to go in that next weekend as well. We knew there wasn't anything we could really do, but we thought we could cheer them up. Lend moral support.

Our plans were made in the old calendar, Calendar One, but they took place in Calendar Two, Cancer Calendar, which had no fixed beginning or end, no set months or days. This was the calendar that governed now. Here, things happened at the same time as other things, preceded other events, superseded or even erased them. It was like trying to keep track of time on an Etch A Sketch. Dr. Brenner and Megace and the call my father got back from Mayo from the oncologists who reviewed her scans and the multiple phone calls to multiple experts that friends of friends knew at Sloan-Kettering or at the Farber—all these took place in Cancer Calendar, which, though none of us would admit it, was not only unstable but somehow inverted, a counting away from what we all knew as real.

Sometimes, the two calendars overlapped: Northwest Airlines, Boston to Detroit, Terminal D, Friday, June 12, 11:00 AM. Sometimes they didn't.

Everything changed. It was hard to work or think. When Sacha napped, I sat in the study and stared out the window, books and papers in front of me, but real thought seemed impossible, it had been wiped out, and now all I had left was feeling. Guilt, longing, sadness. During the day, when Sacha was up, I lived in the old calendar: I made appointments (pediatrician, child-care agency); I ran errands (Star Market, CVS, Boston Baby); I worked on syllabi for the fall, I wrote things on the whiteboard in the kitchen. *House on Myrtle Street with Sandi, ten am. Call vet.* When Sacha napped, I slipped back into Cancer Calendar, into worry and sadness.

I called my mother to check in. She had an appointment with Dr. Brenner first thing Monday morning, and she had started taking the Megace right away. You could either pick a lemon-lime drink or pills, and she picked the pills, which she said were big enough to cure anyone of anything.

"How are you feeling?" I asked. "Were you able to sleep?"

Her voice had a crisp, dismissive sound. She couldn't really talk, she told me. She had one foot out the door to meet the head of the history department at Country Day. "End-of-the-year nonsense," she added.

I didn't want to hang up yet. "But—how are you?" I asked again, unsatisfied.

She was fine. In the Kübler-Ross model, the first of the five stages of grief is denial. In my mother's case, this meant she was dealing with the news the cancer had come back in a highly specific way.

She'd decided to put their house on the market and move to Birmingham.

For years, only half seriously, my mother had had her eye on houses "uptown." "Uptown"—Birmingham—consisted of a few square blocks of upscale restaurants and boutiques that sold designer clothing and kitchen gadgets. My mother loved Birmingham—the library, the village park, the sense of things opening. At heart she was still a Chicago girl, and she thought our house—a square colonial on two acres— was too isolated and too much work.

First, we assumed she was kidding. Then, we decided this was a chemically induced lapse in judgment, a rare, previously undocumented side effect of the Megace.

Megace, my mother told us, was a miracle drug. Just a few days on it, and already she was feeling better.

She was in high-planning mode. "It's time to live life," she told us. "Seize the day."

"She sounds like the Lifetime Channel," Julie said, when the three of us checked in with one another later to compare notes. "Soon she'll be talking about silver linings."

None of us was used to conference calls, and it felt funny. Jockeying for airtime, the way we used to around the dinner table when we were little. We'd all start talking at once, then all fall silent.

"Well," Sara said uncertainly. "It's not easy, dealing with all of this . . ." Sara, either by temperament or training, isn't as ironic as Julie is. She's softer. Julie is the "funny" one. Sara is compassionate. And I'm in the middle. Seeing both sides, and sure of neither.

"I think she's losing it," Julie said.

"I don't know," Sara said slowly, defending her. "I think it may be about energy now. Maybe she thinks if she throws herself into moving, it'll keep anything awful from happening."

Since my mother had told us about the cancer coming back, Sara, Julie, and I had started checking in a few times a week. Julie set up the conference calls, and we traded information. Timelines. Cancer Calendar: Megace Month, Day Three.

How did she sound to you today? What did Brenner say? What was the deal with changing the dose of Megace? Sara was looking into organic therapies. She'd read somewhere soy could be helpful. A macrobiotic diet. There were pesticides all over those Granny Smiths she ate.

Julie, keen believer in Alpha Medicine, had also been doing her homework. "There's some question," she said, "about how effective Megace is. What about starting something more powerful sooner?"

She'd read an article about a radical approach. If you did a bone marrow transplant early, there was a chance—if not of a cure—of a longer period of remission.

"Or," my mother said cheerfully, when Julie suggested this to her, "it could just kill you outright and you wouldn't have to hang around and wait."

My mother didn't want to talk about macrobiotic diets, or flying out for a second opinion at the Farber. She was confident Dr. Brenner was on top of things. She was doing fine, thanks very much. If we didn't mind, she actually didn't want to talk about cancer. She wanted to pin down the number of condos we needed in Charlevoix over Labor Day weekend. How certain was Julie's doctor about her due date? If she had the baby the first week of August, Julie and Jon could still make it to Charlevoix for Labor Day, couldn't they? My mother knew it wouldn't be easy traveling with an infant, but it would be so great to have us all together.

Apparently, my mother had forgotten her own admonitions about taking a baby on an airplane. Among other things.

"Next, she'll probably suggest scheduling a C-section," I told Julie later, comparing notes. "That way you'll have a date, and she can just go ahead and book the rooms."

"Very funny," Julie said.

Mostly, what my mother wanted to talk about was moving. Every place she looked at got defined by its proximity to the library. Six blocks from the library, there was a Victorian someone was rehabbing. Right around the corner from the library, there was a big colonial being turned into condos. My father didn't want a condo, she admitted. "But the location . . . ," she added wistfully.

"Mom," Sara said, thinking this through. "What about teaching? How are you going to manage putting your house on the market and selling it and getting a new place ready before fall?"

Silence on her end.

"Teaching," she said, "is another thing."

We waited.

"It's too much," my mother said crisply. "I'll miss my 'bubbies'—that was what my mother called the cream of the crop, the most type A of her AP History gurus. The ones who got into Stanford and Yale, on her recommendation. "But I've decided. Your father and I talked it over, and I've already been over to see the head of the department, and I told him I'm not going back this fall." She paused, considering. "I've decided to retire."

We were stupefied. My mother, not working? She'd fought for her job, tooth and nail, having come to teaching relatively late in life, competing with the twentysomethings, the superstars who could coach as well as teach. She'd struggled with the department to let her broaden the curriculum, working her way up to teaching the AP course, which she'd made her own, spending hours every evening preparing lectures, bringing it all to life. The Babylonians. The Hittites. The Egyptians. She turned every part of history into a colorful pageant, filled with personal anecdotes. What Charles the First said just before he was beheaded. Which emperors had venereal diseases. How little boys were given beer for breakfast in early modern England.

My mother adored her students. What was even more impressive was how much they loved her back. They called her "Nails," as in "Tough As," claiming she was the hardest grader in the department, but they got on waiting lists to be in her classes.

She wasn't going back?

This was much more serious than the idea of moving. I had that cold, sick feeling in my stomach again.

Things must be worse than she was letting on if she'd given up her job.

"I've wanted more flexibility for a long time," she told us. "It'll mean I can come out to see you guys more."

We were silent.

"And I'll be able to travel with Dad," she added. "I never get to go with him when he gives papers."

More silence. For once, all three of us were tongue-tied.

"So there's plenty of time for moving," she added, as if the case were closed.

JULIE AND I MET FRIDAY morning at Logan. Never one for traveling light, I had a mountain of baby equipment with me: Sacha's umbrella stroller, her car seat, her new baby backpack (she'd outgrown the Snugli). Not to mention Sacha herself, wriggly and irritable, and an ungainly duffel, its strap digging into my shoulder.

Julie was carrying a bag, too. Plus seven months of baby.

"Do you really think Mom's serious about selling the house?" she asked me, once we were settled in our seats. Last-minute tickets, coach, last row of the plane. We could hear the toilet flushing behind us.

"Maybe she thinks it's her last chance," I said, shifting Sacha on my lap. I'd saved money by not getting her a seat, which now seemed like a bad idea. All Sacha wanted now was to be mobile. She was learning to crawl, and keeping her still was next to impossible. "I think that must be it. It's now or never."

Julie agreed. "I think the suburbs feel dead to her right now," she added. "It's probably all about energy."

Julie was right—nothing moved on Lakewood Drive. Even the dogs seemed listless and immobile behind invisible fences when we showed up hours later in our rented Explorer. It wasn't a lively neighborhood. On Halloween, our neighbors used to leave candy out in baskets with instructions: Take One, please! or Two Apiece! "It's like Herculaneum here," Sara complained during her archeology phase when she was twelve or thirteen. All three of us had left as soon as possible, to college, to graduate schools farther away, out of state, out of the country, *out*. No wonder my mother wanted to leave, especially now.

My father had always been the holdout. For years he'd said no, he loved the yard, he didn't want to be on top of their neighbors, but after my mother's cancer came back he couldn't deny her anything.

When we got to Lakewood Friday afternoon the house was swarming with Realtors, each with a clipboard, and my mother was sitting on the couch icing her leg, which had developed a blood clot from the Megace.

Julie and I fell on her. What was this? What was going on?

My mother was undeterred.

Dr. Brenner said this could happen sometimes. The Megace did something to the circulatory system. It wasn't common, but it happened. She'd always had bad veins, so this just figured. Par for the course.

She was supposed to ice the clot for twenty minutes every hour. That didn't leave much time for real estate, but she was doing her best.

The front door was open and Realtors were coming in a few at a time, peering into rooms, taking notes. This was the Realtors' open house, and apparently it was important to set the right tone so the agents would all like the house and show it to their clients. My mother seemed delighted they were there. It was like she was hosting some bizarre party—she kept calling out to them from her perch on the couch, naming each room in turn: *foyer, family room, kitchen*, gesturing like a flight attendant to the left and right.

She was in fine form. She made a huge fuss over Julie, patting her belly, making her stand sideways so she could assess her girth. And Sacha! So much more grown-up since May!

"She can turn over now," I said proudly, forgetting for a moment why we were here.

My mother was herself, just harder, fuller volume, urgency pulsing below the surface. She introduced us to a Realtor named Sherry who would be taking us all over later to see a new listing in Birmingham. The perfect house for "empty nesters," Sherry told us.

Julie and I glanced at each other.

How was my mother planning to traipse over to look at a prospective house when her leg was so swollen?

"What," I asked, "does Dr. Brenner say about walking on that leg?"

Never mind Dr. Brenner, it was all set, we were meeting my father at the house at four o'clock—"*the* house," my mother said, as if it were now the one and only. According to my mother, the house sounded perfect. "There's a ravine," she told us, "and it drops off at the back, no yard, no lawn, no upkeep." A tiny tributary of the Rouge River ran through the ravine. Apparently you could see it from the back deck. My mother had already nicknamed the house "A River Runs Through It."

"*Your mother*," Sherry said, putting her hand on my arm, "is a stitch." She was wearing a raft of gold bangles, and they chimed when they touched each other, like tiny bells.

Julie and I looked at each other. Under my mother's hard-edged ebullience, we both sensed fear. She was playing at something, and neither of us trusted it.

A RIVER RUNS THROUGH IT had been empty for a while. We could tell as soon as we opened the front door—the rooms echoed, I could smell a faint residue of perspiration and newspaper; there was gray rubber industrial tiling on the first floor and an enormous atrium ceiling that lifted skyward two stories. I had strapped Sacha into her new backpack, and I could feel her getting heavier as I walked. "The previous owners," Sherry murmured, "make exercise videos, which is why so much of the first floor has been turned into a 'gymnasium.'" *Jim-NAH-see-um*, Sherry pronounced it, like an SAT word she hadn't had the chance to say out loud.

My mother's eyes widened.

The house was shockingly ugly. Instead of a living room or dining room, most of the first floor was taken up by a mirrored gym; the kitchen, oddly sited on the second floor, was tiled black, with the look and feel of a glove compartment. Room after room appalled me, but my mother got over her initial shock, managing on her cane with only the slightest limp, seeing potential where we saw problems. She shared the possibilities with my father, who—implausibly—seemed willing to go along with her sense of what a change here or there could accomplish. They tossed around conditionals. *If we just widened that—if that could be lifted—if the ceiling were lowered again to allow—if we just—*

Julie pulled me aside in one corner of the mirrored gym. "They've gone nuts," she hissed. I could feel Sacha getting heavier on my back, suggesting she was falling asleep. In the softening light, my parents seemed like strangers: my mother, with her shrinking body and Lucite cane; my father speaking louder than usual, his voice full of optimism, but his eyes behind their heavy glasses had a lifelessness that suggested agony.

He opened a pair of cupboards in the kitchen, frowning, trying to make sense of the emptiness inside.

"That," Sherry said, tapping pertly with her lilac ballpoint, "is the dumb waiter. You just pop your groceries in from below, push the button, and—*voilà!*"

I waited for my mother to give Sherry the toxic smile for which she was famous and call it a day. But that didn't seem to be happening. Instead, she and my father were going back to look again into the other rooms, taking measurements, consulting, putting their heads together, talking about coming back later with an architect. Sherry was beaming, and Julie and I looked at each other in disbelief.

"You really like it?" I asked my mother as we moved downstairs to confront the "carport" for the second time.

My mother had her back to me. Maybe she was trying to catch a glimpse of the river through the carport's smudged window. A bird had soiled it, a white Rorschach stain. I couldn't help recoiling at the sense of all the effort needed here, and my mother looked so frail on her cane, months of treatment ahead, years, if we were lucky. Was this the time to be taking on something so enormous?

When she turned back to face me, my mother looked defiant.

"It's got a lot to offer," she said. "Three blocks to the library. We could walk there every day!"

All day Saturday, instead of talking about Megace or what to do about the clot, which was getting worse, we sat at the kitchen table and my mother drew blueprints, converting the gym back into a living room, imaginatively expanding the kitchen, reconceptualizing the back deck to "allow for a greater sense of the river," as Sherry put it when she dropped by with various packets of drawings and photographs for her to consult. My father was out running errands, Sacha was trying to pull herself up on the legs of the kitchen chairs, and my mother's own leg was propped up on another chair, the ice in constant use but not working. Julie made delicate and delicious things for dinner, using a great number of pans. When my father came home, bringing fresh prescriptions from the drugstore, all he wanted to talk about was the house.

They were in love with it, excited as newlyweds. Then the architect came over to meet with them to "go over a few numbers" and afterward they were subdued. It seemed the kind of reconfigurations my mother had in mind would cost almost as much as buying the house in the first place. They'd have to take almost every penny they had in savings to make it work, and suddenly the light went out of my mother's face, the excitement gone, nothing left but pain, the cancer tightening its clutch around her spine.

She seemed to be remembering herself. Remembering the amount of effort involved in selling their house, enlisting the architect to work his magic, the months or years spent trying to get A River Runs Through It to work.

Isn't that what we'd wanted, Julie and I?

The house on the ravine seemed like nothing but trouble—the wrong layout, way too expensive. So why weren't we happy she'd finally seen what we saw, that this was impossible, that it was much better just to stay put and rest her leg and wait for Dr. Brenner to suggest what to do about that clot?

My mother was like a balloon with all its air let out. She lay back on the couch, her face ashen, as if the dream of A River Runs Through It had been more potent than Megace, and now that the dream was evaporating she was back in her own space, shrunken, with only the real to look at.

BY SATURDAY NIGHT WE HAD a serious problem: The clot wasn't resolving. My father called Dr. Brenner on Sunday morning. It was after hours, so my father had to page him. As soon as he hung up, my father started pacing back and forth in the living room, waiting for Dr. Brenner to call back. Twenty minutes. An hour. Everything was on hold while we waited. My father, pacing, grew increasingly irate.

Waiting was a big part of Cancer Calendar. We were always waiting now, it seemed. For a doctor to call back. For someone to schedule something. For a prescription to be filled at the pharmacy. For a clot to resolve, for the pain to diminish. Something. Finally, the phone rang, and my father sprang for it like a fireman answering an alarm.

DR. BRENNER WASN'T HAPPY TO hear about the clot. This was a "significant" side effect, he told my father. Given that the clot hadn't resolved on its own, they were going to have to stop the Megace. It was too dangerous to risk letting a clot form in a deep vein—it could end up in one of her lungs, and that could kill her.

"It's disappointing," he told my father. That was the frustrating thing about these treatments. They caused side effects, some of them more dangerous than the cancer itself. They'd have to try something else.

He wanted my mother to come in the next morning to "reassess."

"I can take you," I told her, glad to finally be able to do something useful.

That was another thing about Cancer Calendar. Things changed all the time. You made a plan, you unmade a plan. You thought one thing would work, then you gave it up. Appointments in Etch A Sketch.

Julie had to leave Sunday afternoon to fly back to Maine—she had an appointment Monday morning with her ob-gyn. She'd be back for my mother's birthday in a few weeks. None of us talked about the peculiarity of this, the we're-seeing-one-another-every-second-we-can sense of visits clustered so close together.

As the dream of the house in Birmingham began to fade, the here and now got sharper, clearer. The real estate agents left their glossy brochures on our coffee table, our house photographed in full color, *Ideal for a Growing Family* written in a crisp black font on the cover. My mother slept most of the afternoon, the pain tightening its hold. She didn't even hear Julie's taxi when it showed up for her at four on the dot.

I DON'T KNOW WHAT I was expecting, but Dr. Brenner wasn't it. I was hoping he'd be like Dr. Henneker, smiling and winking and full of surprising good news. Instead, he was young and dark-haired, with oddly little teeth. No smiles. He talked rapidly, very much to the point. "Like a guillotine," I told Jacques later, calling to fill him in. "Quick and sharp."

Dr. Brenner said he was sorry about the Megace. Very sorry. He didn't waste any time letting my mother know that this was bad.

"This is a setback," he told her. "A significant setback. If the Megace had worked, that would have bought us time."

He looked upset, glancing back and forth between the file on his desk and my mother's face.

My mother, the historian, always wanted reasons. "Why didn't it work?" she asked.

He shook his head. "It's hard to say," he told her. "In part, because your tumor isn't estrogen receptive, it's harder to starve it with a synthetic progesterone."

Sacha wriggled around, reaching for things on Dr. Brenner's desk.

"So," my mother said, in a small, brisk voice. "What's next?"

He'd like to get another set of scans, he told her. Then we could go from there.

My mother didn't say anything. Then—"What if the scans look better?"

Dr. Brenner frowned. "We didn't get very far with the Megace," he reminded her. Given the extent of disease progression in the initial scans, he was concerned. The way he said "concerned," it was clear things weren't going well. This was full disclosure, this meeting. No mincing words.

Dr. Brenner explained there were three possible responses to a treatment: complete, partial, or minor. He'd been hoping for the first or at least the second, but since she'd only been able to tolerate the Megace for ten days or so, it was unreasonable to expect much of a response at all. It looked like it was time to move on to something stronger.

You could've heard a pin drop.

"Elaine," Dr. Brenner said, putting both hands on the top of his desk. He straightened her file a little. "I'm sorry."

Dr. Brenner looked like he was no more than forty. He had a tic that made one cheek muscle jump when he lifted his hands for emphasis. On the desk in a frame turned so we could see it, there was a photograph of two young boys on a tow lift, possibly out West. The boys were dark-haired, laughing. Real life, the picture seemed to suggest, happened elsewhere.

I had a pit in my stomach.

"So . . . ," my mother said, feeling her way. "I have more scans done. Then what?"

Dr. Brenner thought the best thing would be for my mother to start chemotherapy right away—as soon as next week, if they could schedule it. He didn't see any reason to wait.

My mother stared at him. Megace—nontoxic, bearable—was one thing. Chemo was another.

I remembered what she'd told us on the phone. The longer she could stay on Megace, the better. Ten days didn't seem like a great start.

Dr. Brenner was jumping into details.

He had a combination of drugs he liked to start with if Megace didn't work. There were three involved, but the main one was 5-fluorouracil, which was called (for short) Five F-U.

F-U? Could that really be its name?

I asked about side effects.

Dr. Brenner tapped with his pencil. Yes, there were side effects. Less from the Five F-U, though some from that, but mostly from the other two—Adriamycin and Cytoxan. He gave me a funny look—what did I think this was, a picnic?—and named a few. Hair loss, fatigue, nausea. Weight loss, depression, lowered immune function.

My mother cleared her throat. "If I stuck with the Megace—"

He shook his head, putting up one hand. He was sorry, but no. Even aside from the clot, which was dangerous, her metastases were advanced. "Elaine," he said, like she was a student who just wasn't getting the material. "There's *significant* disease progression in your spine, ribs, and pelvis. We need to get going."

Silence in the room.

Significant disease progression. I had a notebook with me—my father and my sisters had asked me to take notes, in case my mother and I forgot anything Dr. Brenner said, and I wrote that phrase down, right underneath F-U. *Significant.* I knew that meant *bad.*

"But F-U," Dr. Brenner told us, "can have promising results." He had statistics for us. Fifty to 75 percent of patients responded to the first course of chemotherapy. Even patients with "minor or no response" to Megace, like my mother, sometimes saw noticeable benefits.

My mother's voice was tiny. I wondered if she'd heard "sometimes," the way I had. "What would those benefits be?"

Dr. Brenner was quiet for a minute. "We're looking for reduction of symptoms," he said. "And improved quality of life."

"And cure—?" my mother managed. Straight to the core, unflinching.

He shook his head. One short, brief shake. "Prevention of tumor progression," he said, as if this was the best he could offer.

My mother nodded. As in, *OK. I'll take it.*

That was it. Like they'd made a deal.

He looked at his watch. He didn't have much time to go over the rest of our questions. He could probably tell we were the types who would ask and ask and ask. His waiting room was full ("This is a growth industry," my mother said later to me, wryly. "Business is booming."). He was pushing his chair back, getting to his feet. He was shorter than I'd imagined. I don't know why this bothered me, but it added to my unease: my mother's greatest ally, and my faith in him shrunk with his stature.

"We can talk more next week, at the clinic. Don't worry," he said, more to Sacha than to my mother or me. He leaned forward, as if he were actually about to wriggle his fingers at Sacha, then changed his mind. "We can get excellent results with Five F-U. Some of my patients—"

I noticed we'd been downgraded from "many" to "some." But if my mother had heard, she didn't let on.

WE WALKED SLOWLY TO THE elevator, more slowly out to Central Parking. We were an odd threesome: My mother, aged a generation in a matter of weeks, struggling with her cane. Sacha, bigger and more buoyant with every passing minute, wriggling in my arms, dying to be released to her new mobility. And me, between them, searching for my mother's keys in my diaper bag.

In the parking garage I worked on getting Sacha into her car seat in the back, then helped my mother into the passenger's seat. I wasn't used to driving her car, the steering wheel felt stiff, it took me a few minutes to get out of the tight space. By accident I turned the audio system on, and my mother's *Learn Italian* tape blasted out full force: "*Mi chiamo Marisa!*" My parents had been planning a trip to Siena next spring.

My mother leaned forward and snapped it off.

So much for Siena, I thought.

I've never been there, though I've always wanted to go. The oldest-known representation of an hourglass, by Ambrogio Loren-zetti, is painted on a fresco on the wall of the Palazzo Pubblico in Siena's main square. It dates from the early fourteenth century, part of a mural called *The Allegory of Good Government*. Temperentia, or Tem-perance, stands in the middle of the mural, gazing contemplatively down at the hourglass in her hands. I've seen slides of the fresco, but never the real thing.

I imagined her now, Temperentia, holding her hourglass. Frozen in soft ochres, browns, and burnt reds in Siena's main courtyard, time stopped in her hands.

"I LIKED THAT HOUSE," MY mother said suddenly.

Past tense, I noticed. *Liked.*

I nodded, trying to look supportive. "It needs work," I said in what I hoped was a neutral tone.

She was looking out the window, not used to being a passenger in her own car. "Your father could walk into Birmingham . . .", she said musingly. She wasn't wearing her glasses, and she squinted a little, as if she were trying to see something off in the distance.

Her face suddenly folded in on itself. "I just hoped," she said, half to herself, "that I could get him moved. You know what I mean, Mellie?"

In that one wish, so much was betrayed. The desire to help out. The sense of a timeline she couldn't control. The acknowledgment that the move was not, in the end, for her—her interest in Birmingham, with its restaurants and shops, was not some longed-for, last-ditch return to city living, but instead an attempt to protect my father, imagining him left alone in our house—*Perfect for a Growing Family*. Moving with him, she could have helped him get ready. But it wasn't going to happen.

Mouth dry, I maneuvered her car out of the garage, and we headed home.

F-U

THE SECOND STAGE OF GRIEF, according to Kübler-Ross, is anger.

Anger has always been hard in our family. I was raised to be anything but: to accept, to apologize. Being the middle of three girls didn't help; I was usually the one who tried to fix things, to see both sides. Being middle-class and middle-American didn't help, either, and it didn't help growing up in the 1960s, the daughter of parents who studied conflict but didn't live it. I remember walking somewhere with my father when I was young and two men near us broke into a fight and my father grabbed my arm, eyes down, and told me in a low, urgent voice just to keep walking and not to look at them. I was surprised, without really understanding; surprised by the force of his need to get away from their quarrel, and to protect me from it. Anger, my parents taught us, was dangerous. Like disease—something that can destroy you, eat you up from the inside. Better to keep your distance, walk away.

When something or someone makes me angry, I almost never realize it until minutes or even hours later. Delayed reaction. By then, it's too late to say anything. Not that I'd be likely to let it show.

But Kübler-Ross must have been on to something, because after my mother's second set of scans came back, I was angry all the time. The news, Dr. Brenner reported, was "very disappointing." The metastases were worse, despite her brief course of Megace. It was a good thing, he said—trying to find something positive to say, I guess—that they'd scheduled chemo for the following week. They needed to get going.

Anger for me came out at the wrong times and places. At the Northwest Airlines ticket counter. At the drugstore. Seeing ordinary people doing ordinary things. Once, in a dressing room with Sacha in Newton, trying something on, I heard a mother and daughter in the dressing room next to me. They were laughing and arguing with each other about something one of them was trying on and the whole scene was so perfectly ordinary, so much exactly what a mother and daughter should be doing on a summer afternoon, buying something to wear to some event they were going to—maybe together—that I could feel rage burn in my face. I had to look away so Sacha wouldn't see. Why couldn't we have that? *Why not?* OK, I knew there were worse things. Hurricanes and rape and addiction and homelessness. Horrible things happen, I got that. I knew in the scheme of things I didn't deserve to be so infuriated about this random situation of ours, our preset half-life. But I was.

I even picked a fight with Annie when she called to check in. I had told her about my mother in June, but this was our first real talk in weeks. Right away I could tell we were in different moods—she was upbeat, filled with news and plans; I was quiet and down. She started telling me a long story about a friend of her mother's who had cancer and was doing great, years and years later. Annie was convinced that her attitude really helped. As she put it: "She's just the kind of person who finds the positive in everything, you know?" I found myself snapping at her. "Surviving cancer isn't about *attitude*, Annie! It's about cell type." She was silent, and I apologized—she was just trying to be a good friend—but I couldn't help it. I read too much into everything these days.

I was angry, Julie was angry, Sara was angry, I suppose in their way Jacques and Jon and Geoff were angry, and most of all, my father was angry. Blazing, furious, white-hot anger. We controlled ourselves and tried to pull ourselves together in front of my mother, which sometimes worked and sometimes didn't.

My mother, instead of being angry—or at least outwardly so—was busy trying to squeeze her chemo schedule into her summer plans. There were endless logistics, shifting of schedules. Sara was flying out at the end of the week, and would stay through the Fourth of July, so she could take my mother back and forth to the hospital for the first round of F-U. I'd come back in with Sacha for round two in late July, since Julie would be too pregnant to fly by that point. My father would be on vacation in August, and he could take her to round three. My mother set it all up the same way she organized our tickets back and forth for family reunions. She was in her usual position, at the center of everything, running the show. Her biggest concern seemed to be making sure chemo wouldn't get in the way of her top priorities: having us all together in Michigan for the Fourth of July; going out to Maine when Julie had the baby; getting all of us to Charlevoix over Labor Day weekend.

Like Pope Gregory, she was remaking the calendar, lifting out rituals and holidays, laying them over this new dispensation. She talked about chemo as if it would only impact the infusion days themselves—three days, a month apart. Nine days total. Really only *half* days, when you thought about how long the infusions were supposed to take. Normal life could just go right on.

We took our cues from her, trying to be upbeat. Trying to

work on our attitudes. Maybe it was a good thing about the clot, we told one another, because it made the doctors do the second scan sooner and realize she needed something stronger. OK, the Megace hadn't worked, but the F-U should do it. From the way Dr. Brenner talked about F-U, it sounded like this stuff could kill anything.

"Maybe we should try putting it out on the crabgrass," my mother said, after she'd read the fine print on the clinic's consent form.

My mother hated the idea of chemo—more than almost anything else. In her usual way, she dealt with her fear through black humor. That and avoidance—she tried not to talk about it. But it was a hard subject to avoid.

Before my mother started the F-U, people called to tell her how much better chemo was now than it used to be. There were all sorts of wonder drugs these days to combat nausea, a well-meaning neighbor told her. Almost everyone had an inspirational story or a piece of advice. A former colleague thought my mother should consider hypnosis. She sent a big flower arrangement, too—gerber daisies, day lilies. My mother wanted to know how all these well-wishers had found out she was sick in the first place. When more flowers came—pink hydrangeas this time—she complained the house smelled like a funeral home.

Much better than flowers were the thank-you notes she got from her "bubbies" sharing their AP History scores with her—almost all 4s and 5s. She loved hearing from her students. None of them knew she was sick, or that she wasn't coming back in the fall. "My brother says he can't wait for the Hittites," a boy named Samir wrote to her. "He says he's taking your AP European History class next year even if he has to camp out outside your classroom to get in!" When she read that part, she got a funny catch in her voice.

SARA CAME OUT TO MICHIGAN in mid-June, flying the red-eye from Seattle, getting in at six in the morning on Sunday, in time for the first round of chemo that Monday, June 22. My mother was in good spirits. She brought a tote bag filled with *New Yorker*s with her to the hospital, ready, she told Sara, to finally get caught up on her reading.

Day One started well. They found the infusion room easily. What Dr. Brenner called "the clinic" was really just a big room off its own corridor on the second floor of the hospital, set up with reclining chairs for patients, little clusters of chairs for visitors, and stations with tea and water. You were supposed to drink lots of water while you were getting F-U, to flush away the toxins.

My mother was getting three different drugs, one right after the other—Five F-U, Adriamycin (which was red, and turned her pee red afterward) and Cytoxan, which burned when it went in and made her sick to her stomach. Sara reported that she was "very plucky." She read her *New Yorker*s, mostly, and looked out the window at the parking lot, and when she didn't feel woozy, she flipped through catalogues, flagging potential baby gifts for Julie. It was all weirdly normal, Sara said, at least if you didn't look too closely at the bags of fluid going into her arm, which had stickers saying TOXIC across the bottom and were such shocking colors. If you tried not to think that all your life you'd avoided anything that had so much as a drop of poison in it, and that what was in these bags was pure poison, designed to wipe out "rapidly dividing cells"—cancer cells, of course, but also skin, hair, and white cells. Not to mention all the other healthy cells running around her body. If you tried not to think about that, chemo could be like anything else. A root canal. Whatever. A few hours later, after the last bag emptied and the little machine beeped, the nurse slipped the IV out and my mother was free to go.

The strange part, Sara said, was how tired she was when they got home. My mother had been ready for nausea, and there was some in the late afternoon, but not bad. What was bad—baffling, really—was the fatigue. "It's like—well, it isn't really like anything else," Sara reported. The first night my mother was sitting there with Sara and my father at dinner, and one minute they were talking and everything was fine, and the next minute her face just began to descend, lower, lower, lower, until *boom*, she'd laid it down right in her plate of pasta. It was like something out of Laurel and Hardy—only not funny.

On top of that, she had no appetite. Her mouth tasted like metal.

"The funny taste in my mouth," my mother told me when I called that evening, asking about the F-U, "isn't the worst." Then she was quiet.

"Then what? What's the worst?" I asked.

She wouldn't say.

"That isn't fair," I complained. "You can't start to tell me and then stop."

"I have to go, your father just walked in," she interrupted. She wasn't following any of the rules.

Sara suspected the worst part was the flowers.

"The flowers?"

"Everyone just keeps sending more and more flowers. And fruit baskets. It makes her feel like she's already dead," Sara said. Literally— they got three arrangements one day. Two the next. Weird combinations, Sara said (she was the gardener among us, so she should know). The house stank of lilies. Apparently word about the cancer had gotten out.

"But maybe," Sara said, reconsidering, "the worst part is getting the IV in."

It turns out there are lots of things involved when it comes to getting toxins into the human body, because the body, being how it is, with its intelligence and defense systems, doesn't actually want Fuck You pumping through its veins; the body says, *Whoa, what is this stuff?* And in my mother's case there were protests, cells throwing up their hands, Do Not Pass Here, borders closed. The big issue was her circulation. In the first place there was the clot, caused by a combination of bad veins and Megace. Now the clot was better but the veins in her arms were bad. On Day One, the nurses had argued about the best terms for describing the problem. One said her veins were "small," another, "dry," but the consensus by the end of the day was that it was very difficult to get an IV into either arm. Everyone was worried about this.

Day Two, my mother planned to ask for the nurse she'd already decided was the Good Nurse, Gretchen. Not to compare, but some of the others . . . Gretchen was the best. Gretchen knew everything about veins and their stubbornness. Gretchen was willing to go the distance. Warm compresses to soften things up. A massage, especially a hand massage, which my mother—usually no great fan of being touched by strangers—told us felt wonderful. Under Gretchen's compassionate kneading, my mother's tiny side-street veins opened into boulevards, and the chemo tunneled through, no problem. But Gretchen was in high demand, and the other nurses—

Sara took Gretchen aside, talked to her, and Gretchen agreed to help my mother through the rest of round one.

In her usual way, my mother developed the relationship into something deeper. Day Two, she and Gretchen talked while the F-U dripped into my mother's arm. My mother coaxed things out of her, bit by bit. The names of her boys (Eddie and Josh). Who cut her hair like that, on that sharp angle. How long she'd been at Rougemont. What kind of specialization did it take, being an oncology nurse? And true to form, before long they were talking not about my mother's side effects or symptoms or cancer at all, but about Gretchen's career dilemmas and her secret love of history. Gretchen—full name, Gretchen Moynihan—had been a Victorian history buff since girlhood. Loved Victoria and Albert trivia, watched the History Channel, read historical romances. She'd actually thought about majoring in history at State, she admitted. But her parents wanted her to become a nurse. They thought it would give her lifelong job security.

Nursing was tough. With the boys at home, and the long hours—

and then, Gretchen added, forgetting where she was for the moment, all the anguish—

My mother nodded, commiserating. She'd forgotten that she was part of the long hours and the anguish.

Had Gretchen ever thought about going back to school? Did she know about the master's program in history at Oakland Community College?

Sara reported all this back to us. "You wouldn't believe it. Before you know it, Gretchen has her notebook out and she's writing down all this information—people to call, courses to take." My mother had gotten her master's in history at Oakland. She knew everyone in the department. If Gretchen wanted, she could make some calls—

Only Mom, we agreed, could mentor her chemo nurse right out of nursing.

Sara told us Dr. Brenner stopped by on Day Two to see how things were going. He called my mother a "trooper" and patted her on the leg.

She was more than halfway through the first course. *Just let those fuckers get in her and do their work*, we thought. *Blow those cancer cells to hell and back.*

By the end of the second day, my mother was jubilant. She could do this! It wasn't that bad!

It was almost July. Almost her birthday. She didn't look that great—her skin was pale, she had shadows under her eyes—but Dr. Brenner said that was a good sign. That meant the F-U was doing its job.

Maybe, my mother theorized, she was already in remission. That was what Dr. Brenner was hoping. Knock those cancer cells out and give her back her life. Maybe not forever, but, my mother said, who needs forever? A while, at least. That was all she wanted.

We inched back into making plans again. The Fourth. Charlevoix. My mother called and booked the condos.

"I'm telling you one thing," she said. "This year, I'm hosting

Thanksgiving. I'm making you guys do the traveling—babies or no babies."

SHE DID IT. SHE FINISHED round one and she didn't get mouth sores and she didn't throw up, so now she could move on and look forward to all of us coming in for her birthday. Dr. Brenner told her he was relieved, because now he admitted that some of his patients couldn't tolerate F-U, not even one course of it, and he'd been a little worried after her bad response to the Megace. But she'd done well. This was good news. Round one was done, and they'd let the chemo do its work and in a while—after round two or three—they'd take another set of scans and reassess.

EVEN WHILE SHE WAS GETTING chemo, my mother and I talked every day, somewhere between three and four o'clock, as if by unspoken agreement. We both seemed to think of each other around this time every day—whatever else either of us was doing—and sometimes I wondered if that had to do with the old patterns, coming home from school as a girl, opening the front door, calling out to her—"I'm home!"—or when I was younger, waiting for her outside in the snowy gloom, waiting for her headlights to pick me out from the others, sliding across the vinyl seat into the warmth of the car, the smell of Dentyne and her perfume (Charlie), Carly Simon on the radio. Three thirty, four. Do we associate people we love, *our* people, with certain times of day? Strange, how even the heart has its clockwork. Sometimes I called, sometimes she did. In each case, we'd start up light—"Hi Mellie" (her); "Hey" (me); "So—what'jdya have for lunch?" (her); "Half an organic squash puree" (me); "Tried to eat a Granny Smith and cheese, but it tasted like tin" (her)—back and forth, light, darting, daring each other to see how long we could go before I couldn't stand it anymore and I caved in and asked her how she was feeling.

"Like the cat's meow," she'd say. Or, "Like something the cat dragged in." A surprising number of cat metaphors proliferated, considering there'd had been no cats in the family since the one that died when it ate Sylvia's tinsel all those Decembers ago in Chicago.

My mother hadn't counted on this, but instead of feeling better after the chemo stopped, she felt worse. Dr. Brenner said that could happen sometimes—the chemicals build up, accumulate in the system. She just felt "off," she said, like she was sitting next to herself, somehow.

One afternoon, while she was napping, Sara called and told me they'd gone out that morning to get a wig. Advance planning: My mother's hair was already thinning, and she didn't want to be caught unprepared when it started to fall out for real. "It was horrible," Sara said. They'd gone to a place out in Pontiac, in a neighborhood neither of them knew. They got lost and it took forever to find the store. My mother's back was killing her, and every time Sara hit a pothole, she moaned. But at last they got there, and with the help of the store-owner, my mother found something. "It's made of real hair, not synthetic," Sara said. "Real hair" sounded creepy to me, but apparently that was what you wanted.

"What does it look like?" I asked, trying to picture this. My mother had worn her hair the same way for twenty years. She got it "done" every Friday at a place in Birmingham she called "the beauty shop." Washed, set, and dried. It always made her look a little like Nancy Reagan to me, her hair acquiring the luster and texture of steel wool. I couldn't imagine her any other way.

"It's kind of a pageboy," Sara said. "Picture Thoroughly Modern Millie with highlights, and you've got it." She hesitated for a minute. "It's rakish," she said at last.

SARA WAS GETTING THE BRUNT of my mother's pain, being with her for those weeks before, during, and after round one. On the phone with Julie and me, my mother was resolute, even chipper.

Distance helped. The phone helped. We didn't know she was

losing weight, though we could've guessed from the way she talked about food. Or didn't. She did talk about the wig a little, though. Probably preparing us for the Fourth of July. She said it itched.

By the last week of June, her hair was coming out by the handful. Sara told us her scalp looked like an old sponge. "You know when little wads of the sponge come off, and there's bare patches?" That's what my mother's head looked like.

"She looks different," Sara added, voice low. Trying to prepare us.

I brushed it off. Julie and I had seen her just a few weeks ago! I remembered her Lucite cane. I knew what was what.

A week before her birthday, my mother started feeling better. She had some mouth sores, which made eating harder, but nothing worse. She called Dr. Brenner's office to schedule the second round of F-U for mid-July. Dr. Brenner was proud of her. She was a "trooper's trooper," he told her.

Now that she had a little energy back, she started planning for the Fourth. It fell on a Sunday that year, but the plan was to have our ritual barbecue dinner on Saturday night. We were all coming out on Friday, different times of day, and my mother was command central, setting up meeting points to share cabs at the airport, detailing flight numbers and arrival times.

Next, she had to map out sleeping arrangements. Sara and Geoff liked staying with the girls down in the finished basement, where my mother had set up trundle beds and a sleep sofa. Julie and Jon were getting the Hilton. At this stage, Julie—almost eight months pregnant—needed the best bed.

The Hilton used to be Julie's room, but my mother had turned it into a guest room, wallpapering and adding plantation shutters, packing all signs of Julie's girlhood away and heaping so many odd-shaped throw pillows on the bed we all decided it looked like a hotel room. Julie nicknamed it the Hilton, and the name stuck. In fact, not many actual guests had ever stayed there. Despite the pleasure she took in providing plush towels and miniature soaps, my mother was fundamentally guest-averse. She threw a fit once when a colleague of my father's, passing through to attend a conference in Ann Arbor, stayed overnight with his partner, a dashing lawyer named Allison. They'd been living together for years, and they were both in their fifties, presumably old enough to run their own lives, but my mother was horrified when she found out they weren't married at breakfast the next morning. "How can they *do* that?" she kept asking us—much to our conjoined amusement—and after they left, she aired the Hilton out for days. They didn't get invited back.

With Julie and Jon in the Hilton, Jacques, Sacha, and I would be relegated to my old bedroom, now converted, like most rooms in my parents' house, into an auxiliary study. I tried not to think about four nights on an unyielding sofa bed, wedged between Sacha's Pack 'n Play and an outsized printer.

Once she'd sorted out sleeping arrangements, my mother threw herself into meal planning. Despite her lack of appetite, she'd spent every minute she felt well enough over the past few weeks baking and freezing: two pies, several batches of brownies, and a raft of appetizers. Not to mention the foundation for her annual Flag Cake, which would require Jenny's and Rachel's deft decorations (blueberries, strawberries, and white frosting) on the Fourth itself.

She sounded like her old self.

It was a relief she was cooking. It was a relief she was doling out bedrooms and worrying about towels. It was a relief to have her call me back three times in a row, reminding me incessantly about Julie and Jon's flight number and arrival time. Telling me *again* where to find the airport van. I was so glad she was feeling better, I wouldn't have even cared if she made Jacques and me bring our wedding certificate to prove we should be allowed to share a bedroom.

Maybe this was it. Remission. Number one on the list of things she wanted for her birthday. That, and a new laundry room. She hated having to lug clothes all the way down to the basement, she told me one afternoon on the phone.

Remission came first, though.

"If I'm really in remission," she asked me one afternoon on the phone, "does that mean I can send back all these flowers?"

What We Always Did

———∞∞∞———

THREE NIGHTS BEFORE OUR FLIGHT to Detroit, the phone rang. It was Sara, calling from Michigan. Out of breath. Something was wrong.

"Mom's in the hospital," she said, shaken. "Dad thinks you guys should try to come out tomorrow instead of waiting till Friday."

My heart started to pound. "What is it?" I asked.

"Some kind of infection, I guess," Sara said. "They had to put her on IV antibiotics."

My mother had been feeling fine, cooking up a storm. Then, on Monday night, she'd started to feel awful. Really bad, not like the earlier aftereffects of chemo. She'd felt a little better on Tuesday morning, but as the day wore on, she kept asking why it was so cold in the house. Finally Sara took her temperature. She had to hunt everywhere to find a thermometer—all they had was the old-fashioned kind, with mercury. My mother's temperature was 103. Sara called my father, who called Dr. Brenner, and he told them to go straight to the ER and have her admitted.

"Dad's there with her now," Sara added. Call waiting interrupted and it was my father, who gave me the same story Sara just had, only translated into medicalese. My mother had spiked a fever around eleven o'clock, 102.8, evidence of an infection she'd gotten because her immune system was suppressed from the first round of F-U. She'd have to be on IV antibiotics until the fever came down. That was why she needed to be admitted.

"It's up to you, whether you want to change your plans and come in early," he said. "She's not in any real danger. She's just very weak. But I think she'd love to see you—"

Those were his actual words. But the tone behind them was different. *Emergency! Emergency! Come* now!

"I'll call Northwest," I said. "We'll come out first thing tomorrow."

"Good, that's good," he said approvingly. "Oh. And another thing."

I waited.

Apparently, the chemo had killed off the cells in her throat and she was having a hard time talking. They had to keep siphoning saliva out of her throat, it was unpleasant but not dangerous, but—he cleared his own throat here—he wanted us to be prepared.

So: change of plans. Mom in the hospital. Mom unable to talk very well, if at all.

"OK," I said, numb. I hung up and told Jacques what was going on and we started rearranging things, calling Julie and Jon, calling the dog sitter, calling Northwest to change our tickets. Sacha and I could get a flight out the next morning; Jacques, who couldn't get away from work on such short notice, would still come out on Friday, as planned.

We were back to Cancer Calendar again. All the festivity had gone out of the trip. We were tense, dry mouthed, moving quickly and unhappily through the house, talking tersely about logistics. Julie was going to fly straight from Portland to Detroit this time—she didn't want to drive down to Boston at this stage, she was so pregnant. This was the last time she'd be able to fly before the baby was born. She'd meet us either at the house or at the hospital Wednesday afternoon.

I flew out first thing Wednesday morning with Sacha. After we got off the plane, I rented a car and drove straight to Rougemont. It was hot out. Cars shimmered in the parking lot, light rays bouncing off silver tops.

There was a place in the lobby where they let me leave our duffel bag and the stroller. They gave me a claim check and I left our things there in a small heap.

Next, I stopped at the reception desk, asking for oncology. Sacha smacked the counter with both hands.

"Seventh floor," one woman said. The other, peering up at me through her bifocals, looked at Sacha and frowned. "You're not taking the *baby* up there, are you?" she asked.

I kept hearing that. "This is no place for a baby," a nurse said sharply to us by way of greeting when we got to the seventh floor. Oncology patients wheeled by on carts, gaunt, hairless, glowworm pale. This is no place for my *mother*, I wanted to tell her, but instead I just nodded, like I agreed but was too numb to turn around.

She wasn't trying to be difficult. Of all occupations, I can't think of one that requires more compassion and generosity of spirit than nursing. She meant well. She took me aside, obviously uncomfortable, and explained that even though they did their best, the custodians never really managed to get to every last corner . . . and the floors . . . so many germs . . . She was looking down at Sacha while she said this. "It'll be OK," I said. I wasn't going to let Sacha crawl around on the floor.

How could I come all this way and not let my mother see her?

Sacha, in fact, was the best possible visitor on floor seven. Because everything to her was equally foreign and unknown, she treated the gray-green hallway with the hopeful attention of a potential trip to the zoo: *What have we here? Is this an IV pole? A wheelchair, left vacant? A cart full of used lunch trays?* When we found our way to room 712A, she was content in my arms, wriggling a little, true, but upbeat, willing to see the positives here, *what's that, a circular curtain? A vinyl armchair?*

Maybe, though, there was another reason why I brought Sacha. I saw room 712A through her eyes and it was less unbearable, just a room, OK, maybe a room made up of vinyl, linoleum, and chrome. A room all beige-gray-green, not exactly House Beautiful, not even A River Runs Through It, but Sacha was open-minded and that meant I could be, too. Here was my mother, propped up with about a dozen of those skinny hospital pillows behind her back, the tray table in front of her stacked with plastic cups of varying shapes and sizes, each with a flamingo of orange plastic straw, and if it weren't for the fact that she looked like utter and complete hell, I almost would have thought she was OK.

But of course she wasn't.

Her gown was gaping open a little and I could see her clavicle bones standing out like pins, grim and sharp. She'd clearly lost weight, but at the same time, parts of her looked puffy and swollen—her face, her fingers. She was wearing a terrycloth turban which had slipped to one side, bits of bare scalp showing. I could barely look at her. I struggled to regain composure, knowing she'd see in my face how changed she was.

None of this should be happening. She shouldn't be here. She should be at home, defrosting moussaka, getting the Flag Cake ready.

Bomma, I said out loud, seemingly for Sacha's sake. *Look, here's Bomma!*

I sounded exactly like the host of one of those inane children's shows on TV.

As if to say: Here we are! This was our new reality, this half-hospital room with its circle of curtain for privacy, a corner just visible from the next bed where her roommate was gasping inaudibly into the phone. We overlooked the roommate, Sacha and I, we were model visitors, we had eyes only for my mother. In fact eyes only for my mother's eyes—we ignored the rest, the tubes coming out of her arms, the confusion of machines on either side, things squeezing and humming and dripping. We focused on her eyes, no, actually, we focused on her *glasses*, shining out at us, and tried as hard as possible to shut out everything else.

We. Sacha and I formed a unit. "I'm so sorry, Mellie," my mother said, or tried to say, because the lining of her throat was literally coming off inside and choking her and every time she tried to talk she gagged. It was horrible. I could see tears in her eyes as she spat and wiped and spat again. Tears of anguish and shame.

Maybe the infection had done some of this, but it looked like the first course of F-U had crashed over my mother like a tsunami, leaving only wreckage behind. Deathly pale, cheeks sunken, blue-green shadows under her eyes, like a caricature of herself. Huge head, shrinking body. Because of what was going on with the lining of her mouth, she couldn't talk. Her beloved voice, that voice I heard every single day, was thick as a plug. I could barely look at her; my stomach churned. I hated myself for the churning. Compassion battled in me with revulsion, and I leaned forward, trying to find a part of her to grab and squeeze that wasn't taped or tubed, and I could feel tears splashing down onto her arm.

"Oh, Mellie," I said back, brokenly. "I'm the one who's sorry. I'm—"

She wasn't the only one whose words got stuck.

Unlike me, Sacha was an ideal visitor. She was oblivious, didn't know what was normal and what wasn't, was doing some of her own spitting and coughing, saw nothing unusual in the slowly deflating IV bag dangling over my mother's swollen arm. She swung out from my waist reaching her arms straight toward my mother like a tiny diver, humming and spraying, while my mother struggled upward to meet her grasp, her cheeks sunken, her eyes dull, her skin stretched taut and shiny, her breath sour. I was a coward because they were right, the nurses, this was no place for a baby, but Sacha covered for me, kept my mother from seeing how horrified I was. She was like the part of me that could stand all of this, she stood between me and this ghost of the woman who was shuddering upward toward us from her hospital bed, reaching for us as if this were life itself I was holding toward her. As if all she had to do was reach upward and be saved.

BACK AT LAKEWOOD DRIVE, JULIE was upstairs in the Hilton, unpacking. Sara was getting things together for dinner. Sacha had fallen asleep in the car on the drive home from the hospital, and I let her stay asleep in her car seat in the front hallway. Julie inched her way downstairs, clutching the railing for balance—she was much bigger, even in just three weeks—and before long the three of us ended up in the kitchen, sitting at the table. I couldn't remember the last time it had been like this: the three of us. Alone, with my father still at work. For eighteen years, this is how we'd lived, the three of us, in this immaculate, isolated four-square colonial, eating dinner every night at six thirty (each in our designated spot) around this same Formica table. Telling about our days. Then we left, one by one—first Sara, then me, and finally Julie. Light-years ago. Now, grown-up, we came back less and less frequently—instead, my mother and father "made the rounds," flying around the country to visit us, seeing us one at a time. Over holidays—Fourth of July, Thanksgiving—we came back, but we were always surrounded: Geoff, Jon, Jacques; Jenny and Rachel. Enough din to cover the rattle of old ghosts.

Now, being just the three of us again felt bizarre. Stripped down to our essence, facing one another. With Sacha asleep and Jenny and Rachel not coming until Friday, it was literally just us. *Girls*, my mother used to call us—a collective noun. *The girls are away at camp. The girls quit piano. The girls are in college.* Three of us, like strands of a braid woven together. Then pulled apart.

Now, we alternated between being on our best behavior and falling back into the old patterns: oldest, youngest, middle. Sara, who had been back here for almost two weeks already, had almost effortlessly taken charge. She knew where all the frozen things were for the Fourth. Where things in the kitchen had been moved to make way for new things: my mother's pain medications. Brochures from the infusion center.

Julie and I tried to fit ourselves in. I noticed we'd taken our old spots at the table.

My mother, never one to hold on to souvenirs, had scoured the house of our childhood, and all our old things had been packed away. The rooms were spare, streamlined, but the house still felt crowded by the past. I could feel our old selves watching us—leaning over the balcony, looking down, the way we used to crouch and spy when my parents had parties, whispering slyly to one another. Two against one. One against two. The tricky triangle of sisterhood—who said what to whom. Whose feelings hurt hardest.

We knew the old roles were there, waiting for us. The endless competition. Who was more organized? Funnier? Who did my mother think was the most "pulled together"? That was one of my mother's prized judgments—the Pulitzer of personality. Being "pulled together" meant you could cope with life, whatever got thrown at you. If you didn't have that, so what if you published your thesis or edited law review? You could find life on Mars and it wouldn't matter.

We all still wanted her approval, much as we hated ourselves for it. Being back home was like tiptoeing across quicksand. We saw the old sinkholes, and much as we didn't want to risk them—not now, with so much at stake—there was only one way across.

To distract ourselves, we kept busy. We threw out old newspapers, cleaned the fridge, made the beds. Put stacks of towels in various rooms, the way she would have. Watered her red geraniums. Eighteen pots, spaced all around the deck, all in need of pruning. "Why can't she ever plant anything else?" Julie muttered, circling with the green plastic watering can my mother had owned forever.

My mother. Queen of what-we-always-do.

JULY APPROACHED WITH THE SMELL of burnt grass and barbecues. Lakewood was quiet, the Realtors gone, the glossy brochures advertising the house still lying (with a certain embarrassment) on the front hall table. Julie cooked—apron distended over her rising belly—while Sara and I organized: cookbook back in its spot on the shelf, cans and bottles rinsed, sorted in the appropriate recycling bins in the spick-and-span garage.

The house was imperceptibly changed. Even in just three short weeks, it had become the house of a sick person. Everywhere there were signs: vials of pills next to the toaster. A kidney-shaped spittoon in the bathroom.

My father went straight from his office to the hospital. When he came back, he seemed glad to see us, but you could see the panic in his eyes.

"They think she'll be ready to come home tomorrow," he told us on Wednesday night.

Thursday, though, the fever was lower but still not gone. More antibiotics ordered.

We took turns. We had a relay going: my father at work, one of us at the hospital, the other two rotating things at home. We took turns cleaning the house, taking Sacha for walks, and thawing various dishes for my mother's birthday dinner, which we were still hoping to have on Saturday night. On Friday morning, we decided to set the table in advance. "Let's do it inside this year," Sara said, a concession to what we didn't want to admit: My mother shouldn't be outside, not in this heat. She was too frail. We used her favorite plates, the ceramic ones they'd gotten one year on a trip to the Amalfi. I made festive menus, naming each course: *Artichokes Toujours. Moussaka Lakewoode. Salade Extremely Verte. Tartine de Flagge.*

We told one another it was important to be funny. Not just normal anymore, but funny. Humor seemed our best weapon now.

Jacques was coming in Friday evening, around the same time Jon was arriving from Portland. Friday afternoon I went over to the hospital alone, leaving Sacha with Julie, since Sara was on her way to the airport to pick up Geoff and the girls. My mother was asleep when I got up to her room, which I hadn't expected, and her roommate was on the phone again—was it possible this could be the same conversation?—so I flipped through the pages of a *Good Housekeeping* magazine from February, waiting for her to wake up. There was something bleak about seeing all the recipes for Valentine's Day cookies and creative ideas for making cards out of red and white tissue paper. Last February looked strangely innocent now, from the sad perspective of early July. My mother had been well then. Or at least if she was sick, we hadn't known it. We were still back in DC then, getting ready to say good-bye to Julie and Jon. A lifetime ago.

That felt like such a big deal then: who lived in which city. I pushed the magazine away.

Hospital Time. Neither summer nor winter. Neither February nor July. There were no seasons here. No light or dark, just a perpetual artificial glow. It was like being inside of an enormous clock: You could feel the cogs moving, the wheels turning over and over, and every second a kind of sighing sound, as if to say, *again, again.* Or, *not yet, not yet.* Machines whirred. The oxygen meter beeped out its forlorn warning: *broken! Broken!* There was the ineffable sadness of three o'clock, the day nurses packing up their things, their pace quickening, moving out, toward fresh air, the out-of-doors, the release of evening, the long holiday weekend ahead, and the patients still lying here, trapped in their beds, while the world orbited, away, away. On

the grainy television sets implausible news programs showed miniature catastrophes blooming and fading. I closed my eyes, trying to
name the sounds I heard, each creak and whirr.

Not now. Not now. Or *soon, soon.*

I must have dozed off for a few minutes, because when I opened
my eyes, my mother was awake, and Dr. Brenner was visiting.

He didn't seem as short as I remembered, or as hearty. "Hey," he
said, noticing me. The colloquial greeting took me by surprise. He
wasn't all that much older than I was, after all. Seven or eight years,
maybe. In another life, we might have been friends.

"You have a visitor," he said to my mother, as if this needed
pointing out.

He patted my mother's leg under its heap of blankets.

"Not such a great day, is it," he said. He sounded sympathetic,
and I wondered if I'd misjudged him when we met in his office.

My mother was listless, eyes flicking on his as if she were trying
to read a book in a foreign language.

I asked Dr. Brenner why the side effects had been so bad.

He explained she'd gotten an infection—not unusual, it happens. "We're going to hold off on the second course of chemotherapy
until she's stronger," he said, tapping with his pencil on her chart.

"What do you mean, 'hold off'?" I asked.

"We just want to wait awhile," he said. "We'll see how soon this
infection clears up, then make a decision about when to resume."

I stared at him. How could we stop? We needed everything we
had to throw at the cancer cells! If we stopped—

He sensed my worry. "This can happen," he told me. He was
being nice. "The best thing is for Mom to get a little stronger, then
we'll start it up again." I knew it was irrational, but I hated that he
called her "Mom." It seemed so awful already, her being here, wearing
this dreadful hospital gown, in this ugly room with no privacy, when
it was Friday and everyone was flying in and her birthday was on

Sunday. Her favorite day of the year. At the very least he could give her back her pronoun. *Your* mom. That would be better.

The good news was, the fever was down. She could stop with the antibiotics, he said.

A nurse came in, there was a general flutter around my mother's bed, unhooking her IV, taking away the bags of fluid. The work was all in the details now, cleaning, propping, swabbing, getting her ready to be discharged.

I hated the idea of delaying round two. Cancer Calendar was rearranging itself in front of us again, days evaporating, weeks being erased. I felt like the big picture was being lost, like something was being pulled out from under us. I followed Dr. Brenner out to the hallway.

I was afraid they were giving up on her.

"Isn't there something else she can try in the meantime? Something less toxic?" I asked.

The look that he gave me was hard to describe. It was a mixture of patience, sadness, and ineffable fatigue, and briefly—just for a second or two—I wondered what it must be like to be Dr. Brenner, with those little boys at home, having to deal with so much suffering every day. I pictured a door opening, one of the boys calling out. *Dad! How was your day?*

He explained that once my mother was stronger—he gave her back her pronoun this time—she could get a drug called Neupogen that would boost her white cells. It was expensive, but worth it. Until then, any form of chemotherapy would be too dangerous. She was just too weak.

"It's her birthday on Sunday," I told him. It seemed faintly ridiculous, saying this, but I kept going. "She made a special dinner. The whole family's coming in tonight."

What I didn't say, what I couldn't describe, was the feeling of my mother's birthday. How it always was. Sitting outside, the grass dewy against our bare feet, sparklers singeing our fingers. The arcs of light they made—Jenny and Rachel dancing with them out in the grass. The smell of coals burning down to ash. "It's a big deal to her, her birthday," I added lamely.

Dr. Brenner nodded, taking in this information.

"Let's get her home, then," he said.

So we did.

Help (II)

LATER, LOOKING BACK, I SOMETIMES played a terrible game with myself, trying to decide which good-bye was hardest. There were so many of them, layered on top of each other, and each seemed more difficult than the others. It was like listening to music that reached a crescendo only to build and build until you were certain you couldn't bear it anymore.

The hard thing about saying good-bye on July Fourth was that we didn't have fixed plans to see one another again until Labor Day. And even then, we weren't sure Julie and Jon would be able to make it. So much depended on everything else—when Julie had the baby; when my mother's blood counts went back up so she could start chemo again. I was planning to come out when she was ready for the second round of F-U, but when would that be? Even the trip over Labor Day seemed tenuous—would Julie and Jon be able to come? Would my mother be well enough to make it happen? Julie, starting her eighth month now, wouldn't be allowed to fly again until after the baby came. Sunday afternoon before she and Jon left for the airport, my mother clung to her. Against Julie's pregnant girth, she looked as tiny and shrunken as a child. Both of them were wet-faced when they pulled apart.

No tickets booked. No chemo schedule. No firm plan of what came next.

When it was our time to leave, my mother pulled herself together.

"Don't worry, Mellie," she told me, patting me on the arm as Jacques and I loaded up the rental car, getting ready to head to the airport a few hours later. "The minute Dr. Brenner gives me the all clear, we'll get those tickets sorted out and you and Sacha will come back."

So far, though, we were all in a holding pattern, like circling in a plane before you get cleared for landing. Her blood counts were still too low for more F-U.

Back in Newton with Sacha, I resumed cycles of my own. Walking with Sacha and Bacchus in endless loops. Circling in the car with Sandi, looking at houses. Calling my mother, waiting for her to be able to talk, calling her back. Cycles eclipsed other cycles. Orbiting back and forth from the house to my new office, pushing Sacha in her stroller. Calling Annie to talk about what I'd be teaching in the fall. Waiting for something to change.

MID-JULY, I STARTED RUNNING AGAIN. Around the same time, Sacha stopped nursing.

I don't remember which came first, the end of breastfeeding or the beginning of running, but somehow, in those weeks after the Fourth of July, I started to become aware of my body again. My veins, how blue they looked on my wrists. The way my fingers moved when I typed. How good coffee smelled in the morning. The nap of things against my fingers—cardboard, rose petals. Flowers sprang up in the garden of the House with the Green Shag, weedy but lovely: tiger lilies. Coneflowers. Flowers of midsummer. Hot and humid as it was outside, I was suddenly ravenous for the out-of-doors. When Jacques came home from work each night, I'd run upstairs, peeling clothes off as I went—T-shirt, shorts—and grab my running clothes out of the bottom drawer of the dresser we shared. I'd take Bacchus with me and we'd bound out the front door, banging the screen door behind us, tearing down Middlesex Road and over the bridge to the reservoir. I could feel energy and nerves and something else coursing through my veins, and I wanted—needed—to run. By the time we hit the path around the water we were going full stride, he and I. Bacchus wasn't very well trained, but if I ran fast enough, he left the squirrels and other dogs alone and more or less stayed with me, and because I needed to focus on him, I'd run without music, listening to the sound of footfalls, of his panting, of my own breath quickening and slowing. It had been eighteen months or more since I'd run, and for the first few times, my chest ached and my breath was ragged, but I pushed through, ignoring the muggy heat and the cyclones of tiny midges that swarmed near the water. I'd run for half an hour, forty minutes, sometimes even fifty, then I'd fall back through the door, sweaty and winded, my face red, my clothes sticking to me, and Sacha would look at me with bright, curious eyes. *Who are you?* her expression seemed to say, *and where's the mother I know?*

Running, I was free of thinking or worrying. It was the only time I wasn't anxious or angry. For that stretch every day, I could just *be*, swallowed up by motion and exertion. Running, I had a body again—legs that ached, calf muscles that tightened when I ran up the trails into the woods. Eyes that swam with tears.

Then I'd come back and take Sacha from Jacques, and bit by bit we'd slip back into being ourselves again. Except that little by little I noticed Sacha wasn't interested in nursing anymore. She'd try and I'd try, but there was a subtle change; she'd fidget, lose interest, and before I knew it, we were down to twice a day—first thing in the morning, last thing at night. Then, only once a day, and not always even that.

Once I read a column in the newspaper called "Last Things," by a woman who wrote features about being a parent. We make such a big thing out of every first, she wrote. First smile, first step, first word. Why don't we record last things? She was trying to remember the last time she'd carried her daughter (now eight or nine years old) down the stairs. I remembered that column and I could feel Sacha's interest in nursing slipping away and I promised myself I wouldn't let that happen: I'd know when the last time came.

But I didn't. Sometime over those last weeks of July it just stopped, with no fanfare or recognition. One morning I got up late, and Jacques gave Sacha a bottle; one night I stayed up late, working on my book, and he gave her a bottle again; or I was on the phone with Julie, or with my mother; one night Annie called and we talked for hours—and somehow, it had been a day, then two days, and Sacha wasn't nursing anymore. A last thing, and I had missed it.

"It's probably time," Julie said, when I called to tell her. "Seven months—that's about right, isn't it?" She was deep into the baby books, getting ready.

I wasn't sure. There wasn't a timeline for this in *What to Expect.* It's easier to chart out the beginnings of things, I suppose, than the ends of them. I looked at Sacha, whose laser focus was now beamed on crawling. It was hard to put into words how peculiar it felt, watching the efforts she made, shooting away from me. Our drive to separate seems so much stronger at times than our drive to connect. Or maybe, separating, we just need to find new ways to come together.

WHEN I WASN'T RUNNING OR talking on the phone to my mother or calling Julie to see how she was feeling—the baby was just weeks away now—most of July I spent looking for child care.

Here is how I pictured the person we would eventually hire to help take care of Sacha in the fall:

She'd be younger than me, more energetic, less moody. Less bound by day-to-day details (laundry, plane tickets), more willing to get down on the floor and play with Sacha. Like a devoted niece I never knew I had.

When I described this hypothetical person—usually to Julie, on the phone—it was mostly in terms of binaries: Playful, yet responsible. Firm, yet flexible.

"Sounds like an ad for paper towels," Julie said.

My mother—feeling pretty much the same, thanks, and still hoping for good news about her blood counts—called every afternoon to weigh in with her own adjectives. Energetic. Organized. (Did this surprise us?) Careful. This is *Sacha* you're trusting someone with, she reminded me, in case I'd forgotten.

Truthfully, the only person my mother could imagine leaving Sacha with, other than my sisters or me, was her.

Jacques took an afternoon off work so we could meet with Eileen Diamond, the owner of the agency in Newton Centre we'd been sent to by Annie's older sister, who always knew where to go for things like this.

"Listen, if DeeDee recommends this place, it'll be great," Annie told me, when she called me back with the number. DeeDee lived in an imposing house in Brookline and ran her life like a small corporation. She was the one who'd sent me to Dr. Millis, Annie reminded me.

"Right," I said, remembering Dr. Millis's brisk, no-nonsense tone, her cold hands. Maybe I should've listened to Jacques, and run our own ad in the classifieds.

"'Diamond' can't be her real name," Jacques said, maneuvering our car into a parking space in front of Centre Nannies.

Real or adopted, the name fit. Everything about Eileen was sharp and faceted—she was tall and angular, wearing chunky metal jewelry.

She looked like she was in her late forties, her own children off for the summer volunteering somewhere in Central America. Pictures of them were propped up on her desk facing outward, at dramatic angles.

Eileen brought us seltzer and glossy brochures and wriggled her fingers unconvincingly in Sacha's direction, the whole time explaining to us how the agency worked. We would pay a (hefty) deposit, take a cluster of file folders home with us, and start selecting candidates who looked promising—"it's all about *fit*," Eileen reminded us. The agency ran clearance checks on everything from candidates' psychological stability to driving records. We could choose up to five people to interview at a time. Once we'd settled on someone, we'd meet again and draw up a yearlong contract. If the person didn't work out, we'd get some money back, as well as a "replacement nanny."

It all sounded so contractual to me—like mail-ordering a bride. On the other hand, how did I think this was going to happen? Did I think I was going to meet a babysitter on the train?

"Now," Eileen said, getting down to business. She peered at Sacha, who was chewing the corner of the brochure. "Were you thinking of live-in, or out?"

"Out," we said in unison, then glanced at each other, embarrassed by how quickly we'd answered. And how loud our voices were.

Eileen frowned. "That's a little harder," she told us. "Most of our girls are looking for a place to live."

She tried to pitch the live-in idea, but Jacques put up a hand to stop her. "We're pretty private," he told her. "We like to have evenings and weekends to ourselves, just us."

That was an understatement. No sane, likeable child-care person would want to stay with us for a minute if they saw us on a typical evening, nine-ish. We didn't even like seeing ourselves then, let alone each other. Evenings and weekends were subject to crankiness, half-dress, and eating takeout straight from the fridge.

I could barely imagine having a stranger around during the day, when we supposedly needed help. How could I talk to my mother and Julie and sob every afternoon into Sacha's back in front of someone I didn't know—even someone discreet, yet confiding?

"Live out," I confirmed weakly.

It didn't seem possible that we had already reached this point. July was coming to an end, and Sacha would be eight months old in a few weeks. She was crawling now. How long before she took her first steps?

The future was blank. All I could manage was to try not to plan, to focus on the here and now: mashing up steamed veggies and fruit for Sacha, taking her for walks, going running. My book had ground to a standstill in the middle of horoscopes, as if prognostication every-where had come to a halt.

My mother—

I felt like I should say something about my mother to Eileen Diamond. I had a strange compulsion to tell everyone I met about her, like the speaker in "The Rime of the Ancient Mariner": *My mother has metastatic breast cancer. Stage 4, in her bones. Incurable, actually. We're hoping chemo will buy her time, but she hasn't been able to start the second round of treatment yet. We don't know for sure when she can. She's in a lot of pain from the cancer, and sometimes it's hard for her to stay awake or concentrate—*

Eileen was passing us each a questionnaire to fill out.

And this whole thing is so hard to understand, because even though we come from a cancer family, it's not breast cancer, it's ovarian cancer. We were always so worried about our ovaries, and so careful, and then this happened, and it just doesn't make sense—

But there was no time here for family history. We had these forms to fill out. Parenting style, schedules, hobbies. These details would help us find a "match," Eileen said.

Our hobbies.

Sacha wriggled around on my lap, trying to grab the pen from me. I had a brief flashback to senior year in high school, looking at the big space on college applications for listing major activities. Honors, national awards.

I didn't really have hobbies.

Maybe it wasn't too late to pick some up. Maybe my mother would rally. Maybe we'd find a great nanny, get the house issue settled, I'd get back to working on my book, we'd have a schedule—

I could study Farsi.

"What should I say?" I whispered to Jacques, who was busy writing. I read his entries for Hobbies over his shoulder. *Squash. Biking. Sudoku.*

Sudoku? "That's not a hobby," I objected, tapping on the word with my pencil.

He looked offended. Then he frowned at my blank page. "What about running?" he asked, looking me over like we'd just met. Only this time, he wasn't planning to ask for my number.

Running! I'd forgotten about that.

Running, I wrote in one of the blanks in rounder-than-usual print. I thought for a while. One hobby didn't seem enough. *Hobby* seemed to demand a plural. *Travel,* I wrote next.

Did flying back and forth to Detroit count as travel? I pictured the magazine racks in the Northwest Airlines, Terminal D. The last row of coach.

Apparently, we were out of time.

"Terrific," Eileen was saying, taking back our forms. "Now, maybe we can just chat about these for a little while—"

Jacques was getting annoyed. He didn't mind filling out a short form, but he was missing a meeting and didn't want to talk about hobbies (real ones included sleeping late, scouring the classifieds for used trucks, and watching reruns of *Law & Order*). He wanted to find out what we got for our nonrefundable deposit. We were post-hobby, and we needed help.

All it took was a few terse questions, and Eileen—she had an

MBA, after all—jumped into action. Of course, we could move on—of course, if he had a *meeting*—

She scattered a few brightly colored folders on the desk between us and disappeared into her inner office, where the contracts were kept. Jacques, frowning, took out a checkbook.

I looked over file number one. Annika Nilson, a sweet-faced girl relocated to Boston from a Midwestern farming community, straight A student, active in her church, her own hobbies (volunteering at a soup kitchen, stargazing) suggesting compassion and a love of nature. Her essay—"The Importance of Family"—centered on a tribute to her grandmother, who'd taught her to bake before dying of congestive heart failure when Annika was twelve.

I pictured myself opening the front door after a day of teaching to see Annika's shining head bent over Sacha's, nudging tiny fingers around a rolling pin.

When Eileen returned, I cleared my throat. "*Annika* looks like a nice girl," I said, trying to sound noncommittal.

Eileen frowned, looked at the folder, reddened. "Oh—I've made a mistake," she said.

Annika, it seemed, had already been placed. A couple in the Back Bay had just hired her. A pair of headhunters, Eileen said ap-provingly, taking the file back. With two-year-old twins.

In my envious imagination, the headhunters were doubles, with two of everything. Two toddlers. Two high-powered jobs. Twice as prepared to swoop in and grab Annika.

We were behind again.

"Don't worry," Eileen assured us, "there are other candidates"—maybe not quite Annika, her tone implied—"but it's true, this is a *very active* time in the nanny-hiring season."

End of July. Everyone, it seemed, wanted to get their child-care situation squared away before Labor Day. We should get back to Ei-leen with our top choices as soon as possible.

Jacques seemed to guess how I felt.

"They probably keep Annika's file as a decoy," he said under his breath as Eileen ushered us out. I could tell he was trying to cheer me up. "Just to scare people into choosing someone else quickly. Annika probably doesn't even exist."

We drove home a different route than usual, letting Sacha drift off in the back. Musing over our options.

"Look," Jacques said, stopping short on a street about a mile from the House with the Green Shag. "There's a FOR SALE sign. Why hasn't Sandi shown us this place?"

I squinted up at the house: big, dark stucco, a little close to the road, which was pretty busy. It was hard to tell what the house was like. Ivy crawling up the walls. Not in spectacular repair. "I'll ask her," I said uncertainly, wondering what grabbed him about it.

You couldn't even see the yard from this vantage. Was it "useable"? Who could tell? Maybe the need to get settled was starting to hit Jacques, too.

Seize the house, as the Romans might have put it.

Words for Things (I)

ONCE THERE WAS NO JULY or August.

The Romans had a ten-month calendar, with months named for gods and numbers. March, from Mars. November, from nine; December, from ten. The fifth month used to be called Quintilis; the sixth, Sextilis.

Then Julius Caesar got the fifth month named for him—so Quintilis was changed to July. Eventually his great-nephew Augustus wanted a month of his own, too, and Sextilis became August.

What if months were named for feelings, instead of numbers or emperors or gods? Remorse. Terror. Ire. Today is the seventeenth day of Remorse. Ire has ended. Can you believe it's Terror again already?

Or maybe you could use Kübler-Ross's stages. Denial, Anger, Bargaining, Depression, Acceptance.

In that case, we were in Bargaining now. Or maybe somewhere between Bargaining and Depression. It was the last week of July. Full summer. Heat burned behind the retina like an eclipse, I couldn't remember a season other than this. The warmth moved up inside of us, dulling us, slowing us to a crawl. Some nights I woke up, soaked, to the split and crash of thunder, and in the next room Sacha slept, working her thumb in her mouth, undisturbed.

We were all on hold, waiting. Julie was due any day now, and I called her constantly, the two of us evaluating signs of imminent labor over the phone. *What exactly did the pain feel like? Low? Sharp or dull?*

"Your cousin is coming, Sachabelle," I crooned, holding Sacha on my lap. Julie had stopped working after she got back to Maine from the Fourth of July, and spent most days now out on their screened porch, talking to me or to my mother on the phone, dabbing herself with ice water, trying to find a comfortable position.

Between calling Julie and calling my mother, I read files from Centre Nanny. It was time to get ready for the fall. I tried to get things done—I got a referral from Dr. Muto for an internist who said she'd be happy to take me on as a regular patient. Her name was Dr. Pierce, and she wore funky glasses and had a cockeyed smile that put me instantly at ease. My version of our family history didn't seem to faze her.

"Let's see what's going on here," she said, putting my chart down and coming over to examine me.

Nothing was going on. Normal breast exam. Normal blood pressure, normal weight, normal blood work. Everything was normal, except that because of my mother, nothing was.

"Still nursing?" Dr. Pierce asked me, looking down at Sacha, who had come with me, the way she always did.

I shook my head. *Last things*, I thought, trying to remember now what nursing had felt like.

THE LAST WEEK OF JULY, Dr. Brenner gave my mother the all clear to start round two of F-U. Her blood work looked good. But now my mother was the one to stall: She was determined to go to Maine when Julie had the baby, and she wanted to put the chemo off until she got back.

"She's nuts," Julie complained, when we talked about it later. "She needs to do the treatment! She can't put it off just for me. Can you imagine how I'll feel if the baby is two weeks late?"

My mother refused to listen to anyone. F-U could wait, she said crisply. Her new grandchild could not. Period. End of discussion.

Julie begged me to talk sense into her.

I tried. Sometimes the logistics angle worked best. "Listen. I can't get my tickets to come out and help if I don't know when you're going to do the treatment," I reminded my mother.

She refused to listen.

Dr. Brenner was OK with the idea of waiting a bit longer. They agreed she'd start round two when she got back from Maine. And my father was going to take time off from work, so she didn't need me to come out, though she appreciated the offer, she told me. Case closed.

So we waited, all of us.

I KEPT SOME ROUTINES, STARTED new ones. I went to the university to get my office set up, letting Sacha chew on the edge of Foucault's *Discipline and Punish* while I wiped down bookshelves. I put books on reserve at the library for my courses. I called Sandi to check in about the house we'd seen. Yes, she knew it, it was a great house inside, but it needed work, and the owner was asking more than we said we could spend—but she'd check with the broker, just to see, because it had been on the market for a while, and you never knew—

Some mornings I sat at the kitchen counter holding my day

planner like it was some kind of sacred text, moving my finger along the edge of one entry or another.

This, and this, and this. This is how we fill up a life.

IN THE AFTERNOONS, I TALKED over child-care options with my mother.

Jacques and I had picked our top three candidates. Cara Reilly from Des Moines, twenty-three, working toward her master's in early childhood education at Simmons. Jamie Brice from the North Shore, who loved children and was hoping to go into pediatric nursing one day. And Annabel O'Rourke from Plymouth—the youngest of the batch, only nineteen, who loved "sewing and 'surprises,'" and had included a photo of herself in her file (a little out of focus) taken on a roller coaster, both arms up.

On the phone, my mother and I mulled over the pros and cons of each. So far, Cara was the front-runner. "What does Cara's mother do?" my mother asked, as if this were the clincher. (If, for example, her mother happened to teach AP History at an elite private school, that would be a plus.) I admitted I didn't know, and there was silence. Maybe she was thinking about that, about the lack of information surrounding mothers, their eventual irrelevance, how they could mean so much for so long, but when push came to shove, they were only bedrock after all—invisible, below the surface, not even warranting a minute of an interviewer's time. But no, apparently she wasn't thinking about that, she was already moving on to other issues. What about siblings? "Sisters or brothers," she mused. "That's important."

I glanced down at Sacha, who was pulling herself up on the kitchen chair, practicing standing up alone. Sisters or brothers.

My mother was right. That really mattered. When on earth were we going to manage *that*?

We met Cara one evening after dinner. I'd gotten ready for her. I changed my shirt, washed my face, inspected myself in the mirror.

I'd never given an interview before, I'd always been on the other side. The interview with the author at the magazine who needed an amanuensis. The fellowship interview where eight unsmiling men asked me what difference poetry would make in the event one country decided to drop a nuclear bomb on another. The interview at the New Orleans–style restaurant where, back from college one summer, I tried to convince the owner I was planning to stay on permanently, claiming I wanted to write menu copy as a career. *Chicken almondine on a tender bed of spring greens.* None of these interviews had gone my way.

Now, I wanted to ask the right questions, not give the right answers. Was that what it meant to grow up?

CARA WAS EASY TO TALK to. I liked her right away. She'd studied literature in college, and we shared favorite authors—Nabokov, Márquez. She had a long list of questions for us about how we liked to handle emergencies. She had a boyfriend (safely back in Des Moines, studying engineering). She seemed perfect: low-key and responsible.

There was one catch. She hadn't spent much time with babies before—all her references were from people with toddlers and school-age children. After we talked for a while—I liked her, Jacques liked her—we tried to get her to engage with Sacha, who'd been pulling herself up on the side of the couch and smacking Jacques and me on the legs with a book the whole time we talked.

There was no sparkle. Cara stiffened up the minute we passed Sacha to her. All her warmth and friendliness suddenly seemed shadowed by something—was it possible?—like fear.

Jacques, who interviews people all the time at work, went for the direct approach. "You seem a little tense," he said after a few minutes. "Are you comfortable with babies?"

"Yes," Cara said hesitantly, passing Sacha back to him like she was made of glass. Of course she liked babies! She thought about that, reconsidering.

"Anyway," she pointed out, "they grow so fast."

"Not the right person," Jacques said, once we'd thanked her for coming, and Cara had closed the door behind her.

I defended her. A literature major, after all! "She just needs time to get used to Sacha," I insisted.

But it was moot. Cara called us an hour later to say she'd decided to accept a job taking care of a three-year-old in Brookline.

We met Jamie the next night, and she seemed fine. A little on the unimaginative side, but she was a "good, solid choice," in Jacques's estimation.

I still wanted to meet number three.

We'd bumped Annabel O'Rourke down to third place because she was only nineteen, which I thought was too young, and she didn't have a college degree, and everything in her file suggested a mixture of schemes half realized and still in transition. "Just what we need," I said to Jacques, "another child to raise." But now, I wanted to meet her. Just to compare.

We scheduled an interview for the next evening. Jacques and I were both out of sorts. We had so little time to get things done anymore! Sacha was fidgety and cross, dinner dishes piled in the sink, and Annabel seemed inconceivably young to me, more like sixteen than nineteen, her long hair the color of a leaf in flame. She was ten minutes late, not having realized our street was a one-way. She was nervous, her plans came out all in a jumble: Nick, her boyfriend (who wanted to make films) had just gotten into art school; they were looking for apartments. Every part of her life seemed in flux, still forming, bordering on chaos, her history crowded with names of aunts and uncles and cousins I was already forgetting even as I heard about them. But her manner with Sacha took my breath away. It was like the moment in *The Wizard of Oz* when the screen goes from black and white to color. Annabel asked to hold her, we said OK, she scooped her onto her lap, laughing, and Sacha gazed at her in fascination, eyes opening, arms opening, like a bud exposed to some kind of spectacular light.

Annabel was a talker. What she really wanted was to design and make clothing, she told us, but in the meantime, she needed to make money to support herself so she could join Nick at art school in a few years. She loved babies. She'd practically raised her three younger sisters herself—no self-pity here, just straight up—because her father left home when she was little and her mom had a bad car accident when she was fifteen, so as the oldest, it was up to Annabel to take over. She loved houses. She loved fixing things. She understood what we meant about the House with the Green Shag. No comment, just a complicit shrug. When she handed Sacha back to me, wriggling and laughing, her hand was unusually warm.

When we offered her something to drink, she asked for milk.

Annabel was wholesome—granted. But was she calm, I wondered. Would she have staying power when Sacha refused to nap?

Was she mature enough to handle all we threw at her? All life threw at us?

Her references, I had to admit, were more effusive than any ever written about me.

In one job, she'd taken care of four boys under the age of seven.

Cooked them lunch, did their laundry—"We made a game out of it," she said, with that self-deprecating shrug. The sorting game. Kids, she pointed out, like games. Barely done being a kid herself, it was clear Annabel liked games, too. Took mattresses off the beds and turned staircases into slides. Threw "unbirthday parties." Or "hide the lunchbox." The boys would run around the house, looking for their lunches—once she hid them in the washing machine. Once, she tucked them behind a pair of boots in the mudroom.

Patience?

In another job, she'd taken care of a seven-year-old girl with special needs. Took her on long rides through the neighborhood in a makeshift cart Annabel constructed out of a wheelbarrow and blankets. Wrote stories for the girl herself because the books her parents got for her—Annabel grimaced—were too difficult and boring. Braided her hair every morning and helped her wash herself. "*You know*," she said with that deal-with-it-life-is-wonderful-even-so expression, and she teasingly referred to herself as Annabel Poppins, confessing that the year her father moved out she watched *Mary Poppins* thirty-seven times.

In case I wasn't won over already, next came the clincher: the story of the cassettes. She mentioned it on the way out the door, having caught sight of one of Sacha's car tapes, snaggled up in Jacques's in-box. I'd forgotten to throw it out after it had gotten mangled in our tape player earlier that week. Annabel eyed it, smiling. She told us she'd used her mother's iron, lowest setting, to smooth out her sister Meghan's cassettes when the little tapes got kinked up and wouldn't play.

"Did it work?" Jacques asked, interested. We had plenty more tangled tapes, if we could just find them.

Annabel nodded. "You just have to be careful with the heat. I used a really thin piece of cloth between the tape and the iron," she told him.

Wow.

What drew me to Annabel was her life force, the sheer ruddy flush of energy in her, like an electric charge. Not to mention it seemed like there was nothing she couldn't fix.

I was pretty sure she was the one. But later, Sacha asleep, I cradled the phone to my ear, dialing, ready to describe her to my mother and ask her what she thought.

Birthday (II)

PICTURE A WOMAN WITH A cane.

She's fifty-eight. She's wearing her Thoroughly Modern Millie wig, pageboy style, with bangs. Shiny and dark, with an artificial gleam that suggests vitality. In the airport you can see the wig from way off because it's the only part of her that looks alive.

She's rail thin and her gait has the stagger of someone who's become incapacitated in a hurry. Age slows you down bit by bit: Arthritis eats away at a hip, maybe, and the rest of the body compensates or doesn't, but it happens slowly. This is different. My mother has aged dramatically in the last month, like Sondra Bizet in *Lost Horizon*—the minute she leaves Shangri-La, a century hits her all at once.

The ordinary can become treacherous so quickly. A stalled escalator, metal stairs frozen, seventeen steps down to baggage claim. It may as well be the Antipodes down there. What about the cramped women's bathroom, rosettes of discarded tissue sticking to the bottom of her Lucite cane? How to balance the cane in one hand, the handbag, how to lean against the stall's door, panting, *he can't come in here to help, you have to do this alone, this was your idea, you insisted on coming against everyone's advice and orders, to see this baby.* Every step is agony. Pain pillows the vertebrae now, knives for clavicles, two hundred and six bones in the human body and so many of them hurt now. A match of small pain ignites the bigger pains nearby, until it's all in flames, rib, spine, hip, neck, *the neck is the worst, who knew it was so hard to hold up a head, the head is so heavy, the wig is so scratchy, keep them from seeing, keep them from knowing, if I can just get these pants down this shirt up this seat down this body what was it Yeats said, about the soul being fastened to a dying animal . . . was that Yeats? Remember that class at Michigan freshman year, the one on Irish writers, the professor what was his name, big burly man from Ireland, with that wonderful accent. After Yeats, we read Joyce. Ulysses. Leopold Bloom. A book for every hour of the day, wasn't that it? And there was a key. Every book was organized around an organ of the body . . . liver, he was eating liver in the first book . . .*

LLBB. Liver, lung, bone, brain. Brenner thinks it's in the liver now too, the cancer. If it goes to the brain—

'I don't want the girls to know that. Let them stop worrying so much for a while. I'm starting the chemo again, let them think it will help. . . .

Dale brought his oncology textbook home from his office and I read it when I can. He doesn't want me to, but I've held my ground. I want the real story, the one Brenner gets. It's important to know what's coming, right? "Would you let me go to Siena without a guidebook?" I asked him. Dale looked away, inconsolable. We were supposed to go in the spring. There's a road that connects Siena to Florence, the 222, I think it's called.

The Wine Route. You can stop in Chianti, Greve, all the small wine towns.

The textbook describes what happens with metastases to the brain. May cause blindness, paralysis, depending on how the cancer spreads.

When I was little, when my parents fought in the next room, I used to squeeze my hands tight and play a game I called The Worst. This isn't the worst, I'd tell the cat, who sometimes liked me and sometimes didn't. Hissed when he didn't. What would be the worst? I didn't have brothers or sisters, so Snowbell had to answer. My friend Linda was born without a hand, she had to wear one made of plastic. That was worse, but not the worst. The worst would be no hands or feet. The worst would be to be tied up in a room full of something horrible—snakes, I told myself. Or maybe hideous spiders, the huge kind I used to see in National Geographic.

These nights sleep comes hard and Which Is Worst plays all the time, like a TV channel I can't shut off. Which would be worse: paralysis or blindness? Blindness, I think, because then I couldn't read. Now I can still read, a little of the New Yorker *each night. But maybe paralysis is worse because you couldn't reach for anything—the table—the book about dying with dignity—*

I keep the textbook in the Hilton, on the table next to the bed, I read when I can focus. Not much. I have the other book too, the one from the Hemlock Society, but the girls don't know about that. Don't know about either, actually. Don't know that I sleep in the Hilton now, I can't stand bothering Dale, can't stand either to be alone down the hall or with him, sick, disrupting him; he needs sleep so he can work. When we get back home we're thinking of hiring someone to help at night, so I don't have to wake him.

After my father left, Jennie moved into my room with me, but I never played The Worst with her. I don't know why.

I want to see this baby. OK, put the mask back on—I promised him I'd wear it. But I know better than to look at myself once it's on.

Maybe in the end you keep The Worst to yourself. Like people do with prayer.

———

PICTURE A WOMAN IN THE bathroom at the Portland airport, look-ing at herself in the mirror. Adjusting her wig. She's flown in to meet her new granddaughter, born three days ago. Madeline Joelle. There is nothing she wants more than to hold this baby.

Picture her. She looks like a scratch, not a person.

A wire woman, a curio. A shadow where a woman used to be.

JULIE KEPT HOPING SHE'D CHANGE her mind, or Dr. Brenner would change his mind, or my father would prevail on her to stay home.

"Can't you convince her?" she begged me.

Julie and I were on the phone. It had been hard to talk to my mother lately. She seemed like she was in a different place. "Some of the pain meds—" my father said.

"I'll try," I said uncertainly.

But there was no stopping her. Dr. Brenner said she should wear a mask to protect herself from germs on the plane. But if she felt up to going, she could go.

Julie, two centimeters dilated and ready to go to the hospital any minute, was beside herself. "I can't believe this," she said. "How on earth does she think she's going to get on a plane and fly out here?"

There was a round-robin of calls. My father fixated on equipment—the right kind of car to get them to the airport, medical-grade masks, travel versions of all her medicine. Who could tell what he thought? Maybe he'd just given up trying to argue with her. Be-sides, what *didn't* seem insane now, when you stopped to think about it? Why was this trip different from any other ludicrous aspect of what they were enduring?

"This is a horrible thing to say," Julie told me. "I want her to come, I really do. But—" She took a deep breath. "I also want to focus on having the baby, you know? I'm worried about having to worry about her."

I knew what she meant. Ironically, the one person who would have understood even better than me was my mother—back before all of this happened. She would've hated the thought of being a burden. What she wanted was to help—like she had when Jenny and Rachel were born. Like she'd helped with Sacha. She must have known she couldn't help much this time. But she couldn't stop herself from trying.

Deep in the middle of all of these negotiations, Julie went into labor and gave birth to Madeline Joelle before any of us could get there. A beautiful, healthy, eight-pound baby girl, born in the first hours of August.

The next day, my parents flew to Maine. My father sprung for business class so there'd be fewer people around her (and fewer germs), and Jon arranged for them to be met at the airport with a car and a driver who could help them with their bags. They were like a visiting royal convoy. She had to use her cane again, not because of the clot this time but because she was having so much trouble walking.

She looked, Julie said, kind of like a folding chair. All bent in on herself.

They stayed two days. My mother was wiped out, but they made it back without mishap.

"What's Maddy like?" I asked my mother, but she didn't want to talk about the trip. Instead, she made an excuse to get off the phone.

We drove up that weekend to meet Maddy for ourselves, and I asked Julie about the visit. I hesitated. "Was it at all good to see her?" I asked.

Julie couldn't answer. I don't think I'd ever seen her at a loss for words before. This time, she couldn't get past the knot of tears.

Drawbridge

———⌾⌾⌾———

WE'VE NEVER BEEN RELIGIOUS AS a family. None of us believes in God. When I was growing up, this used to mystify my classmates, who thought they could bully me into an admission of faith. What if you were being burned alive at the stake? (Mr. Lunn, my seventh-grade social studies teacher, had been giving us detailed descriptions of the deaths of Reformation martyrs.) Wouldn't you pray then? We had six different options for churches within as many miles: Catholic, Lutheran, Methodist, Presbyterian, Episcopalian, and even the Mormon Tabernacle right up the road from us. There was also a synagogue in the vicinity, though in my elementary school, there were only a couple of Jewish families. After a brief bout with Sunday school at Temple Beth El, we retired religion the way some families give up

membership in a country club or stop watching TV. We had a family
meeting, weighed in, and gave it up.

Everyone else I knew belonged to a church, the same way they
all belonged to Blizzard, the ski club my parents wouldn't let us join
because they were sure we'd kill ourselves. In fact, since most kids
spent weekends up at Boyne Mountain, not many of them actually
went to any of these churches. But they knew which one was theirs.
They would know, for instance, what to fill out on the hospital form
that asked—with a faintly worried air—for the patient's chosen religion. Then, as now, we drew a blank.

It didn't help that when it was time to say what our fathers did
(this was back in the day when nobody asked about your mother)
every kid in my grade said something related—directly or indirectly—
to one of the Big Four car companies. Either their fathers worked for
GM or Pontiac or one of the others, or they worked for companies
that made little parts that went into things like seat belts or steering
wheels. When it was my turn, I tried out different terms for what my
father did. "Doctor" went over better than "psychoanalyst." But everyone knew anyway. "He's a shrink," Lucas Hammill would say,
groaning and holding his sides, as if this were the final ignominious
blot on our family's good name. In Newton, where the House with
the Green Shag was, every other house seemed to be owned by a
therapist. But in suburban Detroit in the 1960s, it was better to work
for Ford.

Back then, in the days when emergency drills served to prepare
for Cold War bombs as well as tornadoes, not having a religion was
seen as distinctly un-American, and it didn't help, in addition to my
father's job, that I had other anomalies. I was bad at sports. I was
nearsighted, dreamy. My mother didn't play tennis or ski or fund-raise
for local charities, preferring to spend her free time alone, reading
history books out on our back deck. She didn't like inviting kids over
or driving us to lessons. I didn't mind. I had Sara and Julie, and I loved

reading, especially antiwar novels. For the first half of seventh grade I
spent afternoons mailing angry invectives to President Nixon about
our country's actions in Vietnam. My father worried about these letters, afraid I might end up on some kind of CIA list. He also worried
(as my mother did not) that we were being raised without a moral
center. Instead of religious services, we had family dinners—this was
before food became chic in America, so we ate a lot of multicolored
and finely ground things, casseroles and something called Chicken
Surprise, stuffed with butter, breaded, and fried. During dinner, along
with thousands of calories of high-cholesterol food, we had passionate
debates about abortion, Nixon, impeachment, women's rights, and
the importance of poetry. We were an unfolding experiment: thought
instead of faith.

In high school I fell in with a fringe crowd. I still read F. Scott
Fitzgerald and memorized sonnets, but at school, I hung out with a
group of boys who planned to join the army instead of going to
college. They all wrestled and got Cs and lived in one of the
neighborhoods—literally across a set of train tracks—where the houses
were tiny and people drove pickup trucks instead of new cars from
GM. My boyfriend, Ray—a stocky wrestler with an air about him of
testosterone and doom—took me with him one Christmas Eve to
Catholic Mass in Hamtramck, but the Mass was in Latin and I
couldn't make out a single word. Catholicism was just another thing
about Ray that made him different from my family, from everything
I was trying to escape: I saw the gilt crucifix in his bedroom more or
less the way I saw his wrestling trophies, and all those Cs. But it didn't
last: It was like Just Visiting jail in Monopoly. Afterward, I went back
to agnosticism and villanelles.

Still, I wanted to belong. At college, I was invited to join a sorority filled with Midwestern debutantes. Once a week we ate dinner
in the sorority house, a white colonial that looked like a northern version of Tara. At dinner we were served by scholarship boys dressed as

waiters, and before we ate, the housemother folded her hands piously and everyone said grace. I didn't know the words, but I mumbled along, eyes decorously lowered.

One night, the entrée was ham, slightly shiny, the color of a sunburn. On the side, mashed potatoes and peas. I hated meat—I was on one of my intricate diets, living primarily on Tab, string cheese, and Doublemint gum. I hadn't eaten meat in months. Or potatoes. I busied myself pushing the peas around with my fork.

"Ham," a senior at the head of the table said, in the tone of voice that suggested she was introducing a profligate relative. She studied her plate. "What would happen if we had *Jewish* girls in this sorority? What would *they* eat tonight?"

This was not a topic I was glad to hear introduced. I didn't exactly advertise the fact that I was Jewish. My goal was to be as much like everybody else as possible.

This particular senior—her name was Mandy—was more feared than loved. She was from a wealthy Chicago suburb, and dated a guy from the naval academy who was always sending her bouquets from FTD. She wore rosy mohair sweaters and seemed to drift around in a haze of L'Air du Temps and static electricity. (Once I brushed against her when we were lining up for a meeting and got a shock.)

As luck would have it, that night I happened to be sitting across from the one person in the university who'd known me since elementary school. Her name was Ellie Whitmore, and we'd never liked each other. She was a watery-eyed blonde studying chemical engineering, and we'd kept our distance, even after we found out we'd picked the same college, and (by sheer bad luck) the same sorority. It figured I'd get seated near her tonight.

"I don't get it," another girl said, sipping her water.

"Jewish people don't eat ham. Nothing from pigs," Mandy told her.

"They don't even eat *lobster*," another girl piped up.

Everyone thought about this.

I knew this was my chance to speak up. There were a hundred and four girls in the sorority and only two of them besides me were Jewish. The night I pledged, I'd been taken aside by a stunning senior named Dani—one of the other two—who broke that news to me. The other girl, Lane, was a sophomore. "Nobody knows we're Jewish," Dani had whispered, "except some alum who keeps track for the national board. And us."

Sometimes the three of us stood together during Greek swearing-in ceremonies. But usually we fanned out, went our own ways. Tonight, Dani and Lane were seated far away from me, each at different tables. As far as I knew, neither of them kept kosher.

I was the one avoiding meat, though the irony was, that had nothing to do with religion. My mother used to put bacon in those Morning Cookies on Christmas! More to the point, we actually *celebrated* Christmas, even down to singing carols. I just happened to be going through a no-meat phase. College meat looked unappetizing, and I suspected it was full of toxins.

I pushed the peas back and forth on my plate, head lowered.

Ellie fixed her eyes on me. "*Amy* is Jewish," she said, after a long pause.

Everyone turned. These were very polite girls, raised in the best neighborhoods, the best schools. Nobody said anything. They were all afraid of being rude, which in our sorority was considered worse than flunking. And flunking was a big deal. Once a month, we all assembled and they read our grades out loud. Anything less than a B plus and you risked getting "library hours."

"Really?" Mandy said, putting down her fork. She looked at me with interest. Not unkindly. "What's that like?" She seemed genuinely curious. I guessed she'd never made it as far as Skokie.

I don't remember what I said, but I know it was something cowardly. I didn't want to be a native informant. I'd worked too hard to look like everyone else—I blew my hair dry so it was straight and shiny, even if it always smelled slightly burnt. I was wearing what all

the other girls wore: a kilt, a sweater with my monogram on it. I didn't
want them all thinking I was different. I probably mumbled something along the lines of: "Oh, my family is barely even Jewish. We
don't even go to temple or anything." I didn't look at Ellie, but I could
feel her cool, reflective eyes on me. Just for good measure, I took a
delicate bite of ham. It tasted a little salty, but it wasn't bad.

All I wanted then was to be like everybody else. Having just left
home, I wanted to distance myself from my family, to forget about
our photographs and our troubled medical history and our anxieties
and our endless attempts to thwart the future. Part of what I loved
about college was the chance to leave all that behind.

I didn't get it. Not yet, anyway.

Did I think I got to choose? That believing I was one thing or
another made it true? As if, even as I spoke, my genes weren't spelling
out the real story. Deep inside my cells, despite my kilt and mono-
grammed sweater and my flat-ironed hair, Sylvia and Pody and Gail
and my mother were weaving themselves back and forth in me, warp
and woof. Bone of my bone.

My history had its finger on me, whatever it was I thought I
wanted.

WHAT I WANTED THEN WAS not what I'd been given. I wanted a different set of stories. I liked the Christian ones more than Jewish ones,
which were filled with begetting and smiting and names I couldn't
keep straight: Nimrods and Davids and Shems and Noahs. I liked the
Christian story better: one big tragedy with a transcendent ending.
Easter Wings. I wanted to be a poet, and there was such a great tradition of American poets converting to Anglicanism abroad.

When I started graduate school at Oxford, I decided to give the
Church of England a try. Under the thrall of Donne's ornate sermons,
stone cathedrals, and sweet-faced choirboys at evensong, I tried to
prompt myself into a conversion experience. My old life was so un-
decorated, so unlofty. I went faithfully to evensong all that first year,

and in the cramped, cold pews, tested myself for inner stirrings. All winter I held out hope. I felt something, I was sure I did! I'd stare with experimental reverence at the choirboys, their gray eyes lifting as they sang. Was that devotion I was feeling? I tried, driven by my passion for everything British and elite and saturated with tradition, but as the days grew longer my enthusiasm dimmed, and I began to suspect what I'd been feeling was closer to loneliness than religious fervor. By spring I gave it up, keeping only the religious poets as souvenirs. I got religion secondhand through them: Donne and Herbert and Milton, reading their poetry out loud to my students with so much emotion my voice would hang in the linoleum gloom for a minute or two after I finished. No God, only poetry about God. Maybe for me, that was enough.

I was thinking about all of this now because when people found out my mother had metastatic cancer, a lot of them said things about prayer. Sometimes this was direct: "I'll pray for her," someone would say, and you just had to say thank you. Sometimes you couldn't help thinking to yourself, *OK! Now we're getting somewhere, someone's rooting for us.* It was like a fresh band of cheerleaders fanning out across the field even though the score wasn't looking great for the home team.

My mother, I happened to know, didn't believe in God. History, yes. Family. Stories. Sheer good luck. But not God. And so, I guess, not prayers.

I liked it when people prayed for her, since I couldn't do it myself without feeling like a fraud. I was happy for any kind of help these days, whether it had scientific backing or not. Who were we to be choosy? Anyway, I much preferred people who prayed to the ones who talked about friends of theirs who were pulling through and beating this thing because they had such a positive outlook. I know this may sound like sour grapes on my part, because so far my mother was proving to be a nonresponder, but the positive-thinking school of cancer cure really bothered me. Even Annie fell prey to it. Each time

Annie called me now, she kept coming back to the story of her mother's friend and her remission until finally I begged her to stop. It's not that I don't like miracle tales. I've always liked the idea of the exception, light cutting through a dark curtain. My problem is that if you claim positive attitude really makes all the difference, what does that say about people who aren't doing well—and at this point, my mother appeared to be one of them? Doesn't that mean by definition their attitudes are bad?

Of course, the whole argument is circular. It's much easier to have a positive attitude when the treatment works, even for a while, and you seem to be getting the upper hand. When your doctor explains to you—patiently, patiently—that your cancer cell type is very rare and very aggressive and doesn't seem to want to respond to any of the initial kinds of treatment—no to the Megace, no to the Fuck You—none of this necessarily inspires positive thought.

The second week of August, I flew back to Michigan with Sacha and kept my mother company through round two of F-U at Rougemont. My father joined us, and he and I took turns sitting with my mother and taking Sacha for walks down in the lobby.

THE TREATMENT SEEMED TO BE going OK, but my mother looked terrible. Smaller, much more frail. I brought her glass after glass of water, trying not to look at the places where her bones were sticking out like pins. In the evenings my mother napped upstairs in the Hilton and my father and I pushed Sacha in her stroller around the darkening streets and tried to talk about other things. Teaching. Annabel. Charlevoix.

I came back to Boston. The Monday Annabel started working for us, my parents went in to review the latest set of bone scans with Dr. Brenner.

"What did they say?" Julie demanded, in that ragged, out-of-breath voice of postpartum sleeplessness. We were on the phone, comparing notes. I'd been able to get through to my mother before Julie did. But there wasn't any news yet.

"She doesn't want us to keep asking her about it," I told Julie. "She said they'll call when they know something."

My father called back later to tell us what we'd more or less guessed. He set up a conference call so he could talk to all three of us at once. The scans showed the cancer was worse.

I could hear from my father's voice how bad this was. Physically, of course, because she'd had absolutely no response now from either round of F-U. But also psychologically. It was horrible. The worst possible outcome.

"It sucks," Julie said, starting to cry. "If she could just get *one* little bit of good news—"

My father didn't want to stay on the phone long. "We're trying to get a handle on this," he told us. "Trying to figure out the next step."

I WAS THINKING ABOUT THIS during a lull in a moment that might, from the outside, have looked like a photo on the front of a holiday greeting card. It was the first weekend of September, Labor Day weekend, and we were sitting, all twelve of us, on a small sandy beach in Charlevoix, a resort town on Lake Michigan. Surrounded by the detritus of an afternoon at the beach: a large umbrella; bottles of sunscreen, sand sticking to the caps; an upside-down novel with a gum wrapper stuck inside for a bookmark. The cooler, open, filled with the remains of lunch: skeletons of grape twigs; wads of silver foil; lonely sandwich crusts. Soda bottles with pastel droplets at each base.

It had been a haul to get down here from where we were all staying, in a row of just-painted condominiums overlooking Lake Charlevoix. The whole town seemed to have been scrubbed and renovated since we'd been here last. Baskets of impatiens hung from every lamp pole, and boys with wagons of water and specially outfitted hoses came around twice a day to keep them fresh. All the tatty stores we'd loved as children had been replaced with upscale boutiques selling pink and green sandals or coffee tables studded with shells. Everything was freshly repainted, barely recognizable from the dim lakefront town we remembered with its shabby Fudge Shoppe and shuffleboard courts on the green. Now it was all redone, resplendent, and somehow we'd managed to get ourselves here, even Julie and Jon and Maddy, the way we'd planned months back, when the things we thought we'd do still held.

Now, of course, this was more than an ordinary get-together at the lake, and we all knew that. We'd arrived late the previous day and spent the better part of the evening helping my parents unpack the car and set up their condo. After we helped Julie get Maddy in, we unpacked my parents' car: the black-and-white hamper stuffed with before-dinner delicacies; cold bottles of wine sweating from exposure to the late summer air; folding beach chairs; the familiar striped towels we'd brought up here summer after summer as girls. Back when we stayed in a rooming house instead of condos, back when two weeks up here felt like an eternity, each day opening into the bright blue eye of Lake Michigan, the lighthouse throwing off its long pale beam, when my sisters and I lay on the burning sand, scooping up the silvery grains and letting them run through our fingers, dreaming of something vague and imperceptible—some kind of happiness that might, if we squinted hard enough, resemble the place where we were right now.

Getting things inside had been easy enough. Even getting Maddy set up went well. But getting my mother up to the condo had been hard.

She stayed in the car till the last minute, resting. We could see how much the drive had taken out of her—it usually takes four hours from the airport, but yesterday, given that we'd driven in caravan, given Sacha's need for changing and stretching and being released from her car seat, given Julie's need to find a comfortable position to nurse Maddy, given my mother's need to find something cold to drink that didn't make her feel worse, and my father's conviction that stopping for lunch was a good idea, just to give everyone a chance to pull themselves together, it had taken over six hours. By the end my mother was extremely pale, breathing harder than usual, but each time one of us asked if we could help her inside she just said no, she was fine, go on in, she'd just be a minute. A teeth-grit of a smile.

There'd been endless discussion about how to manage this. The pros and cons, for instance, of renting a wheelchair from Rougemont, none of which was shared with my mother until my father had all the details worked out and then she was furious. She was *not* going anywhere in a wheelchair, thank you very much, and if it came to that we could just *cancel* the entire trip. So we backpedaled, of course we didn't need a *wheelchair*! We'd be fine! I was struck by the irony that this was the first trip Jacques and I had taken with Sacha without feeling completely weighed down by equipment—maybe we were beginning to lighten our load. But now, my mother needed things. Her cane. Extra pillows. Painkillers packed in a cooler. Two kinds of folding chairs my father hoped would make sitting on the beach easier.

Charlevoix had always been my mother's favorite place.

At the center of town, the main road formed a drawbridge over the channel between Lake Charlevoix and Lake Michigan—the road giving way to a section of metal, hinged in the middle so it could lift upward and let the boats through. Every half hour the bell rang, tollgates dropping with a series of graduated warning chimes, and the metal bridge lifted open, bit by bit, until it stood implausibly ajar, like a jaw, letting the taller sailboats through the channel and out to Lake Michigan beyond. When we were little, we used to dare one another to run across the bridge after the first warning bell. I can remember my heart in my throat, panting, running across with terror as my sisters cheered me on. For years I had dreams of something going wrong, the bridge opening while we were still on it, grabbing at the edge of one section of road as we lifted skyward, screaming for rescue.

None of this ever happened, but one year—I was eleven, I think, or twelve—Mr. Larson, the man who owned the rooming house where we stayed, had a heart attack, and my father (psychoanalyst, yes, but MD first, and the closest thing to a cardiologist at the rooming house that week) was allowed to ride with him in the ambulance to the hospital. I heard my father explain when he got back that the bridge had been open and they'd been stuck behind the tollgate for almost ten minutes, waiting, with the insufferable chiming of the bells. Mr. Larson survived, but he was never the same. We still came back, summer after summer, and some things were still waiting for us: the rooming house with its old sloping floors, the lake smell, the flocked wallpaper, and Mr. Larson rocking slowly back and forth on the porch, eyes on the lighthouse, as if he needed the rhythm of the rocking chair to remind his heart to beat.

Now, the Larsons were gone—the rooming house sold, turned into condos. We couldn't stop saying how different it all was. Where had the bead shop gone? Remember the place that sold fishing tackle? But of course, the biggest difference was in us. Not girls anymore. We were all in our thirties now, with husbands and children. We'd grown up, and now there was a whole new generation: my nieces; Sacha; and brand-new Maddy, who had endured two flights at barely five weeks to be here.

Some things were still the same—the restaurants we went to, one per night, each layered with memories of having eaten there every other time we came: the all-you-can-eat-shrimp place, where my father insisted we turn down the offers of homemade bread and steaming fries in order to buck the system and eat shrimp, shrimp, and only shrimp; the elegant inn an hour away with its buffet fantasia, white-clothed tables groaning under hand-carved melons, platters of iced tortes, and mayonnaise-y salads; and our sentimental favorite, The Park Side, a small restaurant with sparkly Formica tables and a view of the harbor's bobbing boats.

But so much else had changed. The inn had closed. Mercury

levels had contaminated the trout at the "other" seafood restaurant, The Fish Pier; at The Park Side, the hostess with the blue-rinsed hair had retired, we needed a high chair for Sacha, a place out of the draft for Maddy, and Jenny and Rachel were somber and reticent, shy with my mother, sneaking furtive glances at her eyebrows, thinned to self-conscious question marks of hair above her pink-rimmed eyes. We were all determined to have fun and we *were*, but in a self-conscious, look-how-much-fun-we're-having kind of way, anxious not to fuss over her, and fussing just the same—wasn't she cold under that air-conditioning vent, did she want a sweater, we could just *ask* them to lower the AC a little, was she sure she couldn't try just a little sword-fish, it wasn't local but it was delicious, and so on, each of us locked in an anxious solicitude we couldn't shake.

Then came the day at our old beach.

It took an effort to get all of us there because the "best beach" was near the old rooming house, blocks from the condos, down a precipitous set of steps, the wood rotted, difficult to manage in the best of times and now was definitely not the best of times. Up at the top, staring down at the crescent of sand, I remembered every other time I'd stood up here, looking down: six or seven or eight years old, my feet cold from the damp gritty sand, my bathing suit clinging to me, the pail's plastic handle digging into my palm with the freight of our booty: mounds of pale gray Petoskey stones. Now Jenny and Rachel were inching their way down, and I could see their pale feet clenching and recoiling, their thin shoulder blades pulling back like wings as they hunched and stooped and scrambled, and I was just behind them, Sacha warm and sticky in my arms.

Sara and Geoff had one hamper between them, Julie had Maddy in a Snugli, Jacques had the towels and the beach chairs, and Jon and my father were helping my mother balance, each of them holding one side of her as they inched their way down the stairs, pausing when she needed to catch her breath. We weren't completely sure what was causing this breathlessness, whether it was anemia from the cancer or her ribs constricting her lungs, but even so, she made it down, and there it was: the little oval of beach winnowed away by time and tide, but still there, pungent and glowing. Jacques set up the folding chairs facing the lighthouse, and we took things out of the ungainly black-and-white hamper. Same hamper, same beach. It was almost like we were little again, crouching here and staring out at the lake.

My mother used to tell us if we looked hard enough we could see Chicago on the opposite side, but we could never see anything but lake as far as we looked, the *Beaver Islander* trudging slowly across the horizon with its burden of tourists. Sara was teaching Jenny and Rachel how to find Petoskey stones, with their octagonal crenulations. It took patience. You had to walk slowly, stooping down just at the point where the waves lapped the stones and darkened them, and between the shiny dark greens and the quartzes and the opalescent whites; if you were lucky you'd find one, gazing up at you like a magic eye with its octagons of fossil veins.

Julie laughed, watching them. "Remember how we used to paint the ones we found with clear nail polish so they'd look like the ones they sold in town?"

I remembered. You couldn't see the fossil lines when the stones were dry. The polish, we thought, would preserve the lines forever.

A family scene. Three generations. Blue water, white boats, the sun still hot. Now and then a cool breeze raised gooseflesh on our arms, and you could smell the slightest whiff of autumn in the air.

It was a good day. It had taken enormous effort, but we'd done it. We'd had lunch, kidded around, Jacques and Jon were throwing a football back and forth, in an aren't-we-like-the-Kennedys kind of way, all bluff and boyish humor. And there was a nice sense of being, just for this little while, free from worrying about anything having to do with the body, with being hungry or tired or hurting, with being too hot or too cold or needing to go to the bathroom. . . . Even my mother seemed relatively comfortable, at least for the moment. We were actually all, stupefyingly enough, OK, and then—

Which one of us asked about the F-U? Was it because, woven into one another's lives as we were, we were even in that sunlit moment imagining the next step, the next visit, the effort, the plans, the coming back? We were each of us so tied to what was coming next: school starting for Jenny and Rachel; the semester of teaching about to begin for me; Maddy's first sets of shots. Like anchors, tethering us to the and-then-and-then-and-then of next month, and the month that followed.

In any event, someone asked, "When's the next round of F-U?" Simple question. Could be answered with a date, or a number: two weeks from Tuesday, for example. Or, we're not sure yet, we're waiting to see how the blood counts look.

But that wasn't how it went. My mother, lying back in her folding chaise, her Jackie O glasses on, said—casually, as if she'd just remembered something she'd forgotten to mention, something insignificant, maybe, like a change in plans for where we were eating that night, but it wasn't that, it was something else—"Actually, I'm done with the F-U."

Silence. The loud horn of the *Beaver Islander.*

"What?" I asked cautiously, like I didn't want to break something fragile. It was funny how this happened, how someone said something and for a minute you literally didn't understand. Then you did, and the lack of understanding opened up into something worse.

She was stopping the chemo.

Why? What did she mean?

"Does Dr. Brenner want you to try something less toxic?"

She shook her head. I could see the veins on the side of her neck. She was so thin, it hurt to look at her.

Here's how we were sitting when she told us this: my father to one side, my sisters and I to the other. Jacques, Geoff, and Jon had moved farther down the beach, a pantomime of throwing and catching. We couldn't see the ball. Julie was nursing Maddy, trying to keep her screened with a tent of towel. Sacha was asleep in her backpack, which we had opened up and jammed upright in the sand. Head wobbling to one side, mouth open, a rivulet of drool forming at one corner of her lips. Jenny and Rachel, squatting on thin haunches, were yards away, out of earshot, poking at an emerald fringe of seaweed.

"No," my mother said with a gentle shrug, "no, we're just going to take it as it comes, that's all. No more poison." She was looking out at the horizon, at the *Beaver Islander*, at the place where we couldn't (whatever she said) see Chicago.

"So," Julie said, feeling her way. "You're saying—"

My father put his hand over my mother's. They'd talked all this through, I realized; they were telling us something that had already been decided.

"Girls," my mother said, and in that collective noun I imagined the hundreds of moments, back when we were girls and she was Mom, calling upstairs to tell us dinner was ready or urging us to hurry because we were running late for school. A hundred memories crowded one another: I was lying on the floor of Sara's bedroom, watching her pick snails off the wall of her aquarium, we must have been late for something because my mother was calling us, irate, *Girls!*, or we were in the mudroom kicking our boots off and one sailed across the kitchen, leaving an arc of slush across her perfect floor; she was furious with us (*Girls*), or withholding, or folding herself up in her reading chair with a frown; or she was holding up a thermometer with a puzzled glare, assessing our illnesses—she hated us being sick; or she was braking behind some crazy driver (to her they were all crazy) and her arm flew up instinctively, across the space in the passenger's seat where one of us either was or ought to have been sitting. *Girls*. Only now, of course, we were no longer girls. Sara was here with Jenny and Rachel; I was with Sacha; Julie, with Maddy. Or if we were girls we were girls only to her, and a lump began forming in my throat, as half comprehending what she was trying to tell us, I realized that inside of her there was still our girlhood. When she went, that went. When Sacha woke up and opened her cat-gray eyes and blinked herself back into consciousness and looked around for me, she saw something else, someone in the process of becoming the person she'd one day think of as her mother, but no girl. Never a girl.

The girls were going.

"I don't want to spend the time I have left that way," my mother said, not looking at any of us. My father still had his hand on hers. They were in cahoots—they had planned this.

"It was awful, taking that stuff. Having that poison drip into me." My mother shook her head. "It made me so much sicker . . . and Dr. Brenner says . . ." She took a deep breath. "He says for me, it isn't helping." She lifted her shoulders. They were so thin. A month ago she weighed ninety-two pounds, and my father threw out their scale. "Not much quality of life after all, I'm afraid. Not in my case."

Julie started to sob. Her shoulders heaved, and I could see Maddy trembling against her with the motion. Julie understood before I did: My mother was telling us it was over. She was giving up. I barely heard the rest of what she and my father were saying, the importance of having time left with dignity, with her faculties intact, with some chance of enjoying—this was the phrase they both used, as if they'd scripted it—"the time we have left."

Time left with dignity. Terminal Time. This was like no time I knew. It was time that was finite— *Isn't all time finite, aren't we all mortal*, my mother was saying. Yes. But this was different. This was time cut off from hope. With nothing left to try, not even the fiction this could work.

I wanted to argue her back into sense. There were other things, experimental things. Hadn't Dr. Brenner said that, when I was there with her at the clinic earlier that month? If the F-U didn't work?

Yes, my mother said, patient, using her teaching voice. But if the F-U only got a "limited response," the chance of the next level of drugs working was slim. Dr. Brenner had told her that. And by this point she was so weak from the F-U, or from the cancer, or both, that he was worried she couldn't tolerate anything stronger.

It was just a question of time, she said. "Quality of life" and time. Dr. Brenner had met with my mother and father last week and laid it all out for them. They were all on the same page. They were shifting now to what he called "palliative care."

"What does that mean?" Sara asked.

Palliative care, my mother said quietly, meant they would try to keep the pain to a minimum. Taking care of the symptoms, basically, instead of trying to slow them down.

So, in essence, keeping her comfortable. Waiting for her to die.

I just stared at her.

There was nothing to say. Nowhere to look. In the distance, the *Beaver Islander* blew its horn again: a signal to the drawbridge. *Get ready. We're coming into the harbor.*

My father wanted to help her back up to the car and then to the condo. She was exhausted and needed to rest.

The steps looked different, standing at the bottom, holding her by one arm, staring up. The spaces between them wider. So many times as a kid I'd run up and down these steps, stopping (maybe) to wriggle out a splinter, the damp wood cold under my bare feet. But now, seeing them with her, they looked unwieldy. From behind she looked so sick, her back hunched, shoulders stooped, her sweatshirt billowing around her emaciated frame like a sail. Like a hieroglyph, where once a person had been.

BACK IN BOSTON, I HAD a Charlevoix dream.

We were on our way to The Park Side, all of us. My mother was well, tanned, healthy, way ahead of us, impatient because we were dawdling (*Girls!*) and we were going to lose our reservation. She had her laundry bag slung over one shoulder, kind of like Santa Claus, because she liked to drop it off at the village Laundromat before we ate. Such a multitasker, my mother, even in dreams. She crossed the bridge first, hurrying across as the bells begin to ring, turning back to us, urging us on, *hurry, hurry*, but it began to lift just as she reached the other side.

"Girls," she said, chiding us. We could hear her perfectly, it was like she was right next to us instead of all the way across the bridge, then she was shrugging, smiling, a what-can-I-possibly-do-about-this? expression on her face, and at the same time a don't-worry-it's-fine-we're-all-fine look, too. She was on one side and we were on the other, and the drawbridge kept lifting higher and higher, its metal jaws locking us apart.

Going Back (II)

NOW THAT LABOR DAY WAS behind us, you could feel it. September: cooler in the evenings, the shadows longer, shop fronts crowded with mannequins in sweaters, paper cutouts of leaves at their feet. You could smell fall in the air.

Next week I'd be teaching again.

I'd been preparing for weeks—getting my office organized, Xeroxing things to put on reserve in the library, meeting colleagues. Since we'd come back from Charlevoix, I'd been going to my office most mornings, but we were so close to campus I could still come home for lunch to see Sacha. I didn't feel like running, for some reason— I must've gotten some kind of bug while we were traveling, because my stomach felt funny. But in the afternoons, while Sacha napped and Annabel was still with her, I took walks—usually to Newton Centre, a mile and a half away. I liked walking around the center of town, watching people, going in and out of stores, trying on clothes I thought looked like what I used to wear: skirts with a rumpled, linen feel, loose sweaters, boots with flat heels. Once I stopped in to see Sandi at Centre Realty to see if she'd heard back from the owner of the house Jacques liked. "Yes!" she said, setting her pencil down; she'd actually just heard, if I could believe it—the owner had been away, but had just gotten back from the Cape. And apparently she was more flexible on price than she'd been previously. She'd come into some inheritance money, and that meant there might be "some wiggle room" on the asking price. Would we like to go over and take a look and see what we thought?

"Yes," I told her. "We would."

Sandi said she'd call and set it up, and get back to us.

Later, I walked back to the House with the Green Shag.

It felt funny not having Sacha in my arms or in a stroller—I'd forgotten what I used to do with two free hands. Annabel and I were starting to fall into a routine, but it was all still new to me. At about nine each morning she'd come in, smelling of shampoo, carrying a batik bag bulging with a paperback novel and a huge water bottle. She'd call out enthusiastically to Sacha, put her things down, and right away, they'd start playing.

Annabel was great. "Cautious, yet fun," I told Julie, mocking myself, but in fact, it was true. She lit up the house every time she came. Maybe it was the sheer ruddy joy of being nineteen, having just recently left home, living with her boyfriend, earning her own money—even if it wasn't a king's ransom. Or maybe she was just a joyful person. We all loved her; we soaked up her energy like parched plants absorbing water.

Every day was different: one day a game in a makeshift fort; another day a stroll up to a place Annabel had seen that she thought would be perfect for a picnic. Annabel mapped out every detail—she daubed Sacha with sunblock twenty minutes before departing, to let it "sink in"; she hinted—ever so gently—that there was an organic brand she could pick up from Whole Foods that was gentler than our brand for baby skin; she found an adorable hat Sacha had never tolerated and now accepted without a murmur; she prepared a snack (unsweetened Cheerios; a sippy cup of water with a splash of juice); she brought not one but *two* books to read with Sacha "under a shady tree," as she put it; and she infused the whole outing with such a sense of possibility and fun that I was temporarily mournful when they were gone. I wanted to be under that tree.

Great as she was, I felt a kind of sadness wash over me every morning when Annabel came. Keys in the lock, ebullient voice, that scent of shampoo—it made me ineffably blue, though I couldn't quite say why. Maybe partly it was the acknowledgment that the summer was over, that Annabel's presence signaled the end of my year alone with Sacha. I'd hear them laughing together when I was upstairs, putting final touches on teaching notes, and I'd press my fingers to my temples, straining to hear them, straining not to.

One morning just before I started teaching, after they left for a walk, I stood in the kitchen and looked out the window. A flash of sadness crossed me. I still wasn't feeling great—I'd probably been eating too many protein bars, skipping too many meals, because my stomach was still bothering me. Or maybe it was just the stress of getting ready for teaching. Our yard—I was beginning to think of it as "ours"—was parched and sere. I decided to call my mother to check in, but she was groggy, half asleep, could she call me back later?—and briefly, dizzyingly, I had neither of them, neither baby nor mother, I was neither mother nor daughter.

I hated that my mother slept so much now. Sleep was stealing her from us. We had so little time left with her, why was it so hard for her to stay awake? One of them, it seemed, was always sleeping. Sacha, my mother, my mother, Sacha, the naps blurring into each other, except that Sacha was more alert with every passing day, and my mother less so.

In this and so many other ways, they seemed to be crossing each other, moving in opposite directions. Chiasmus, that's called in literary terms, for the letter *X*. Poems that begin and end with the same word, but cross in the middle. Characters who change position halfway through a novel. My mother slept more, Sacha, less; my mother moved less, and suddenly Sacha was pulling up on things, taking steps along the couch while she hung on. She crawled so fast now it was terrifying. By this point, every second of the day one of us was chasing after her, yanking her back from the edges of things, calling after her to be careful.

LIKE US, MY PARENTS WERE also getting used to having help at home. Just before the trip to Charlevoix, they'd made two decisions. First, they'd asked their contractors to convert their upstairs linen closet into a laundry room. They were starting this week.

"You remember Hank and Jimmy," my mother said slurrily.

This news was greeted, on my end, with silence.

"Tell me more," I said, feeling my way. If she weren't so sick, if she hadn't given up on the F-U, I'd tell her the truth: She should be committed, instantly. What on earth was she thinking about? Even setting aside how absurd it was to have a bunch of guys traipsing in and out of the house with her so sick, what was the *point*? My parents had a perfectly good laundry room.

"Down in the basement," my mother said, as if she could read my mind, "is a long way to go just to throw in a few towels."

Now I remembered: She'd wanted two things for her birthday— to go into remission and to build an upstairs laundry room. Now, only the second looked possible.

I pictured my mother up in the Hilton. The basement, two long flights down. I remembered the stairs in Charlevoix, the way she struggled to hide each wince as she heaved herself up, riser by riser.

My mother had a thing about laundry. She did it daily, compulsively, folding shirts with neat sharp corners, the way Sylvia used to wrap parcels in the hat shop. We used to complain her signature scent was Tide. But these days, was she up to that? I was afraid by the time this new room was finished she wouldn't be able to use it.

"Well," I said uncertainly. "That'll be more—convenient."

She was already filling me in on domestic decision number two: the hiring of nurses.

Her voice slurred a little as she explained to me the distinctions between nursing agency one, staffed by RNs who charged a fortune, and agency two, with LPNs, who were only *half* a fortune. Why did her voice keep slurring? "Are you OK?" I asked sharply.

"I started taking some stronger stuff, Mellie," she said. Her voice sounded like a high school drama student playing a drunk—an impersonation of slurring, rather than slurring itself.

It turned out the "stronger stuff" (liquid morphine) was one of the main features of "palliative care." It was also the reason nurses were needed now, because my father was at work during the day (he'd been back since they returned from Charlevoix) and my mother needed enough morphine that she couldn't be alone. My mother didn't tell me any of this—I found it out later, from my father. Instead, my mother described for me in great detail the nurses' personalities and the ins and outs of their extended family members. Ray, the day nurse, was tidy, organized, but hard to talk to. She "ran a tight ship," my mother reported. Dora, the night nurse, was "mellow," "kindhearted," and a superb knitter, which my mother found impressive, never having mastered this skill herself. Dora could even knit cables. It was a good thing my mother liked Dora, because my mother was up a lot at night, wanting to talk.

"Why—" I tried to puzzle through this. "Why are you up a lot at night?"

"Oh, one thing or another." Slurring. "You know."

I didn't know. But this was yet another thing that fell into that category for me these days.

———

MY FIRST DAY OF TEACHING fell on the second Tuesday in September. Lapis blue sky, leaves brushed with gold, a day brimful with color, like a page out of a medieval Book of Hours.

We'd rehearsed this for weeks, like emergency workers preparing for evacuation. Annabel arrived an hour ahead of schedule so I wouldn't "stress out" (her term). She had a whole artillery of distractions for Sacha, not that Sacha—who adored her—needed distracting: three battered Dr. Seuss books; a vial of bubbles with a little wand; and—somewhat disturbingly—an heirloom Barbie, hair frizzled in simulated dreadlocks, wearing only a beach thong and one stubby high heel. Jacques was already at work and there was no time to discuss the pros and cons of Barbie before I left.

I WATCHED SACHA CRAWL INTO Annabel's open arms with a bitter taste in my mouth. There's nothing generous about love, I decided, as I ran upstairs, pulling off pieces of my stay-at-home-mom clothes—leggings and T-shirt—as I went. Lying on my bed, carefully spread out, were the clothes I'd picked out last night. Without me in them, they looked like a flattened-out version of a person. The new linen skirt from Newton Centre. An oatmeal-colored sweater, loose fitting, lovely. I'd even set shoes in place, low-heeled, sober. Grown-up shoes.

Annabel wore Keds.

Nothing felt right. I had the weird sensation of pulling socks on after a summer at the beach. I looked different when I sneaked a look at myself in the mirror. Lines at the corners of my eyes. A kind of heaviness of expression. When I clattered downstairs, shoes sliding around, Sacha was chewing on Barbie's leg, which bent forward implausibly at one knee. Annabel, serenely oblivious to the unwashed dishes in the sink, was lying on the green shag rug in front of her, plotting out a day of adventures.

I had that bad taste in my mouth again. Wicked stepmother, I mentioned—only in the most casual and offhand way—the dishes, Sacha's laundry. *Just if there was time.* Annabel couldn't have been more cheerful and less promising. Babysitters, like oncologists, are masters of the conditional. *We'll see! It's such a pretty day! So fun to go out!*

I kissed Sacha on the top of her head, with its fading aroma of babyhood. I went over the numbers for big and small emergencies. Rehearsed the what-ifs. Pediatrician. Poison control. Spare cash—just in case. I'd been practicing this for weeks. Why was it any different today, just because I'd actually be teaching while I was gone?

Annabel was shooing me away, smiling, sure of herself, *go, go, we're fine!* and I was out the door, walking to work, halfway to my office before I realized I hadn't told Annabel where we kept the fire extinguishers.

First day. Funny how it never changes, from place to place, time to time—that feeling of butterflies in your stomach, sweaty palms, worrying if you're wearing the right thing, if they'll like you—whoever "they" are. Or you.

It was baffling to be here. The same in some ways, so different in others. I had a plaque with my name on my office door. In my office there was an ugly brown desk with a drawer that locked, two metal file cabinets, a view of the quad. It had been almost eight months since I'd been at Georgetown, but it felt more like eight years. At Georgetown, classes started at ten minutes past the hour, and without even realizing it, I showed up for my first class at ten minutes past. The students had clearly been waiting for me, pencils tapping on desktops, eyes narrowed. I felt like a substitute, and they could tell— eyeing me as if to gauge how long it would be before I snapped.

BECAUSE I WAS NEW, AND because most classes filled based on word of mouth, I had only eleven students in Stuart Literature and Culture: 1603–1649. On my file folders I'd nicknamed it "Slac." I was surprised by how nervous I was facing them, four boys and seven girls.

The girls all looked like Annabel. They seemed barely awake, hair still wet, the room smelled like apricots and lavender, their skin was so fresh it looked like it might burst open, lashes matted with moisture as they stared vacantly out the window, guys with their hands jammed in their pockets, caps on their heads turned backward, breathing softly as if they were still asleep and I was some weird apparition in their dreams. I called their names one by one, the syllables like stones in my mouth. Michaela. Christina. Nicholas. All multisyllabic, sonorous. They didn't look at one another or at me, they sat in a semicircle, drowsy, young. Who knew what they were daydreaming about as I pronounced or mispronounced their names?

To settle myself down, I told them what I knew about the seventeenth century. It was like describing a country I'd visited years ago: Each detail reminded me of another detail, line after line taking shape until I remembered or thought I remembered it vividly. It was strangely comforting, ruminating on the defects of another era—the rotten sanitation, the barroom brawls, the rapiers, the illiteracy rates and sex scandals and political debacles. Our current scandals seemed less abhorrent in light of James I and his paunchy favorite, Buckingham. Against the soothing mantra of some other country's debauched miseries, we seemed so sturdy and oversized, so buffeted by overhead projectors and the cool glow of fluorescent lighting.

They had their copies of *Hamlet* out on their desks, waiting. In this class we would be covering the period from the death of Queen Elizabeth (1603) to the execution of Charles the First (1649). Forty-six years, two reigns, but a whole revolution in politics, science, representation. *Hamlet*, written just after the death of Elizabeth, was the consummate tragedy of mourning. It was also, I told them, a play situated in an anxious political moment. Elizabeth had just died. Who was in charge? What happened when one ruler died, leaving a gap in power?

I asked them to open their copies of *Hamlet*.

We were starting with the first act. With the changing of the guard. One watch giving way to another.

"What do you think of the word *watch* here?" I asked them. "How do you think it's being used in this context?"

They looked at one another, uncertain.

"Well—it means to look at," Michaela suggested. Self-conscious for speaking up first.

I nodded, remembering how much I liked this, asking questions, waiting for answers, and one of the guys, Nicholas, added something about alarms and lookouts, and we went from there.

An alarm, a signal, a lookout. One guard leaving, another coming in; one Hamlet dead, another bound to revenge him.

I asked if they could think of any other meanings for the word *watch*, and when nobody could, I pointed to my wrist. Mine was from Nike, black rubber, twenty-six dollars.

Oh, they said—*that*.

We talked for a while about the word *watch* and I told them that it was just beginning to be used in the early seventeenth century to mean a portable timekeeper you could wear or carry. For a long time, I told them, *clock* and *watch* were used interchangeably. Bit by bit, the word *watch* started to replace the word *clock*. I asked if they could think of any associations with the word *watch* that weren't there with *clocks*, and the atmosphere loosened up a little.

"Well," Christina said slowly. "You look at a watch."

There was some dissent. You looked at a clock, too, a boy named Jason pointed out, but we went back to the OED and the ways in which watch was associated with the visual, and I told them a little bit about timepieces in the seventeenth century and how they were becoming increasingly part of visual culture: things seen, instead of things heard.

Then we talked about Jacobean conceptions of dying.

A memento mori, I explained, was a small material object intended to remind people of the brevity of life. Literal translation, from the Latin: "remember you will die." In Stuart England, there was a whole cult of memento mori—people wore watches shaped like skulls, or had their portraits painted with candles half snuffed out, or with death's-heads in them. Pretty much everything that was animal or vegetable or mineral could be construed as a memento mori. I had a few slides to show them for examples: Dutch still-life paintings of half-eaten fruit; a *vanitas* diptych of a portly woman overshadowed by a leering skeleton.

Maybe this was too much for the first day.

They were quiet again. Michaela unwrapped a piece of gum and put it in her mouth. Jason started doodling in the margin of his notebook. Everyone else was faithfully writing down what I told them: "The fear of death was sometimes sanitized or managed by the production of material objects. Consumerism was a way of staving off the sense that life is transient, fleeting."

Inside my notebook I found last week's receipt from Northwest Airlines and half a shopping list: Pampers, size 5; fat-free peach yogurt; Equal; sesame bagels. My own attempts at staving things off.

The conversation slowed a little. I was almost ready to let them go a few minutes early—it was Day One, right?—when a boy who hadn't said anything yet raised his hand. His name was David. "I don't understand why he's like this," he said. He seemed to mean Hamlet, not Shakespeare. "I read this play in high school and I still don't get it. Did they really believe in ghosts?"

I stopped short. They were all looking at me expectantly. I was the professor; I was supposed to know the answers.

There were lots of ways to answer him. I'd been reading an interesting book that suggested that when the Protestants suppressed the idea of purgatory in England, the belief in ghosts emerged as a way to preserve the sense of the in-between. Ghosts showed up everywhere in the Renaissance. Donne's poems are filled with men coming back from the dead to haunt their lovers. Ghosts paced the stage, crept behind chairs in Dutch paintings.

But did people actually believe in them?

"Some people did," I told David.

Some people, of course, still do, but I didn't say that.

I couldn't pretend to understand *Hamlet* completely. I'd read it many times, and it was always a different play for me—even though it was always December, always midnight, always Denmark, the air frosty, a cock crowing, a bloated, melancholy prince traversing the same lonely landscape, a world of corpulent and corrupt uncles, of madness and sorrow. It was even harder to make sense of it now, sitting in this sunlit room with these wholesome students, each so seemingly sane, so securely anchored to the late-twentieth-century world of antibiotics and vitamins and exercise, a million light-years away from the dim Jacobean world of poison and death's-heads.

"Ghosts," I said slowly, "are in-between things."

I didn't believe in them, of course. Not me, the consummate nonbeliever. Give me something out of the ordinary, and I was all set to doubt it.

On the other hand, this past year there had been these ghosts. Emily, who was there, and then wasn't. And what about Sacha? Every month she changed—stronger, bigger, doing new things—and some older version of her disappeared.

Then there was Jacques and I. We were so different a year ago. It wasn't that I wanted it back, the way we used to be. Lately, especially at night, before sleep, Jacques held me and we talked about my mother and sometimes I cried. But somewhere, who knows where, the ghosts of the people we used to be were trolling some dim horizon.

My mother . . .

My mother was becoming a ghost.

There are more things in heaven and earth, Horatio, than are dreamt of in your philosophy.

I had tears in my eyes.

I blinked them away. Luckily they weren't looking at me anyway, they were riffling through pages in their Norton Critical *Hamlet*s, sneaking furtive glances at the clock hanging over my head, thinking about their next classes, maybe, or about getting something to eat out of the vending machines, and I told them that I thought in this case, the ghost was a sign of all the things the culture wanted to understand, but couldn't. I tried not to think about my mother, tried instead to focus on these eleven students. It was time to get going, we were saying good-bye, I was assigning another act for them to read for next class, and before I knew it, they were floating away like so many bubbles.

The Moon Ring

—⊗⊗⊗—

BY MY NEXT VISIT HOME, I could see things had gone downhill
fast.

It was a hard weekend. I'd left Sacha back in Boston with Jacques,
after endless deliberation, and as soon as the plane took off, I was
sorry. She cried when I left, and I felt worn out: sick of crying, of worrying, of Terminal D, of back-and-forth. Sick of being in-between. I
wasn't feeling great. The plane ride was bumpy, and by the time we
reached Detroit I was tired and queasy.

It was hard to believe my mother had made it to Charlevoix just
a month ago. In just a matter of weeks she had become a full-scale
invalid, moving only very slowly and with intense deliberation from
one to another of three "stations" set up for her in the house that just

a few months back had been filled with real estate agents. *Perfect for a Growing Family.*

Now, either she was in bed upstairs in the Hilton, pillows propped behind her, *New Yorkers* fanned out on the bedside table along with an increasing battalion of sick-person's things—paper cups, drinking water, vials of pills, tissues, ChapStick (her lips were always dry, my father thought it was the morphine)—or she was downstairs in the family room in the big chair with the ottoman, a similar coterie of objects on the table beside her, with (maybe) the addition of the cordless telephone or the biography of Churchill I'd gotten her for her birthday. Or else she was at the kitchen table, sitting in front of the greenhouse window, a yellow melamine plate in front of her, holding (depending on the meal) a sliver of banana bread, untouched; or a few slices of Granny Smith and some whisper-thin slices of Jarlsberg cheese. Dinner was often skipped completely, erased by naps. She had no appetite, which might have been from the morphine, or from the pain, or maybe just from the cancer itself. Who knew?

Once in a while, she wanted a cup of tea. Or a sip of ginger ale, especially if the bubbles had gone flat. But most of the time, she didn't want anything.

When I got to the house late Friday morning, Ray, the day nurse, met me at the door. She was a small woman, mouse-brown hair, a strong aroma of peppermint and Dial soap. "She's upstairs," she told me in a crisp, offhand way. My mother may have told her who I was—"the middle one." Maybe my mother talked about us now, to the nurses. Hard to know.

I'd never opened our front door and had a stranger answer. It was unnerving.

Even more unnerving was the sound of pounding upstairs. The contractors were working on the laundry room. Actually, they were still in demolition phase, smashing apart the walls in the linen closet that was going to become a laundry room one day. The noise got louder as I climbed the stairs. Outside the Hilton, it was deafening. How was my mother able to sleep through this?

I wasn't sure how my father had managed to get the contractors to come with so little notice. Maybe he'd prodded them into action, or maybe it was a windfall for them, a job small enough to fit in between bigger-scale remodels. So far they mostly seemed to be making noise and dust, clattering through the closet in the upstairs hallway with sledgehammers. When I got upstairs I saw they'd taped sheets of plastic to the place where the closet door had been, like one of those dividers you drive through at a car wash, and miraculously, most of the plaster dust seemed to be staying inside. I could see them in the closet, masks on their faces to keep the dust out. They looked, through the cloudy partition of the plastic, like the shadowy figures in Plato's cave—dreamlike, handing each other tools, reaching for things.

The laundry room was the first thing my mother wanted to talk about when I came in.

"Hey, Mellie," she said, patting the side of the bed next to her. "Did you see what they're doing?"

Her voice sounded different. It was the morphine: It made her slur her words, and along with that, the effort not to slur them made her overly careful. It was like she had something in her mouth she was trying to conceal.

Tactful, I tried to pretend everything was normal. Like I was used to being shown in by a nurse, traipsing into the Hilton past carpenters, finding her sitting up in bed, emaciated, a glass of ice chips next to her with a sad straw poking out.

I sat down to look at what she wanted to show me. The laundry room plans.

She had plotted out every detail. She showed me magazine clippings and grid paper drawings. The space was tiny, there was only room for a stacked washer and dryer—in the past, healthy, she had derided these—but I was too careful with her now for anything but affirmation. I praised it all, trying not to notice that in the sketch she'd drawn, morphine-inflected, the lines were ragged. Across from the stacked washer-dryer, there would be a wall-mounted ironing board.

"Very nice," I mumbled. Something in the Hilton smelled funny to me—was it the medicine? The airlessness?—and I felt my stomach lurch.

"They're getting a lot done," she told me, though it was hard to know how anyone could tell that yet. Maybe they gave her progress reports at the end of each day.

The whole conversation felt surreal. Did she really care as much as she seemed to about the choice of cabinets, the color of the laminate on the counters?

How could this be what a life came down to in the end? How, after everything she'd planned—courses, histories, phenomenal excursions, babies, careers, lives—could she be plotting and replotting a room (four feet by six) to hold a supplemental washer and dryer?

While my mother showed me the plans, I sneaked surreptitious looks at her. She looked even thinner and frailer, if that was possible. She was wearing an unfamiliar robe over her pajamas that looked like the kind of thing someone must have sent her as a get-well present—expensive, not her taste. I could tell she'd gone to trouble getting ready for me. She had her wig on, and she'd taken pains with her makeup. Ray must have helped her. She'd drawn eyebrows on with a brown pencil—like scratches of graffiti on a white wall—and she'd put mascara on the two or three pale stalks of eyelash that somehow, miraculously, had survived two rounds of Fuck You. Her cheekbones, always prominent, now stuck out unfathomably far, and her face was all bone and angle, more like a pelvis than a face, really, with only her big owl glasses to provide a familiar sense—oh yes, it was her—like a jut of well-known jaw under a Halloween mask.

Her face looked bigger than usual, because the rest of her was so wasted. It gave a stronger than ever impression that she was all head.

Like poor Yorick.

She wanted, she told me, to hear *everything*. She patted the bed again, signaling that I should inch closer, it was the last vestige of hospitality she could offer, like this was some kind of bizarre pajama party, and I moved forward, uncertain. My stomach felt terrible. She wanted to know about Sacha, what she was doing, did she like Annabel? Was she crawling?

I started. How had my mother, who always remembered every detail, forgotten? Sacha had been crawling since July. My mother *knew* that. She'd seen for herself, in Charlevoix!

"Yes, she's crawling," I said, unnerved. *Between earth and heaven*, I thought, remembering the lines from *Hamlet* I'd been reading on the plane.

If she caught her mistake, she didn't show it: She was moving on.

How were my students? What about my department, what were the other professors like? Who—this was so my mother—was I having lunch with?

"Oh—different people," I told her. I mentioned a few names.

Actually, I liked my colleagues—the ones I'd met so far. I just hadn't been eating lunch with them. Instead, I ate at my desk, facing a gray plaster wall with lighter gray squares on it where somebody else's posters used to be. I underlined passages in *Hamlet*. Some days I called home and asked Annabel if I could talk to Sacha. Annabel was always willing to try and make this happen, but Sacha would thwack unhappily at the phone with her hand and whimper to get away. My voice when I wasn't in the room with her confused her and made her cry. Sometimes I called Jacques and we talked in code. "How is she today? Any better? Did they change the morphine dose?"

One day I called Julie, and she said my father was thinking about canceling out patients for a while so he could spend more time with her during the day. We knew that was a bad sign. He'd wanted to save that until absolutely necessary.

I didn't tell my mother that I went to campus on Tuesdays and

Thursdays and prayed (except being me, I didn't pray, it was more like intense wishing) that I could get through my classes and make it home before I fell apart.

None of my colleagues knew what was happening with my mother, except my chair. I couldn't exactly ask for time off—I'd just started. I'd just had eight months off! I'd already had to ask my chair to see if we could slow down my tenure clock. When I'd taken the job back in February, I'd asked for credit for my two and a half years at Georgetown. Now, I wanted to give the credit back.

I didn't tell my mother any of this.

I'd been rehearsing anecdotes to tell her, bringing stories for her the same way I'd brought photographs, dozens of them sticking together in my book bag, almost all of them identical shots of Sacha, pulling up on things, stepping on the feet of her terrycloth onesies so they stretched out behind her, but before I could show her, she was beckoning again for me to come closer, struggling to get something out of the drawer of the bedside table. Her eyelids lowered, she was suddenly fighting off exhaustion, it seemed to have dropped over her like a parachute, she couldn't fight it, but there was something she wanted to do before she fell asleep for what must have been, even just that day, the dozenth time.

THIS VISIT, SMALL THINGS BOTHERED me. The fact that Ray, who my parents were paying seventy-five dollars an hour, couldn't even make my mother a new cup of tea when she asked for it. I found her microwaving the same wretched cup of brown water when I came downstairs, and I wanted to strangle her.

"How about some *fresh* tea," I said. Who knew how much time my mother had left? She almost never wanted to eat or drink anything, and when she did, why couldn't she have a cup of tea that was drinkable?

Ray put her lips together, looking past me.

It was easy to get mad at Ray, to take things out on her. But in fact, Ray wasn't a bad person. In fact, she was pretty compassionate, in her own way. Later, when I found her down in the kitchen while my mother was napping, she explained that my mother's biggest enemy now was pain. If she took enough morphine to be "comfortable"—Dr. Brenner's new goal—she felt like she was completely out of it. Couldn't read or write. Couldn't stay on the phone for more than a few minutes. The morphine made her unbearably sleepy—she dropped off, just like that—and it turned her mouth to paper and didn't so much get rid of the pain as—this was Ray's version of my mother's description—"put it next to her, somehow." So she tried to tough it out, struggled with Ray over every ounce—no, no, she didn't want that much—it was liquid, a funny shade of gold—but then she hurt so badly she cried and begged for more, only to get hysterical again (Ray's description) when Ray brought it, begging her to pour half the dose down the drain.

It wasn't fair blaming Ray, trying to make things all one way or another. *Good and bad*, my mother used to say, joking about the ways in which people divide life up so neatly—the good nurse, the bad nurse. All one thing or another. But of course it wasn't that simple. When we weren't here, my sisters and I, Ray helped my mother in ways we couldn't fathom. Already, impossible as it was for me to understand, my mother—who could always do everything (except knit)—couldn't do most things for herself. She needed help going to the bathroom. She couldn't get in or out of the bath by herself. It was Ray and Dora who were there now, lifting her, helping her, listening to her stories, and maybe that was why I was so irritated with Ray, not because she kept reheating the same cup of tea my mother sipped but wouldn't drink, but because Ray stayed, permanent, paid, and all I did over and over again was come back here just to leave.

MY MOTHER SLEPT ON AND off all that afternoon. When she woke, sometime after five, the workers were gone, the hallway was quiet. Dora, who I hadn't met yet, was parking her Toyota in the driveway, and Ray was packing up to leave. One watch giving way to another. The changing of the guard.

My mother was calling me. She wanted to talk to me before Dora came. In this tiny space between nurses, this space left for us to be just us, alone.

Mother, daughter.

Nobody else here. No sisters, no baby, no husbands. Not even my father. Just my mother and I: the two of us. Early evening light coming through the shutters. Her wig had tipped to one side while she slept, and if I had been another kind of person, I would've scooped her up in my arms and held her tightly against me and sobbed. Instead, I stood uneasily in the doorway, still feeling sick to my stomach, my eyes swimming, wishing there was something I could do to make any of this better.

"Ame," she said, her voice hoarse. Her voice sounded like it was coming from somewhere else.

Hamlet's ghost.

"I have something for you. Do me a favor—" She shifted, pain flashed across her face. To be alive for her now was to hurt. She gestured in the direction of the bedside table. "Open up that drawer and see if you can find a little box—"

I walked around the bed. The drawer, like all her drawers, always, was painfully neat. On the shelf below the drawer, there was a thick blue volume. An oncology textbook. My father had told us she'd asked him for it sometime this summer. She didn't want the dumbed-down version, she'd told him. She wanted to know what was coming, the official version, not Cancer Lite.

In the drawer, there was a tube of ChapStick. A black velvet box. A paperback—something from the Hemlock Society, whatever that was. This is what she kept next to her now. I took the box out, held it, waited.

"Open it, Mellie."

Inside, there was Sylvia's ring. The gold ring with the moonstone set in a bezel. The stone had a face carved in it. I knew this ring by heart—we'd always called it the "moon ring." My mother had kept it in her jewel box, with several other family heirlooms. Sometimes, when she was getting dressed to go out on a Saturday night, sitting at her dressing table in her bedroom, she'd let Sara, Julie, and me take her jewelry out and lay it out on her bed. She kept the moon ring in a special box, way at the back of her jewelry case. It was always the one I begged to try on.

The ring had a special history. Sylvia had gotten it for her sixteenth birthday. She wore it every day, my mother told me—never took it off. Her godfather had it made for her in Africa. Other rings came and went—her engagement ring, her wedding band. But the moon ring was the one she always wore.

"I want you to have it," my mother said now, and before I could protest, she told me she was giving an important piece of jewelry to each of us. Sara was getting the diamond ring Jerry's father had given his mother when he was born—to celebrate. A boy, after three girls in a row. Julie was getting a ruby: my mother's birthstone. All three rings passed down from one of my mother's parents. Something of hers for each of us to have.

I stared at the ring.

I remembered how I used to beg her to let me hold it. I loved the way the light shone through the gray-mauve stone, the kindliness of the carved face.

Now, I wanted to close the box and hand it back to her. It was hers, and though I knew my mother had always been preemptive, a planner, that she wanted to give her treasures away while she still could—that this was, in some last, implausible way, a chance to see a glimpse of the future, to see her ring on my finger—I didn't want to take it.

Maybe I thought if I didn't, this moment would hang, suspended, that I could stave off what was coming. I wanted to tell her I couldn't accept this, I couldn't do what she was asking me to do. But her eyes were already starting to close. In a minute or two, she'd be asleep again.

I took the ring out of the box and slid it on my finger. The gold was slightly warm.

And it fit. Like all these years, it had been waiting for me.

Safe as Houses

THE BRITISH HAVE A SAYING, "safe as houses." I remember hearing it while I was studying at Oxford, and it stuck in my mind. When Sandi opened the front door to the stucco house we'd been waiting to look at—there was something fiddly about the lock, it took a minute—that saying came back to me, because the overwhelming feeling that washed over me was one of safety.

Maybe it was because the house was made of stone, maybe because it seemed so solid—bigger than any of the other places we'd looked at, with higher ceilings. I'm not sure. I only know that as soon as we opened the door, a feeling of relief flooded through me. We stepped inside a vestibule inlaid with intricate red tiles. Beyond, we could see into a front hall filled with light.

In actual fact, the house needed lots of work. It had been built in 1910, and lived in by only three families, each for a quarter of a century. None of the previous owners had been ready to undertake the house's most pressing projects, and by the time we saw it, it was a mess of bad wiring and desperately needed a new roof; we wouldn't be allowed to open the side door that led out to the porch until we could afford to have the bricks relaid, and there were signs of water damage in the basement. We took all of this in, but none of it mattered.

It might have been partly exhaustion that led us through room after room, wide-eyed, touching the tips of each other's fingers, breathing out to each other little phrases of admiration. "High ceilings." "Another fireplace." This was the house Jacques had asked about a while ago, a square stucco house set just a bit too close to a street just a shade too busy—that's why we even had a chance of being able to afford it. That, and the fact that the owner, a tall ebullient woman with a shock of white hair and penetrating eyes, had recently determined she was done with the suburbs and wanted to move downtown. The owner had seen as many buyers as we'd seen houses. Rejected on all counts. Sandi and the other agent whispered speculatively to each other—the difficult buyers meeting the difficult sellers. Who would have believed it? And who would have believed that we'd like each other right away, all the difficulty on both sides evaporating?

We loved the house. We loved the old bell system that let people buzz different rooms from the kitchen. We loved the old stone porch, the wide staircase. The house was closer to the university than I might have liked, and Jacques, list in hand, was stricken by how much work it needed, but there was a tacit understanding between us that these things were tolerable, that what mattered were other things—how solid the floors felt. How the back door opened into a garden that was level, if overgrown. At the top of the stairs and to the left was the room that settled it for me. It had belonged to the owner's daughter before she went to college; she'd scratched her name in one of the many windows that lined the room on two sides, overlooking the bramble-filled garden. I knew right away this would be Sacha's room. We were done looking, this would be home.

It worked, the way things sometimes do after lots of effort spent elsewhere, with surprising ease. The negotiations were amiable, the owner fair, the lawyers polite, the closing date speeded up, and because the house was less than half a mile from the House with the Green Shag, the owner let me come with my blueprint paper and my measuring tape and my video camera, and I took notes on dimensions and hired painters in advance and took videos for my mother, room by room. Sometimes my hand shakes when I take pictures, and that day it shook even more than usual. I still seemed to have whatever stomach bug had been bothering me off and on for the past few weeks—I was probably fighting off the flu—so I knew the movies were coming out a little fuzzy, but at least she'd get the main idea.

My mother had had a better week—Julie had been out visiting with Maddy, and she'd sounded brighter, almost good. I thought of days like this as Optical Illusion days. If I squinted one way, I saw a lady with a hat instead of two vases. Seeing it like that, I thought, she could rally. Listen to her! Maybe we could get her out here somehow for Sacha's first birthday. Maybe we could bring her here to see the house, the big squares of sunlight moving in patterns on the old tile floor, the beautiful weedy garden, the bushes with their tawny, unplucked crop of hydrangeas. Then there was something—a coughing fit, a pause—and the lady with the hat was gone and all I could see was two vases and I couldn't believe I could have seen it any other way. She was sick, unbelievably sick, she could barely make it down to the *kitchen* anymore let alone navigate an airplane trip to Boston.

The owner accepted our offer in early October, and we signed the purchase and sales agreement. We hired electricians, going back and forth between the House with the Green Shag to what we now called Our House. I still wasn't feeling well, and finally, squeezed in between everything else, I went to see Dr. Pierce, who prodded my stomach, listened to my lungs with a stethoscope, and drew some blood.

"Periods regular yet?" she asked after I told her I'd stopped nursing in July, and even before the words were out of her mouth, I realized what was wrong. Why I'd been feeling so crummy.

Of course.

I was pregnant again.

It all made sense. Fell into place instantly—how could I not have realized it earlier?

"I think I know what's going on," I said shakily, not sure whether to laugh or cry, immediately starting to count backward. August? July? She leaned over to pat me on the shoulder before going out to ask one of the technicians to bring me a pregnancy test. But I was sure of the results even before I took it. I was trembling slightly all over, trying to add and subtract months in my head.

When?—

Two emotions flooded through me as I asked her if I could use her phone to call Jacques. One was utter joy. A second baby. Unasked for, but so deeply wanted—a gift of life in the midst of the deepening sense around us of death and dying.

The second feeling, wrapped around the first, was sorrow. This baby would be born, and my mother would never know her (or him).

I pushed the sorrow down.

Maybe she could make it. Six more months. Half a year. It was possible—

It depended when the baby was coming.

When. That had always been the first question in our family.

"But," Jacques said, when he came home early that night to celebrate, "there's another way to look at it, too."

I had tears streaming down my face. He was the only one who knew. Tomorrow, I'd call Julie and Sara. Annie. When I worked up my courage, I'd call my parents. Maybe my father, first. And then my mother.

I looked at Jacques, waiting.

"You feel like you're trading," he said in a low voice, picking up my hand. "I know you. You think, because you wanted another baby so much and now this is happening, that somehow you've made some kind of deal with the fates." He shook his head. "It isn't like that, OK?"

I kept crying. Hormones, along with everything else.

"It doesn't work like that," he said.

For an ultrarationalist, Jacques had a strangely mystical way of looking at this. He thought the new baby would somehow be connected to my mother. A reminder of renewal, of new life beginning.

To my surprise, Julie said more or less the same thing when I called her the next day. She blew her nose for a while, cleared her throat. Then said, "It's a good thing, Mellie. Really."

I still didn't want to tell my parents. I kept putting it off. One more day. I found an obstetrical practice—a friendly group out in Wellesley, half midwives, half doctors—and one of the doctors gave me an exam, and told me my due date. March 15.

AS LONG AS I COULD remember, my mother was the one I told whenever something good happened. In college, I used to call her to tell her when I did well on a test or paper. "Remember that history final I thought I messed up? Well, it turns out I did really well—" And she'd be there, riveted, glad for me. "You're kidding! An A? Can you read me his comments?"

Did I call her when things went wrong? I don't remember. I don't think so—not usually. But she called me every day anyway, so if no good news was forthcoming, she'd probe. "What is it? You don't sound right." Or she'd remember to ask. "Did that guy ever call? What happened with that interview you were supposed to have?"

Now, I had this wonderful news, and I couldn't bear the idea of telling her.

I went up into the study and closed the door behind me so I could focus. Dialed, heard that familiar ring. Ray answered, saying (sounding aggravated) that she'd have to go upstairs to see if my mother could talk. I thought I could hear the workmen hammering in the background.

Finally, my mother picked up.

She sounded extremely slurry. Either more morphine today, or she'd just taken it.

I got right to the point. "Mellie," I said. "I have news."

"Hang—on—" she said. I could hear her breathing. Struggling with the pillows. More breathing. "OK," she said at last. More a whisper than a voice. "Go on."

I closed my eyes, tilted back in the office chair, trying to slow myself down. "I have—" My voice broke up, like on a radio station you can't pinpoint. "There's something—"

Her voice sharpened. Mother's intuition. "Are you OK?" she asked, suddenly focused. "Is everything all right? How's Sacha?"

"I'm fine, she's fine," I mumbled, starting to cry. Hormones. I was a mess. "Mom." I almost never called her that anymore. I went right in—no lead-up. "I'm pregnant. We're having another baby."

There was dead silence on the other end. Then—it cut between us like a knife—she said it. The word that has always been our mantra.

"*When?*"

"March 15," I said. The Ides, they used to call it. Caesar gets warned about it in Shakespeare's play. For the Romans, it was a festival day. They considered it auspicious—a day of good luck, of fortune.

We hung there on the phone together and neither of us spoke, and for some period of time—a minute, a few minutes, I have no idea—we both cried.

Ashkenazi Jews customarily name their babies after relatives who have recently died. My parents had their own version of this: They kept the first letter. Sara was named for Sylvia. I was named for Alexander, my father's grandfather. Julie lucked out: Nobody died, and they picked her name just because they liked it.

This new baby would be named for my mother, Elaine. We both knew that. An *E*.

"Are you thinking about names?" she asked slowly.

"A little," I said. I took a deep breath. "I wonder . . . which names *you* like." I didn't want to say anything before she did about the letter *E*. I didn't want to admit out loud to her what that meant. That by March—

Of course, her planning gene kicked in, trumping everything. "If it's a boy," she said, tentatively, thinking out loud, "I like Edward. Do you?"

I took a deep breath. So we were admitting this, then. We were actually admitting—

Like my mother, I tried to stick with the name, tried to put aside what it meant. *Edward. Eddy, Ed, Ted*. I couldn't picture a boy.

"If it's a girl . . . ," I began, coaxingly.

She was silent, pondering.

"If it's a girl . . . ," she murmured.

If it's a girl, I thought, *I'll love her with all my heart, whoever she is.* Maybe there was something to what Jacques said, mystical or not, because sad as it was to tell my mother about the baby, I was also glad she knew. Glad that as long as I lived, as long as this new baby lived, I would look at him or her and know: My mother knew about this. Just by talking about the baby together, it felt to me like my mother was giving it her blessing.

"You don't have any girls' names?" she asked, mulling this over.

I mentioned two, testing for her reaction: *Eleanor. Eloise.*

But there was no chance to get her feedback. It sounded like someone had come into the room. I heard something scrape; a low sound, either a cough or a muffled groan. "Ame, Ray's here, she has to help me with something. I need to take some medicine," my mother said. "I'll have to call you back. . . ."

Another shift of position, some mumbling.

"Is that OK?"

"Of course," I said. I set the phone down, looked around the study, and lay my head down on the desk, listening to the faint blood-beat pulsing in my ear.

"Elisabeth," I whispered. The name I loved most, but hadn't dared to say.

IT WAS LATE OCTOBER, AND Sacha was almost eleven months old. I was busy with teaching and meetings and we were closing on our house in just a few weeks, and I was at the end of my fourth month now, starting to show, and all of it felt real and affected me in important ways, but through it all, there was only one thing that really mattered, and that was how sick my mother was. People kept asking me how I was doing—the few of my colleagues who had found out. Annabel. I kept smiling and saying fine, I'm fine, but I felt like a sleepwalker. I got up earlier each morning—we'd set the closing for mid-November and the move for the end of the month, so we didn't have much time left in the House with the Green Shag Carpet. This alone seemed to wake me, this sense of time running out. We were packing again. Rolls of tape, string, stacks of cardboard boxes leaned up against things. Bacchus hunched in the corner, chewed up rolls of tape in his mouth; the afternoons were brimful with golden light, the trees a color I'd forgotten could exist in nature. Eighteen-carat gold, rimmed with lapis.

Awake, Sacha watched everything. She dangled from the swing we hung from the doorway, eyes steady. She pulled herself up in the playpen in the living room, her eyes sober, fixed on ours. As she watched, her mouth opened and closed, mimicking ours. She was trying, I told Jacques, to speak.

It was words that separated her from us, words Jacques and I volleyed back and forth while Sacha, eyes big, fastened on us soberly at dinnertime, mouth shaping a little as her gaze flew back and forth. As October drew to a close, her syllables and sounds began to round

into recognizable forms, almost words—*ta-ta-ta-TA!; da-da-da-DA!*—
and I'd take out her alphabet book of laminated family photos and
we'd pore over them endlessly: all of the aunts first, then Bomma and
Boppa, my mother blooming with improbable health from some
earlier incarnation, beaming mischievously at us from under a curling
red sticky *B*. Some nights we never made it to Cousins or Dogs, so
content were we to linger over our *B*s. We lay on the floor of the room
that had been Sacha's since we moved here and I flipped through the
pages and practiced saying out loud for her the names of the people I
loved most.

"Bomma," I said. "Look! Here's Bomma!"

She could learn words early. It could happen, couldn't it?

Physically Sacha was still small for her age, and in terms of motor
skills, a month or two behind most almost-one-year-olds: She had no
interest in walking yet on her own, she pulled herself up on things
only to sink down again with a sibilant grin, crawled instead of walked,
and at the playground in Brookline where we went on weekends,
other parents guessed she was eight or nine months. Not almost a
year. It was all normal, my pediatrician reassured me. Some babies
walk at nine months; some wait till they're a year and a half old.

Still. I wanted—*needed*—for her to be ahead of herself. She was
going to be an older sister in March. She needed to grow quickly!
Besides, if she did things ahead of schedule—if she talked early—my
mother would know, and it would count. It would be real.

My mother was the historian. She was the one who remembered
things, who made sense of things—the keeper of records, maker of
plans.

I didn't particularly care when Sacha walked, but when it came
to words . . . I wanted her to learn to say "Bomma." I desperately
wanted my mother to hear her say her name.

We were all flying out to Michigan for Thanksgiving. Maybe
Sacha could say her name by then.

I understood at almost every level that what I wanted was impossible. Sacha wasn't old enough yet to speak. "What Your Baby May Even Be Able to Do This Month" didn't suggest this would happen until close to a year. If then.

But I could still try.

I tested Sacha, surreptitiously. When Jacques was downstairs, I sneaked out her book of alphabet photos and quizzed her in the bath. "Who's this?" I asked, all smiles, pointing to my sister. Sacha, solemn as usual, pronounced something unintelligible. *Ba-ba-ba-ba.* When I turned the page, she squinted a bit at my mother's picture, bubbles forming on her lips.

"*Bom-ma*," I said, unrelenting, "that's who this is, darling," and I guided my finger deliberately to my mother's face.

She grabbed wetly at the book, not at the page with my mother's photo, but at the next one, where my father—in happier times, relaxing—was beaming out at us from his position, seated near a desk full of books and papers. His was the image she seemed to reach for, as if a more solid planet had slipped between my mother and herself, rendering my mother's face shadowy, imprecise.

Finally, I put the alphabet photos away.

Some nights I stripped off my clothes and climbed into the bath with her and the upcoming move and the new house and work and everything else seemed to slip away, like so many shells pulled back by a warm engulfing tide, and she wriggled on top of me like a fish—slippery, perfect, her skin glossy with soap, her hair sticking up in little tufts.

Deep inside of me, the new baby circled and dove.

Through the skylight over us I could see the bright, hard eye of the moon. The nights were drawing in earlier, cold as stone, but in our borrowed bath Sacha and I slipped and glided, wordless, fearless, as if winter would never come.

Words for Things (II)

IN *THE CONFESSIONS,* AUGUSTINE WRITES that memory is like a house. You move from one room to another, and each memory fills a space, informing it, ineluctably giving it shape. "The huge repository of the memory," he writes, "with its secret and unimaginable caverns, welcomes and keeps all these things, to be recalled and brought out for use when needed; and as all of them have their particular ways into it, so all are put back again in their proper places." The way Augustine describes it, memory is like a vast storehouse. I imagined crawling back through dim corridors that opened into room after room: pantries, with their bright boxes, canisters of grains. Bags of papery onions. Herbs rustling in the eaves: rosemary, anise. Wheels of bright cheeses; the soft, fermenting aroma of apple and chicory. The secret and unimaginable caverns of what we keep.

OCTOBER. IN NEW ENGLAND, A month of change. From *octo*, "eight," for eighth month. In the Middle Ages people thought that on Saint Francis Day, swallows flew to the bottoms of ponds to hibernate through the winter. Walking back and forth from the university to our new house and back to the green shag again as the month drew to a close, I thought about hibernation. Bears knitting themselves a skein of warmth deep within a cave. The frowsy scent of shared breathing. Being pregnant this time felt to me like that: burrowing inward. Keeping this new life warm.

The last weekend of the month, we turned the clocks back. We went from room to carpeted room, Jacques and I, looking for clocks to change, propelling the hands with our fingers, resetting dials, tapping new numbers into the microwave, the travel alarms.

"I love this," I heard Jacques say to himself, operating on the shower radio. "We could really use this extra hour."

I imagined where that hour would go, in Augustine's storeroom. A small, low-ceilinged room of extra hours, the color of slumber.

NOVEMBER 15, WE CLOSED ON the house—a small, cramped office downtown, thick piles of forms that needed signing, Sandi and the other agent shaking hands, the lawyers shaking hands, the former owner shaking hands with Jacques, with me, with Jacques again, and now we had four tarnished keys, an unfathomable amount of debt, and the house was ours.

We weren't officially moving until just after Thanksgiving. For now we were trying to get things ready at the new house, setting up appointments with contractors and electricians, choosing paint colors. What this meant, of course, was that we were perpetually in between, running back and forth, thinking that while we were heading over we should just take a few boxes of books, a plant, a radio, some flashlights—the former owner, it turned out, hated overhead lighting, and had taken her lamps away with her.

Without any furniture in it, the house looked different. There were lighter rectangles on the sallow walls where paintings used to hang. Bits of wire, the odd picture hook, wires erupting in odd places from the floor, cracks in the plaster. The walls of the room that would be Sacha's were being sanded, and there were piles of plaster on the floor; an old sticker from the aquarium, half picked off, stuck like a tattoo to a windowpane. When I came with Jacques, we were in planning mode. Usually someone came with us, one of the painters or our electrician, and we talked about fixing things, installing recessed lights, sanding and polishing the floors, but when I came by myself I didn't plan much at all. The house was on my way home from work, and often I just stopped in now, getting used to the feel of opening the door with my key, listening to the noises the house made, its stirrings and creaking.

A few days after the closing, I came alone. I was meeting the painters, who had finished the walls in Sacha's room—robin's egg blue—and wanted to get started on the dining room. I had a fan of paint colors with me. They were painting everything white, but the dining room had complicated woodwork, and we were supposed to have made six or seven different choices I could barely remember now. Which white went where. Which finish. I had a list of shades for the painters to try: Atrium White. White Dove. Navajo White. It was almost four o'clock, the house was already getting dim, the painters were late, and I remembered Jacques had told me the phone service might have been turned on that afternoon.

I tried out the cordless phone Jacques had gotten from Radio Shack. I was standing at the kitchen counter, looking outside, and I saw it was beginning to snow, one of those bizarre squalls that come out of nowhere sometimes in New England in the late fall, millions of tiny flakes of white that whorl around, not sticking, like the inside of a snow globe, and in the dwindling light everything was white and gray. Shades of white. The first snow, early. I dialed my mother, and—amazingly, this almost never happened anymore—she picked up right away.

This was the first time I'd been able to call her from our new house. No owner there anymore but me. I caught her awake and unusually lucid—lately the morphine had been making her groggy and looped out, but this afternoon, she sounded almost like her old self.

Four o'clock, the end of a teaching day, and I was calling her, and she was there, answering. Just like always.

"Hey," I said, walking into the dining room. "You're not going to believe where I am."

I heard rustling, a bit of heavier breathing. "Wait a minute," she said. "I'm getting into position here."

I closed my eyes, picturing her in the Hilton. Her stuff around her. Her owl-eye glasses, the ubiquitous pack of Dentyne. The most recent *New Yorker*. The oncology textbook on the nightstand next to her. "Want me to tell you what it says may come next?" she asked me one night, her voice bitter. Not like her. No, I had said. I didn't want to hear.

I knew some of what was coming. I looked it up myself. But other things could still come next, I reminded myself. She'd told us when we were together in Charlevoix that as long as she could still get pleasure out of reading and taking baths, it was worth hanging on. Those things she still looked forward to.

"And talking to you guys," she'd added.

Lately, Julie told me, she'd admitted baths had become torture. The nurses had to help her in and out, stay with her the whole time. And her body . . . "I can't look at myself," she said. "It's horrible. I'm nothing but bones."

But she still had reading. That, she told Julie, would be the last to go. Like the Cheshire Cat's smile. This week, there was a story in the *New Yorker* she was reading. It was good, she reported, but not the author's best.

Words, words, words.

"I want to know everything," she told me now. "Blow by blow. Room by room." I could hear her breathing hard. It cost her now even to speak.

I tried my best. I made it through the first floor with what I thought was the right mix of jocularity and satire. I described the brown walls in the dining room (soon to become some shade of white). I mocked the linoleum floor in the so-called powder room. I described the burnt orange sixty-year-old wool carpet in the former owner's study. Kelly green wallpaper in the kitchen. I kept it light, I was on to the patois of the real estate world, I had the buzzwords, the descriptions, and then I moved upstairs, the cordless still cradled under one ear, but when I reached the guest room I stopped short.

"In here—" I said. My voice broke.

There was nothing in here. It was four walls, dingy white, but as I looked around, I imagined how we would change it: We would paint the walls ivory, put up plantation shutters, cover the bed with white cotton sheets, refinish the heart pine floors, hang photos on the wall. The guest room. As I looked into the soft-hued future I was imagining, it was only a room at best, a room that would hold guests and none of them her.

"What," Lucas Hammill had goaded me, back in sixth grade, "would make you pray? If you were being burned alive? What would it take?"

This, I thought now, holding the door jamb with one hand and holding the receiver away with the other. The words formed inside me almost on their own. Half prayer, half wish. *Let her make it here. Let her make it. Let her see the new baby (Elisabeth; Eloise). Let her live.*

I started crying and couldn't stop. I knew she would never set foot in this house. The house, through no fault of its own, was a storehouse not for the past but for the future, for the life we were trying to build for ourselves and the family we were making. And it wasn't the house or the room that mattered but everything else she wanted so badly to witness and wouldn't: Sacha's first words. Maddy sitting up. Our new baby. Just when we needed her most (as if we hadn't always needed her most, through every minute of the lives we'd lived right up to that moment), we were losing her.

I wanted desperately for her to hang on. But to hold on to her—to want her to keep going—was to condemn her to suffering.

I didn't say any of this. Instead I sobbed, holding the phone away from me so she couldn't hear, but of course she heard and she started sobbing, too, and she was saying, "I want to know what it's like, tell me, I want to picture it, even if I can't be there too—" and in the middle of this the doorbell rang and it was the painters and she and I, both still crying, had to muddle through an ordinary good-bye in the middle of the larger good-bye that housed us.

A FEW DAYS AFTER THANKSGIVING Sacha stood alone for the first time.

As usual, I was on the phone with my mother. Thanksgiving had wiped her out—it had been too much for her, we admitted now, all of us going in at once. She was paying for it now. Most of the time when I called she was asleep now, and some days I had to call back four or five times to get her when she was awake. But then there'd be an afternoon like today (funny, how it was always three or four o'clock, the good times) when there'd be a minute or two of pure lucidity.

Jacques was playing with Sacha on the green shag, building blocks, and she pulled up on him and let go and didn't fall. Eleven months and three weeks. The look on her face of amazement was partly comical, partly moving—this sense of her own autonomy, her capacity to do this miraculous thing without our help. And then, a few days later—as if language really is nourished by autonomy, or created by it—Sacha said her first recognizable word.

That word—my legate, my skeptic—was *no*. Only she said it, inimically, ponderingly—backward. "Ohnnnn." Shaking her head, as if there could be any question what she meant, whether it was prompted by the proffered organic squash or the toy that just the week before she had reached for. "Ohn." At bath time. At bedtime. Firm, unequivocal, and I thought I knew what she meant, as I traced my path back and forth from the House with the Green Shag to my office to my class-room to the new house and back home again, going to the ob-gyn, calling my mother, learning she was asleep and couldn't talk, or in pain and couldn't talk, or in the bath and couldn't talk, or talking with her and realizing she wasn't herself anymore, or that we weren't really talk-ing, that somehow Sacha was learning, growing, pulling up, standing, shaping words, and my mother was slipping away. That this could be happening was unbearable, untenable, I thought of that famous line from *King Lear*, the line of pure negation: "*Never never never never never*," and all I could do was hold Sacha and brush my cheek against hers and agree that this could not and should not be. Ohn.

Then—I had only words to play with—I turned Sacha's word around and around like a Petoskey stone in a tumbler, polishing it, lacquering it. Ohn of my ohn. She was my own, my only, this gray-eyed child. My mother-in-law worried I'd let all my sadness seep into her, that she would carry the weight of this first year inside her and be changed by it.

I couldn't say this wasn't (maybe) true.

There had been hard days. There had been ghosts. I remembered it all: the sad smudge of Emily's tiny heel. My mother playing the Comparison Game. A River Runs Through It. Charlevoix. The Green Shag. We'd said good-bye to parts of ourselves and other parts had taken their place. I remembered Sacha's small arms stretching down like a diver's for Bomma in Rougemont Hospital, and I thought—no. (*Ohn.*) If sadness had seeped in, and I was sure it had, hadn't love also seeped in, hadn't she also learned what it means to feel?

Did I wish Sacha's first word had been something else, or that it had been forward instead of backward?

No. I didn't. She was so adept by now at turning things over, herself included, this girl of ours. Our hourglass.

I liked her word *ohn*. It was like she had faced the vertiginous dome of the universe and met it with the only possible word that could match it. Isn't that all any of us can do—face what we face, accept the fact that time is finite, that we get only so much—it's never enough, but still—and just keep trying? Isn't this what my mother would teach her if she could, what history will keep teaching her, to say, facing what we face (each in our own particular way, with our own inflection, backward or forward)—"no"?

What We Know (Now)

EARLY IN DECEMBER, JACQUES AND I met with my new doctor, Dr. Muto, at the Farber. We were there just to talk, not for any kind of exam.

It was an unusual meeting. Here I was, six months pregnant, Jacques with me, holding my hand, and I was asking Dr. Muto to take my ovaries out right after the baby was born.

"Not *right* after, of course," Dr. Muto said, looking at me with concern.

"As soon as it makes sense," I countered. I reminded him I'd be thirty-four in May. We could wait until summer, even late summer. But I wanted to have the surgery before I started teaching again. While I was still thirty-four.

"Remember," he said, "thirty-five is just a target. There's nothing magical about that number."

He brought some charts out to explain to us how doctors had arrived at thirty-five as a recommended age for my sisters and me to have surgery. "It's not an exact science," he said. He explained that since genetic cancers often occur younger with each successive generation, doctors liked to subtract ten years from the age of the closest affected relative when she got sick. Sylvia had been forty-three; Pody, forty-five, Gail, forty-seven. After considering the average age of onset in our family (Sylvia, Pody, Gail), they'd decided thirty-five was a safe target for our family.

"But remember," Dr. Muto said, "thirty-five has always been just a target. Suppose you waited until thirty-seven, for instance." He drew a graph for us. "Your lifetime risk may be high—forty, fifty percent. But for each individual year, that risk remains relatively low. Let's say, one or two percent for each year between thirty-five and forty. Then it might go up a bit after forty." He looked at me, as if he were worried that I couldn't quite picture this. "For every hundred women in your exact situation who did *not* have the surgery this year, that means only one or two of them would get cancer. The rest wouldn't."

Jacques, who does this kind of analysis all the time at work, found this fascinating. He loves graphs, models, statistics. But I couldn't focus on the numbers. I'm a story person. I was still turning over what Dr. Muto had said about subtracting ten years from Sylvia's age when she'd gotten sick. Forty-three. I was already thirty-three-and-a-half. That meant I was past the deadline, if you were a stickler. I didn't find the idea of 1 percent or 2 percent at all reassuring. One or two women! That could be Julie and me. (Sara, long past surgery, was already on the safe side.)

"Now, your mother—" Dr. Muto began.

Jacques put his hand on my leg. I couldn't go there right now, and Jacques knew it.

This was a week where I hadn't been able to get through to her. Not even once.

"That's a different situation, of course," Dr. Muto said. His eye was on the pad of paper—he couldn't see my face. Then he looked up at me. "Breast cancer," he said, shaking his head sadly. "One out of eight women is the latest statistic." He reminded me that while there was some suggestion that having your ovaries removed reduced the overall chance of breast cancer, it didn't (of course) remove the risk.

And now that we were talking about remaining risk, Dr. Muto said he owed it to me to point out that high-risk ovarian patients continued to be at risk for extra-ovarian cancer. Even after surgery ovarian cancer can still develop in the peritoneum, the lining of the abdomen. There is something called EOPPC—extra-ovarian primary peritoneal cancer—that women can still get, even with their ovaries gone. Dr. Muto himself (sadly) had a patient who'd gotten that, several years after having her ovaries removed. And she had died.

I cleared my throat. I understood nobody was promising me anything rosy. "But the chances go way down, right?" I asked. I was worried we were losing focus. I wanted this meeting to strengthen Jacques's support for the surgery, not to give him the sense it would only be partly effective.

Dr. Muto nodded. "Dramatically reduced." Removing my ovaries would bring my chance of ovarian cancer way down. Still there, yes—but close to nothing.

That was all I needed to hear. I didn't expect guarantees. I couldn't do anything about falling meteors. But I had a responsibility—to Jacques, to Sacha, to the new baby, to my whole family, to myself—to take care of what I could. Bringing my risk down to almost nothing—that seemed like a miracle to me. If I had to remove a limb to get there, I'd have gladly done it. A two-hour surgery, removing two tiny organs I was done with?

The baby kicked.

OK. *Almost* done with, I amended.

This, as far as I was concerned, wasn't a hard choice to make. It was what Jacques calls a "no brainer."

"I'm ready," I said, pushing the graph back to him. "Or at least I will be, as soon as the baby comes."

"Let's talk in the spring," Dr. Muto said, shaking hands all around. He cleared his throat, looking at me. "Late spring, early summer," he revised. "Meanwhile, try to take care," he added gently.

I read a million things into that. There was so little, it seemed, that I could really take care of. I couldn't take care of my mother. I couldn't fix what was happening to her, what my father was going through. I couldn't stop myself from grieving. I couldn't protect Sacha from how sad I was, however hard I tried.

But I could plan the surgery. On the way out, I stopped and made a follow-up appointment for April.

WHEN WE WALKED OUT OF the Farber, it was snowing heavily— snow was already accumulating on the sidewalks. Big, soft flakes. We didn't know it yet, but this was the first of sixteen or seventeen serious storms between now and spring.

That's what I remember most when I think about that winter. Snow. Endless, constant snow, as if the whole world were trying to erase itself. A white blur, an absence.

We didn't celebrate Christmas that year. No tree, no gifts. In the last days of December, the year running out like so many grains of sand, my mother died. Upstairs in the Hilton, my father at her side. Sara, Julie, and I had just been there to visit, and we were all planning to come back again after New Year's, but this time it wasn't up to us to make the plans.

IT SNOWED CONSTANTLY ALL THAT winter. Twenty-two inches one storm. Eighteen, another. Snow covered bushes and cars, sat on sills, lay heaped in mountains at the curbs where the plows left it. Turned gray, then black; froze; seemed part of an eternal frozen landscape. Sidewalks were impassable. In the afternoons I cut swaths through the snow with a shovel, panting, and as I shoveled, more fell.

I missed her all the time. Sometimes, trying to move the wet, heavy snow, I cried so hard I thought I'd make myself sick. There's an emptiness words can't describe and that for me was the emptiness of three and four o'clock every afternoon, when I would look at the phone, and then away. When I would imagine her voice reaching for me. For all of us.

Mellie . . .

Sometimes, napping—being pregnant made me so tired this time—I would wake to my alarm and think it was the phone, and for a minute or two, before I was fully awake, I'd swear I could hear her voice. Bright, sparkly, lucid, the way it used to sound, before the morphine and the pain and the constant sleeping. Like she had something exciting or funny or maddening to say, and she couldn't wait to tell me.

The things I wanted to tell her piled up, like the snow.

BY LATE JANUARY, I WAS hugely pregnant again—dazed, exhausted, heartsick, trying to take care of Sacha, Jacques, myself. Instead of teaching second semester, I did administrative work for the department through February, then took time off. It wasn't great timing— I'd only taught for one semester, and here I was, already asking to be an exception. But I didn't have much choice. The baby was due smack in the middle of the semester. As I was coming to see, life makes its own calendar, and if you're wise, that's the one you follow.

SACHA WAS SAYING NEW WORDS all the time now. *Slipper-lee. Eenie-meenie. Wow.* One night, looking at her alphabet book in the bath, she ran her wet finger back and forth across my father's photograph.

"*Bop-pa!*" she exclaimed, eyes shining.

I stared at her. "Sach," I said, trying to rein my excitement in. I turned the page, back to my mother's picture. Taken three or four years earlier, over the Fourth. Her eyes sparkling. "Who's this, sweetie? Do you know who this is? Can you say?"

"Boppa," she said again faintly, losing interest.

Words for her came from the here-and-now. She was like a tourist, picking up nouns for what was most essential. *Cracker. Mittens. Snow.* She knew my father: He came regularly to see her. To see all of us.

"It energizes me, being with you," he said one night, looking past me out the dining room window.

"He can't stand being at Lakewood without her," Julie said sadly, the one time we talked about it. "She was right to want to sell the house. It's like—what were those boats she used to teach her students about? The ones the Egyptians used? The house is like that. Filled with her stuff. It breaks his heart."

Even now, all these years later, Sacha calls him Boppa. All the grandchildren do. *Bomma*—

Sacha never said it—not naturally. It never had meaning for her. Years later, in history papers or school reports, my mother got referred to as "my grandmother." Distant, historical. "Bomma" was Jenny and Rachel's word, washed clean of meaning for the rest of the grandchildren, like a Petoskey stone. You had to hold it underwater to see the lines: Otherwise it was bleached and pale, like every other stone on the beach.

JANUARY, FEBRUARY. I REMEMBER SHOVELING. I remember coming inside, tapping the shovel so the snow slid off, Bacchus charging toward me.

Annabel would stand at the window, holding Sacha up to watch my progress as I worked, and from time to time they'd tap on the glass, both of them waving and smiling, but I couldn't look back.

Which child felt it more, the grief I lived in? Sacha, watching me, trailing me, picking nervously at the hemline of my old, worn Laura Ashley jumper, trying out phrases. "Momma—better now? Momma ohh-kay?" Or this new baby, curling and turning in me, with only my sorrow for succor? What did each inherit?

Would we ever get to that final stage in Kübler-Ross's hopeful diagram—*acceptance*?

My mother used to love Dylan Thomas's villanelle, "Do Not Go Gentle." She didn't believe in acceptance (unless it was an acceptance from Stanford for one of her "bubbies"). If rage were a season, my mother would have wanted us to stay in it as long as we could.

And we did. I mourned and raged. I shoveled (endlessly) and the paths filled in around me.

Elisabeth was born March 9, six days early. Healthy, beautiful, with a smile so sweet it tugged at me. At all of us. She seemed to come into the world smiling. I know they say those aren't real smiles—they're reflexes or indigestion—but with Elisabeth, who we nicknamed Libby almost immediately, honest to God, I swear they were real.

Jacques brought Sacha when it was time for Libby and me to leave the hospital. We wanted Sacha there with us when we left, so all four of us could start our new life together. It was raining—one of those days in March when winter gives way to spring—and already dark out by the time we got everything packed up. We set the infant seat up next to Sacha's car seat, experts now, and as we drove west on Storrow Drive, me in the back with the two girls, Jacques in the front, windshield wipers humming, I had an uncanny sense of things falling into place.

I HADN'T FORGOTTEN MY PROMISE. A few nights after we got home from the hospital, I was nursing Libby in the living room, watching the shadows, noticing it was staying light a little longer now. Mid-March. Jacques was dancing with Sacha to one of the CDs she made us play over and over again that winter—*Reggae for Kids*. Calypso beat. The two of them, feet tapping, spinning. Laughing. How long had it been since I'd heard laughter? I could see their shadows crossing on the wall. I looked from one to the other and felt as if something in me were thawing.

"I think I'm ready for the surgery," I told Jacques. "I want to do what we talked about, and have it this summer."

I was surprised by his reaction. After all, we'd gone together to see Dr. Muto back in December. I thought we were on the same page about all of this. But if Libby's birth sealed my determination to go forward, it had a different effect on Jacques. Maybe it was the reminder of how joyful it is, bringing a new life into the world.

Jacques didn't think we should rush.

"You've been through a lot," he reminded me. "And Libby is brand-new. Give all of this time—let yourself be for a while. There's no urgency."

No urgency? I was going to be thirty-four in less than two months. I had two babies to take care of now. They needed me. There was *plenty* of urgency.

Jacques didn't understand. He wasn't trying to be difficult. He just couldn't see the point of rushing. To some extent, we were back in familiar territory—me, with my desire to plan and take care of things; Jacques, who wanted to take his time, to be certain this decision was right. But now, the stakes were higher. Surgery was irreversible, and it would have important consequences for us both.

I called Julie to ask her advice.

"Be patient," Julie advised me. "He may just need some time to catch up with you."

This was the same old mantra—I didn't have time. At least, I didn't feel like I did. But I knew Jacques didn't understand.

These days, the world for me was divided in two: people who had lost a parent (and understood) and people who hadn't. Much as I loved Jacques, he was still in the other camp. His father was alive and well at eighty, his mother, amazingly fit and healthy at seventy-four.

It changed the way he saw things. He felt like he had nothing but time. And by extension, like *we* had nothing but time.

I, on the other hand, felt like I had to act *now*.

For days, we argued. "What if we wanted to have a third child?" he asked one night, out of the blue.

"What if I wanted to be an astronaut?" I shot back. Actually, of all the untried experiences I might regret one day, being an astronaut is not high on my list. I was just trying to give him an example. My point was, there were lots of things we might want to do or try, if we had world enough and time.

But we didn't.

"It's not that I don't think you should have the surgery," Jacques said. "I just think we need to slow down. I don't see the rush."

That was how things stood with us for a while. We were at a standstill.

Then one night, lying in bed together, he put his hand over mine. "You really want to do this, don't you," he said.

I nodded. Then, realizing he couldn't see me, said *yes*. My voice small in the dark room.

"Listen," he said, rolling over and cupping my face with his hand. "I don't see this the way you do. But you're the one who just lost her mother. You grew up with this fear hanging over you. If you need to have this operation to move on and live your life, I'm behind you."

I gulped, grateful and heartbroken at the same time. I hugged him, tried to assure him this was the right thing.

The last roadblock was gone. I was determined to move ahead.

I called Dr. Muto's office to confirm our appointment. April 12. My plan was to schedule the surgery for late summer. Maybe August.

OK: I cried sometimes when I thought about the operation. But that was more relief than regret, I told myself. I was ready.

THEN—OUT OF THE BLUE, IN late March—the letter came from Creighton. Sara, Julie, and I each got a copy. And everything we knew—everything we'd always thought about everything—suddenly changed.

HBOC. Hereditary Breast and Ovarian Cancer.

Fear, Edgar Allan Poe once wrote, is the strongest emotion. He was right. When I read that letter, fear ran through me, like a wick.

HBOC. So it *was* the same thing—what my mother had. What Sylvia and Gail and Pody had.

Was that why my mother's tumor had been so aggressive, why nothing had worked? Nonestrogen receptive, my father had told us. A rare cell type, Dr. Brenner had said. Hereditary breast cancers, according to the letter from Creighton, tend to hit women young, and are often more aggressive and harder to treat than other cancers.

She'd done everything she could—everything known to us—but she'd only dealt with half the risk. None of us had any idea. Not even my father, for all his vigilance.

We talked, disbelieving—Sara and I, Julie and I, Julie and Sara. We all talked to my father, who got a copy of the letter, too. *What are you saying? You mean what she had was the same thing?*

Same thing, different part of the body.

The sharpshooter, after all. Not a different villain.

"Well," Julie said, trying to understand the magnitude of this. "It isn't exactly the same thing. It's a different cancer. It's just caused by the same mutation."

I hated the word *mutation.* It reminded me of spaceships, aliens.

It was hard to turn all of this around so quickly. After almost thirty-four years of thinking one way, suddenly everything was different. Yes, we were a high-risk cancer family. But it wasn't ovarian cancer. Or not *just* ovarian cancer.

And, to make everything even more complicated, now there was a test. Not a hypothetical, maybe-one-day test, but a real, actual test. This was nonfiction. The letter from Creighton told us where to go for genetic counseling. Dana-Farber, where my own doctors were, was right there on the list.

"One step at a time," my father said, though I could already hear the urgency in his voice. "You'll go see your doctors, get advice—"

What about my appointment with Dr. Muto in April? What about August? Should I still go ahead with surgery? Or should I get the test first?

"I don't like the idea of taking this test," Julie said slowly. "I don't know why, but it makes me . . ." She hesitated. "I don't know. I just think we need to think it through really carefully. We need to think through all the consequences."

Sara and I agreed.

What didn't we like about it? Was it that the test was so definitive? That it might be divisive? I don't think we knew yet. We were all confused, trying to figure this out. "New information," my father called it. That was an understatement.

BRCA1 started to hit the media. The *New York Times* ran a story on the "breast cancer gene," and people started talking about it. Talk shows, magazines.

Every story propelled my father back to the phones. Had we heard—? Had we seen the story—? What were our doctors saying? *What were we going to do?*

I didn't know what to tell him. Truthfully, I didn't want to talk about it—especially not with him. Being pregnant and breastfeeding— especially twice in a row, relatively close together—makes your body weirdly public. Complete strangers feel like they can come up to you and pat you on the womb and comment on how you're "carrying." Low, high, boy, girl—it's all up for discussion. People you don't know see you nursing and start giving you advice about your nipples. I suppose some people get used to that. But I've always been private about my body. I'm one of those people who keeps her towel on at the gym. Even when I was young, at overnight camp, I used to get dressed with my back to everyone else, trying to wriggle into my bra before anyone could see anything. Julie and I had perfected the art of changing on the beach in Charlevoix—snaking your underpants down through your bikini bottom. Using your towel as a tent.

I didn't want to talk to my father about my ovaries *or* my breasts.

"I'm seeing Dr. Muto in a few weeks," I told him, buying myself time. "Jacques and I will ask him about HBOC."

Silence on his end.

"Don't worry, Dad," I said, softening a little. He'd been through hell. And I didn't blame him for worrying. Now that I had children, I could empathize. What was it Francis Bacon said—having children is like giving hostages to fortune? That's what we were, all of us. Fortune's hostages. But when you're the parent, you can't help it. You want to get in there and fight.

I was lucky to have Sara and Julie to agonize with. We were our own built-in support group.

I thought of all those circles in the diagrams from Creighton. It was like someone had just taken a dark pen and connected the dots. Solved the crime.

The sharpshooter, circling. Eye to the lens. Only now it turned out there was a pair of them. If you sneaked past one, the other was still out there hunting.

APRIL 12, JACQUES AND I went to see Dr. Muto at the Farber.

Sacha stayed home with Annabel. We brought Libby, since I was nursing and couldn't be away from her for more than a few hours. When we got off the elevator, the department I'd gone to for all those years was gone. They'd merged, annexed now to the high-risk breast cancer group, like a tugboat pulled up onto an ocean liner. Before, there had been two hallways, two departments, two diseases. I remembered the way I used to get off at the elevator bank and turn, looking back at the breast cancer wing, with its shop selling scarves and wigs, and I'd feel a stab of something. Not pity, just that not-me sense (relief?) as I turned and walked the other way, to the smaller, less crowded waiting room where we ovarian people waited with our separate anxieties and terrors. Now, I had a whole other hallway claiming me. A whole new set of options to puzzle through.

This new department (Women's High Risk Cancers) was buzzing. Ten doctors to every one I was used to. Lots of cherrywood and granite. They were trying to set up a protocol for genetic testing, but it was all still brand-new. One doctor (a geneticist) came over to talk to me before my appointment with Dr. Muto. She had a clipboard, a pager, and a watch that looked like the kind runners wear. This was all just breaking news, and none of the support systems were in place yet—the counselors, the routine. It was all frontier. The ink wasn't dry yet on the brochures they gave me. A lot of information had to be ad-libbed, nobody had the story completely straight yet. She explained what it would mean if I carried the mutation. An 85 percent chance of getting breast cancer over my lifetime. A 50 percent chance of ovarian cancer. If I had the gene, that is.

But of course, there was a chance—a 50 percent chance—I didn't.

What would that mean, I asked. If, say, I happened to test negative?

Well, she said, considering. That was actually hard to say. They had found this one gene, but they were very close to finding another. Until we knew exactly what my family had—she glanced at my chart—that is, until someone tested *positive*, we couldn't know for sure. Positive for BRCA1, that is. Not for something else. It was possible my family had a different gene, in which case, we could all test negative, and that wouldn't really tell us anything at all.

Here's the way she explained it: They'd found Dallas, and maybe Houston, but there was still the rest of Texas out there.

"What about your mother?" she asked me. "Was she tested before—?"

I cut her off. "No," I said. Most days, I could manage when people asked me about her. This didn't feel like one of those days.

While we waited for Dr. Muto, my head buzzed. I felt even more confused about the test.

I needed to talk to Sara and Julie, and see what they thought.

What I really needed, though, was to ask my mother. What would she do?

My mother liked tests. Wasn't she the AP guru? On the other hand, this seemed more like pass-fail. My mother had never thought much of pass-fail as an option.

I had no idea what she would say: She'd taken the answers with her. We were on our own.

WE FILED INTO DR. MUTO'S office. Jacques took one chair, I took the other, Libby in my arms.

"I'm sorry about your mother," Dr. Muto said, looking straight at me.

I dropped my eyes.

"Thanks," I said. Jacques leaned over and put his hand over mine.

I told Dr. Muto we wanted to book the surgery. Remember, I said, we talked about it back in November? "I'll be thirty-four next month," I reminded him.

Dr. Muto cleared his throat. "What about getting tested first for BRCA1?" he asked.

I shook my head. "I don't think I'm ready for that yet," I said. "My sisters and I need to learn more about it, figure out our family's strategy. But that's going to take a while. And in the meantime—" I paused. "I don't want to wait much longer for surgery," I added. "Not past this summer."

I wanted my ovaries out, test or no test.

"Why?" Dr. Muto asked gently. (He is a kind, kind man.) "Why wouldn't you want to think about having the test first?"

The most honest answer may not have been the best one. *Because I've always planned this.*

This surgery had always been on the horizon for me. Always. I'd grown up believing this was the one thing that would keep me from ending up like Sylvia and Pody and Gail.

I understood the landscape had changed, tectonic plates had shifted, we were on new terrain. But I was almost thirty-four. In just a year, I was going to cross the line. I wouldn't be on the safe side anymore.

What if I took the test and it was negative and Dr. Muto wouldn't do the surgery? Hadn't the doctors just told me that until they got a positive—for one of us—the negative wouldn't mean anything definite? Neither Julie nor Sara was keen to be tested. Sara, maybe one day. Julie felt the way I did. It could be years before we knew for sure which exact mutation my family had. And I didn't *have* years.

"Well," Dr. Muto said, thinking this through. "There's three of you, right? So the odds are—"

The odds were *one* of us was positive. Maybe two. Only for me, these weren't just three circles on a grid. These were my sisters and me.

"It's a group decision for us," I said. "We've agreed to wait till we're all sure it's what we want."

At least what we had now—new information—was something all three of us shared.

But once we started taking the test, that would change. Given the odds, we wouldn't all get the same results. Picture that in my family. Picture Tricky Triangle crossed with Who Got What. I could barely imagine that. What would that do to the three of us as sisters?

"What do you think of all this?" Dr. Muto asked, turning to Jacques.

Jacques cleared his throat. "It's hard, imagining Amy having the surgery right now," he said slowly.

Dr. Muto nodded, waiting.

"But, knowing her—" He glanced at me. "I think the test would be a bad idea."

I was surprised. We hadn't talked about this yet. Jacques is usually very rational about decisions. I would've guessed he'd want me to be tested, especially since it could delay or even prevent surgery.

Dr. Muto looked thoughtfully at him, considering. "OK," he said at last. "Here's a plan. Why don't we schedule surgery for late this summer, which is what Amy wants. In the meantime, though, you two should keep thinking and talking. I'd like to meet with you both in July to reevaluate before we go ahead and confirm this."

That seemed fair to me. We set the date for August 25. One night in the hospital at most. The whole thing would take less than two hours. Thirty-four years of worrying, over just like that.

No more ovaries. No more Tampax or periods or feeling particular ways at particular times of the month. No more thinking about myself the way I had since I got my period at eleven.

The worst part: no more babies.

But on the other hand, no more CA-125s. No more ultrasounds. No more living from fear to fear. At least not *this* fear. And that was a start, wasn't it?

IN MAY, WE HAD A naming ceremony for Libby. My father came. Julie and Jon came with Maddy. We had some neighbors and friends. One reason for the ceremony was to talk about how we'd chosen Libby's name: Elisabeth.

In Hebrew, it means "God's promise."

Funny, how much I liked that. Even the God part.

I sat up the night before the naming ceremony, thinking about why that was. Maybe it isn't completely true to say I don't believe in God. Maybe it's just that I haven't found the story yet that makes sense to me. Not the Christian story. Not the Jewish one, with all those smitings and begettings. But something that explains the ways

in which we are connected to one another, generation after generation. The things we give each other. The love of poetry. The way it
feels to turn a word over and over, until it glows. Predispositions.
Predilections. Gifts.

SARA COULDN'T FLY OUT FOR the naming—she was teaching, the
girls were in school. But she had written Libby a letter, which I tried
to read out loud. I got through most of it, but my voice broke when
I got to the ending.

*We will always love you with a special kind of love, because you are
our E.*

E: Elfin. Exuberant. Empathic. Energetic. Elegiac.

Elisabeth. Who is almost never called that, but instead called
Libby. For Elaine, giver of nicknames.

Who was herself almost never called Elaine. Mom. Bomma.
Mellie. My father called her "Tude." "Nails." Gail, who couldn't pro-
nounce Elaine as a child, called her "Naincy."

Names—like gifts—connect us. We name each other, and then
name each other again. It doesn't stop.

This wasn't a ceremony for my mother, though. We'd had that.
New Year's Day at Cranbrook. The ground too frozen to bury her
ashes.

This ceremony was for Libby: for life, not death. For the start of
things, not the end.

"When," I asked Julie that night, sitting up with a glass of wine
in the kitchen, "will everything we do stop feeling like a memorial
service for her?"

Julie shrugged. "Never?" she said.

I asked her about August. Would she be able to come down and
help Jacques with the girls when I had the surgery?

"Absolutely," she said.

"I'm next," she said after a moment, thinking. "After the next
baby, whenever that is."

Then we talked about the test. BRCA1.

"The problem," I said, trying to figure out what the problem was, "is that it doesn't just change things for one of us. It's all of us." I looked at Libby, who had fallen asleep in my arms, still half-nursing. "It's them, too. We're deciding, once we know, what they'll know."

I was still in between, still used to thinking more like a daughter than a mother. But that was beginning to change. Jacques and I had talked ourselves blue in the face about this, and though we disagreed about a lot, one thing we both felt strongly was that we wanted the girls to grow up as unafraid as possible. I wanted them to love their bodies, to love being alive. I didn't want them to panic over every rash or mole, the way I always had.

I didn't want them to hear the word *ovary* and think of dying.

When I asked Jacques why he'd said what he said to Dr. Muto—about the test being a bad idea for me—this is what he came back to.

"I just know you," he said. "If you get bad news, you'll never stop worrying. Ever. You could have every surgery imaginable, and you'd still worry."

He wanted to protect me from how he knew I could be.

Julie wanted to know what I was going to do after August. What about the rest of it? Ovarian surgery was only part of the solution. What about breast cancer?

I hadn't thought that far ahead. One body part at a time, I told her.

IT'S A FUNNY PHRASE, "SETTING the date." Like you're putting something in place—a brick in a foundation. Something to build on.

I'd thought about this surgery for so long it was hard to believe it was getting closer. August 25: an auspicious day. Actually, it just happened to be the day that worked best for everyone: Dr. Muto; Julie, who was staying for a few nights to help us out; Annabel, who by some lucky fluke had decided she wanted to keep working with us, even after her year was up. (Neither of us ever wanted to go back to Eileen Diamond.)

"Are you scared?" Julie asked me.

"A little," I admitted. It wasn't the operation itself, which Dr. Muto had explained was fairly simple. Because they could use a laparoscope, there wouldn't be much pain, and the recovery time would be very short. What was unnerving was imagining what life would be like afterward. As Dr. Muto kept telling me, the ovary is a smart little organ. It does much more than just produce an egg every month. Ovaries produce estrogen, helping all sorts of functions in the body: circulation, memory, nerve conduction, energy, libido, skin tone and elasticity. Moisture in the eyes. The body's sense of cycles, of time. It would be a little like taking the mechanism out of a clock, I thought. For months, I'd been insisting it would all be fine, that I was ready. But now that the day was here, I couldn't help worrying. What would it feel like?

I was probably the first patient in Dr. Muto's practice to have this operation so soon after delivering a baby. But I was ready. The timing was good. Waiting till August had given me five months to nurse. I'd be back on my feet, we'd have ourselves settled before I started teaching. And I could make my deadline. I'd be having the surgery before I turned thirty-five.

In some sense, I was doing this in my mother's honor. We couldn't turn our backs on what we knew. We still had our family history, even if it was different from the one we thought we knew. It would be unthinkable, after all this suffering, not to try our hardest to keep this from happening again.

We knew, each of us, that the sharpshooter was still out there, circling. Watching my mother fight for her life moved each of us one step closer to the enemy. She'd been our guard. To the very end, that's how she saw it.

In December, the three of us had gone back to see her, not knowing it was the last time. She was on oxygen, she could barely speak, but she was still trying to reassure us. Wasted, barely able to draw breath, grabbing our hands with her bony fingers, like a claw. She gasped at us: *This is it. I'm the last one. This stops with me.* As if superstition, not science, really had the final word.

But we were all too much her daughters to believe that. None of us could just let this go. She'd gone through too much for us to shrug, move on, forget our family history. To just say, *what will be, will be.*

No. We owed it to her to fight back.

I HAD THE SURGERY AS planned, on August 25. Julie came down from Maine the night before with Maddy, and cooked dinner for us, and we stayed up late, talking about things that mattered. Such as: Is Gymboree a racket, or is it worth it? Why does everyone think men are so great when they do something perfectly ordinary, like cooking a meal or taking kids to the park or (amazing) changing a diaper? We didn't talk about genetic testing or closing doors or what it would feel like, living without the smart little organs that had made my body tick since puberty.

"Don't worry, Mellie," she said before we each headed off to bed at midnight. "It's going to be OK."

"I know," I said. And would have hugged her, if we were a family that does much of that.

The next morning, they let Jacques go with me as far as the point where the orderlies roll the gurney off into the OR. He held my hand as we rolled, walking faster to keep up. Last thing, I gave him my glasses to hold.

"Listen," he said, leaning over close. "I want you alive and well. For a long, long time—till you're old and cranky, OK? I don't care about anything else. You hear me?"

I did. I nodded. And off I went, in the direction of whatever came next.

EPILOGUE

FLASH FORWARD TWO YEARS. SACHA and Maddy were in nursery school, Libby was a toddler. Julie had a new baby. Remarkably, she had a boy—the first in our family. They named him Ben. True to her word, she started planning her surgery. Like me, she didn't waste time.

We were all busy, life moved on in its messy way. So did the world. Researchers found a second gene, BRCA2. Now, when the three of us got together, we added new topics to our ever-changing list: Was Suzuki really the best way to learn piano? Why don't kids actually play outside on their own anymore? Added to this, we wondered about hormone replacement therapy and the risks of extra estrogen for women with family histories like ours, and soon Sara was forty, I was thirty-eight, Julie, thirty-four, and before we knew it, we were talking about surgery again. Breast surgery this time. A bigger surgery, more extreme.

We still said we didn't want to get tested, even now that there were two genes to hunt down. But then we got more "new information." After my first surgery, I tracked down my second cousins in Illinois. Gail's children, Paul and Jill, roughly our ages. We barely knew each other—in fact, I had to get their phone numbers from my mother's second cousin, out in California. But I finally got hold of Jill one afternoon in spring. At first, she had no idea who I was. Then, she was happy to hear from me, very warm.

Yes, she knew all about the gene. She and Paul had both been tested. She was matter-of-fact about it, happy to share the results. She'd tested negative—a huge relief, she told me, especially since she had three kids—but Paul had tested positive. He had the mutation: BRCA1.

So now we had our answer—we'd found our broken gene. This meant if we got tested, the results would be "meaningful."

Julie and I went back to the Farber together. We met with the top people running genetic studies there. We called Sara and debated. What should we do?

Sara had already scheduled prophylactic mastectomies for that winter. She didn't want the test now. She didn't want to risk her HMO pulling their support—there was no way she could swing the surgery (which cost tens of thousands of dollars) without her insurance paying. And honestly, she said, even if she tested negative now, even with this new "new" information, she'd still worry. She'd found a lump the year before, had to endure an awful biopsy, sweating out the results for two of the worst weeks of her life. She didn't want the test at this point. Later, when Jenny and Rachel were older, maybe. But not now. Surgery—again—but no test.

So we moved ahead, one by one. Second surgeries. Physically, these were much harder. Much more complicated, each requiring weeks off from work and day-to-day life—no driving, no lifting.

Sacha was five when I had breast surgery. Libby, three. I had two operations, ten weeks apart. Jacques and I weren't sure how much either of the girls could understand at their respective ages, but I gave them an analogy. Sacha had a favorite stuffed toy, a whimsical Humpty Dumpty my mother had given her from the Met. She carried him with her everywhere, flapping one of his legs back and forth, rubbing his fraying arms, until eventually his stuffing came out and Annabel (ingenious) restuffed him and made him a new pair of overalls out of some old jeans.

I held Humpty up for the girls. "See how his new stuffing helps him?" I said.

They nodded. This mattered. For a while, there'd been talk about having to put Humpty up on a shelf, he'd gotten so frail.

"Well," I said, "the doctors think my breasts would be healthier if I got new stuffing, too. So that's what they're going to do." I explained that for the first surgery—the big one—I would be in the hospital for four nights, and when I came home, I wouldn't be able to pick them up—much as I wanted to.

Libby, literal child, fixated on that—my not being able to pick her up. Whatever I told her, she seemed convinced the problem was in my back.

"You back all better now?" she asked when I came home. She hung back shyly, afraid of bumping me. Apparently Jacques had coached them not to rush at me and bowl me over when I came home, so they stood nervously together in the hallway, holding hands, as if restraining each other.

For days they followed me, running their eyes up and down to assess the damage. Then bit by bit, I healed, and we all forgot. Libby hung on to worry the longest.

"You back a big better?" Libby would ask pensively from time to time that summer, chewing her lip, watching me. "O little better?" Libby never forgot an idea. For months, she would catch my eye, blink, and ask again. "How you back now?"

"Better," I told her, settling for simplicity.

Back. Back in time. Looking back. Setting back the clock. Maybe that's what we wanted, my sisters and I, why we wanted surgeries instead of testing, surgeries as if to prevent the need for testing, because what we really wanted was to move back, to a time when none of this was needed, when we could just live our lives and *be*.

YEARS LATER, SARA HAD THE test done. Jenny and Rachel were old enough that she thought it would be useful for them to know the results.

She was negative.

Was she sorry she'd gone ahead and had all that surgery? No, she told me. Not for one second. Not at all. We were in Charlevoix when I asked her—a reunion of sorts, walking on our old beach, kids scattered. "You know," she said, shrugging, "I think I would've wanted the surgeries no matter what."

The test, it seems, was only part of what we needed for answers. Or maybe it's more that *answers* were only part of what we needed. And that was lucky, because answers appeared to be few and far between.

OUT OF THE FIVE OF us, three of us so far have been tested. Two negatives, one positive. Two—Julie and me—left to go.

These days, I go back and forth. Even with the surgeries behind me, I still anguish about this. If I have the test, maybe I can save Sacha and Libby some of this worry. If I'm positive, they need to know so they can move on and be smart about the choices they make. If I'm negative, they can let go of at least this particular set of fears.

On the other hand, if I find out, they'll be forced to know. That would take away the space that for me has been soul-saving, if not life-saving—the space of not knowing for sure.

The girls are a big part of my indecision. The girls are back, but in a different position. I'm the one now, standing at the bottom of the stairs, calling up into the dim twilight of a winter's evening. *Girls! Gir—rllllls!*

Then there's Jacques. This is his story, too, annexed to mine through the dumb luck of a train ride, a conversation, a chance connection. A good marriage. He loves me, loves our life. He knows how I am, how anxious I get. He doesn't want me to know whether I'm positive for this mutation or not. He doesn't want this shadow lengthening across our lives, the lives of our daughters. Some questions, he thinks, aren't ours to ask.

THERE ARE OTHER COMPONENTS. MOSTLY, though, I think it just comes down to the dawning realization that what we know now isn't the whole truth, any more than what we knew back when I was growing up was the whole truth. There will be more new information. Sometimes I look at the *New York Times* and shudder, thinking, is today the day I'll open the paper up and find out there's another component to this gene? My mother's cousin Sherman has been fighting a rare form of pancreatic cancer for the past ten years. Could there be a connection? What if we find out other organs (pancreas, colon) are implicated? What if it never stops?

I GREW UP SO FEARFUL. Anxiety of airplanes. Anxiety of interior organs. Anxiety of highways, of steep grades, of descent. Anxiety of failure. Anxiety of speaking. Anxiety of strangers. Anxiety of small, closed spaces, like elevators or caves (or spaceships). I had the surgeries. My feeling was: Do anything, but keep me from facing the knowledge I have what my mother had. What Sylvia had. I couldn't have faced that and raised the girls. Or at least raised them the way I wanted. I wanted to be optimistic. Unafraid. To call for them in the kind of voice that reverberated with the sense I would be there when they came bounding down from whatever it was that kept them busy, free, away from me.

———

IN LITERARY STUDIES, WE TALK about "passing." Trying to pretend to be something you aren't. Black, passing as white. Gay, passing as straight. For me, having the surgeries and refusing to have the genetic test allowed me to pass—at least until I began writing this book. For so long, I wanted to be like everyone else. So here I was, a person from a high-risk cancer family passing as "normal"—whatever I thought that meant. Very few friends or colleagues know I had surgery. I did everything I possibly could to protect myself—except to speak the truth out loud. Nobody knew: This was private. I did what I needed to do. And for a long time, that gave me just enough peace to live my life and forget.

Or almost forget. Once, several years ago, Julie had an idea. Why not go back to Rougemont and find out whether my mother's pathology could give us the answer we needed? We could have her tissue blocks tested. That way, we could have our answer, without having to face what we were so terrified to face ourselves. It would be about my mother, then, and not about us.

It was a long, sad story. A ridiculous story, in many ways. Of course she had the mutation! Who were we kidding? But we threw ourselves into the hunt. We spent months trying to wrangle with various administrators at the hospital, who finally admitted her tissue blocks had been lost. Lost, or thrown out—probably the latter. It was like we'd tried to find the oracle, and the oracle wasn't there.

Even worse, we'd gone back—years later, as adults—mothers ourselves—and tried to look for one last, vital thing from her—a way in which she could protect us, offer herself up in our stead. And of course, it was too late. There was literally nothing left of her. Not a single, frozen cell.

AS I WRITE THIS, IT'S fifteen years later. Half a generation. In some ways, the old decision is back again. The surgeries, for me at least, are history. But what about the test? We do what we do, but then time passes. Choices don't necessarily get made once and then go away. What made sense then, what worked for a while, doesn't seem adequate anymore now, because I've moved to another place on the timeline. *The girls* are going now, but in a different way. My daughters are becoming young women. They're growing up in a world dazzlingly different from the one in which I grew up—and for the most part, they're facing it open, honest, unafraid.

We're struggling, Jacques and I, with a question that needs to become part of a larger debate. There is no simple, right or wrong answer. What, after all, would I do with the information if I get it? When is the right time to tell the girls what I learn? What will they do? Two daughters, two possible answers. What difference will it make to each of them? To the two of them together? Finally, these are choices that have to be made—slowly, thoughtfully—one by one. The information we get will change over time, and the decisions will, too. What we'll know in ten years will be different from what we know now. And so it goes.

At times, I beat myself up for having been so fearful for so long. At other times I look at the girls and think, maybe they are who they are in part because I raised them without knowing for sure. Maybe I've given them that, at least—the space to grow up without fear.

I'm not sure. We do what we do, and let the rest go.

Or do we? Do we ever let go of the past?

I started writing this book because I wanted to understand why my family made the choices we've made about testing and surgery. How we've lived with and understood risk. But along the way, I discovered that wasn't all of it.

I wasn't just writing about my family history. I was trying to get that history back.

Once, when Libby was almost three, a friend, Lee, came over for dinner with her six-year-old son. She'd been a roommate of mine when I lived in New York City one year, between bouts of grad school. I wanted to show Libby her picture, and I found a small album from the party Lee had given for me before Jacques and I got married.

Libby loved looking through the pictures. There I was, modeling an eyelet nightgown over my clothes. Holding up a china platter. Years younger, lighter in expression, playing bride-to-be.

"Look," I said, stopping at the last picture in the book. Julie and my mother and I, out on Julie and Jon's deck in northern Virginia. It was a close-up, and it was clear all three of us had drunk more than our share of the sangria. Julie was on one side, I was on the other, both of us with our arms around my mother. All three of us soused and happy. Our mouths open, heads back, laughing our heads off.

"Who that?" Libby asked, putting one moist finger on my mother's face.

I tried to sound matter-of-fact. We still rehearsed sometimes from Sacha's tattered alphabet book, but years had passed. Kids forget. Like the black-and-white photos hanging in the hallway, I thought. My parents' persistent attempts to keep Sylvia alive for us.

Libby was puzzling over my mother's face, her eyes clouded.

I didn't want her to see how much this hurt.

"That," I said brightly, "is Mommy's mommy."

Libby seemed to mull this over. "I like Mommy's *daddy*," she said after a while, as if making a peace offering. "He nice."

I nodded. "Yes," I said, still trying. "He's very nice. But, Libs, Mommy's mommy—Bomma—*she* was really nice, too."

She looked at me, skeptical.

I leaned closer to the picture. "I miss her," I said, as cheerfully as I could. "You know what?" Libby's favorite phrase that year. Her version: "You—what?"

"What?" she said back, interested.

"I'm going to give her a little kiss," I said, and I leaned over and kissed my mother's celluloid, rosy cheek.

Libby watched me, considering. She studied my mother's picture.

"She not talking," she said. And broke my heart.

AN EARLY MODERNIST I ADMIRE, Stephen Greenblatt, wrote in the introduction to one of his books on Shakespeare that he had begun his study "with the desire to speak with the dead." To some extent, he wrote, that's why we study history. To make the dead speak in us.

I don't know what my mother would say if she could sit down with us now, with Sara, Julie, and me. If we could have her back for a day. One day: sunlit, luminous. Or even one hour.

Maybe it's summer. Charlevoix. All the beach toys gone now, the kids are grown, Jenny is in a doctoral program, engaged now. Rachel is in the Ukraine with the Peace Corps. Sacha and Maddy are applying to college, Ben and Libby are both in high school. What would she say about any of this? That a test, in the end, is only a test? That the answers we think we're looking for are only part of what matters most?

They took their treasures with them, the Egyptians, she might say, shading her eyes against the sun. *They loaded their boats with what they'd gathered, and they set off.*

There's no way of knowing. Because, as Libby grasped when she was not quite three, my mother—she's not talking.

And even if she were, even if we had our answer, whatever it was, what would we do with it? How would we fit it into the shaped poem we try to assemble of our lives?

Would we see an hourglass, or wings?

ACKNOWLEDGMENTS

WRITING A MEMOIR MAKES YOU think—and thank—in layers. This book has benefited from the generosity and support of a number of people. My colleagues Elizabeth Graver and Suzanne Matson have guided this endeavor at many stages, and it's no overstatement to say this wouldn't be a book without their help and advice. Richard Parks took on the project at a particularly difficult time in the book industry, nurturing it (and me) with encouragement, sagacity, and insight. From our first conversation, my editor, Rachel Holtzman, has been a kindred spirit, a wonderful reader, and a great source of counsel. I've been lucky for her guidance.

Before the book came the medical history that inspired it. Many doctors have helped my family navigate our way since the research on hereditary breast and ovarian cancers first came to light in the early 1980s. While we have benefited directly from some of the best clinicians in the field, we've also been helped indirectly by others who have dedicated their careers to learning more about BRCA1 and BRCA2. Research done at Creighton University and at the Gilda Radner Hereditary Cancer Detection Program has been particularly important for my family. Closer to home, special thanks go to Dr. Judy Garber, and to my surgeons, Dr. Gadd and Dr. Muto, for helping me to make difficult and complicated choices. Each of these fine doctors has found ways to integrate humanity into their science, and I admire them for it. I deeply appreciate Sue Friedman's work at FORCE, a nonprofit organization dedicated to educating and supporting women at risk for hereditary breast and ovarian cancers. Women (and men) with dispositions for these diseases will find the world of high-risk cancer a much less lonely place thanks to the community FORCE provides.

If the medical world has granted me one kind of support, academia has offered another. Boston College—both the university and my department—has allowed and even encouraged me to move beyond my field in ways that have made this project possible. Beyond that, the English department has been a wonderful home for reading, writing, thinking, and talking about literature, both with colleagues and students. I am lucky to work with so many people I count as friends. Both inside and outside of academia, friends have helped with this book in dozens of ways: talking, reading drafts, giving advice (professional/medical/maternal), sharing (exemplary) works of creative nonfiction, and talking some more. Special thanks are due to Barbara Bierer, Elizabeth Bartle, Barbara Beal, Caroline Bicks, Mary Crane, Sari Horwitz, and Pam Peck for their support and insights. For Lucienne Thys-Senocak, who managed to read and make insightful comments on the manuscript in the midst of incalculable challenges of her own—there are no thanks big enough.

My biggest debts are to the people who have lived with me most closely. Members of my extended family, from Newton to Johannesburg, have talked me through hard choices, read drafts, and provided countless models of humor, persistence, and the power of stories. On my mother's side, I want to thank Sherman Holvey, her only surviving cousin, who taught my mother to dance and has always brought grace and style to our family—and who knows himself what it means both to suffer and to heal. Huge thanks also go to Paul and Jill, my newly rediscovered cousins, who have accepted my efforts to tell my piece of a larger story with generosity and warmth. My nieces and nephew have read and commented on drafts and helped in myriad ways. Thanks to Jenny, Rachel, Maddy, and Ben for this, and for so much more. On Jacques's side, thanks are due to Nasreen Rajab-Budlender, an early fan of my efforts to describe life with a newborn; Suellen Perold, a wonderful sister-in-law and sympathetic ear; and to Charlotte and Helene Perold, who continue to exemplify—in so many ways—the rich connections that motherhood and daughterhood afford.

My father has always been the best of readers, listeners, and guides, not least in this. My sisters, who have made every step of this journey with me, are at once my best friends, my partners, my collaborators, and my allies. They are amazing, both of them, for letting me even attempt to write a story that rightly belongs to us all. In the same way, Jacques, Sacha, and Libby have not only allowed me to write a story that is largely and importantly theirs, but have encouraged me to do so. They are a daily reminder why all of this matters.

My deepest thanks go to those no longer here to receive them. To Sylvia and Pody, who knew none of this. To Gail, who knew only a glimmer of it. And finally, to my mother, lover of history, who taught me that the present is only the smallest neighborhood of the past.